Political Development in Pacific Asia

Political Development in Pacific Asia

David Martin Jones

Polity Press

The right of David Martin Jones to be identified as author of this work has been asserted in accordance with the Copyright, Designs and Patents Act 1988.

First published in 1997 by Polity Press in association with Blackwell Publishers Ltd

2 4 6 8 10 9 7 5 3 1

Editorial office:
Polity Press
65 Bridge Street
Cambridge CB2 1UR, UK

Marketing and production:
Blackwell Publishers Ltd
108 Cowley Road
Oxford OX4 1JF, UK

Published in the USA by
Blackwell Publishers Inc.
Commerce Place
350 Main Street
Malden, MA 02148, USA

ISBN 0-7456-1504-X
ISBN 0-7456-1505-8 (pbk)

A CIP catalogue record for this book is available from the British Library and the Library of Congress.

Typeset in 10.5 on 12pt Ehrhardt
by Graphicraft Typesetters Ltd, Hong Kong
Printed in Great Britain by Hartnolls Ltd, Bodmin, Cornwall

This book is printed on acid-free paper.

Contents

Acknowledgements

I would like to thank Cambridge University Press for permission to use map 1.1 from *The Cambridge History of Southeast Asia* edited by Nicholes Tarling volume 2, p. 80 (1992).

A number of people helped in the preparation of this book. During my sojourn at the National University of Singapore I profited enormously from conversations with Leo Suryadinata, Chua Beng Huat, Diana Wong, James Jesudason and Janadas Devan, who gave freely of their time and guidance through a potentially overwhelming literature. Collaboration on *Towards Illiberal Democracy in Pacific Asia* with Daniel A. Bell, David Brown and Kanishka Jayasuriya, whilst we were colleagues together in the Political Science Department at the National University of Singapore, proved immensely valuable for this project. John Thompson at Polity Press thoughtfully guided the initial idea and his anonymous reader provided a wealth of detailed and valuable comment on earlier drafts of the manuscript. Finally, I owe a debt of gratitude to the people at Polity who so smoothly produced this volume, notably Gillian Motley, Julia Harsant, Sue Leigh and Justin Dyer.

Abbreviations

ABRI	*Angkatan Bersenjata Republik Indonesia*
ADB	Asian Development Bank
AFTA	ASEAN Free Trade Area
AHS	Approved Housing Scheme
ANZUS	Australia, New Zealand, United States (defence treaty)
APEC	Asia Pacific Economic Cooperation
ARF	ASEAN Regional Forum
ASA	Association of Southeast Asia
ASEAN	Association of South East Asian Nations
BN	*Barisan Nasional*
BOB	Bureau of the Budget
BOI	Board of Investment
CPF	Central Provident Fund
DAP	Democratic Action Party
DBS	Development Bank of Singapore
DJP	Democratic Justice Party
DLP	Democratic Liberal Party
DPP	Democratic Progressive Party
DPRK	Democratic People's Republic of Korea
DRV	Democratic Republic of Vietnam
EAEC	East Asian Economic Caucus
EDB	Economic Development Board
EPB	Economic Planning Board
EPF	Employers' Provident Fund
EPZs	Export Processing Zones
FDI	foreign direct investment
FKI	Federation of Korean Industries
FPDA	Five Power Defence Agreement
GATT	General Agreement on Tariffs and Trade
GDP	gross domestic product
GLCs	government-linked corporations
GNP	gross national product
GRCs	Group Representation Constituencies
GTCs	General Trading Companies

HCIP	Heavy and Chemical Industry Plan
HDB	Housing Development Board
HICOM	Heavy Industries Corporation of Malaysia
HPAEs	High-Performing Asian Economies
ICA	Investment Coordination Act
ICMI	*Ikatan Cendekiawan Muslim Indonesia*
ISA	Internal Security Act
ISI	import-substituting industrialization
JDB	Japanese Development Bank
JECC	Japan Electric Computer Company
JPCC	Joint Public–Private Consultative Committee
KADIN	*Kamar Dagang dan Industri*
KCIA	Korean Central Intelligence Agency
KEDO	Korean Energy Development Organization
KIET	Korean Institute of Electronics Technology
KLSE	Kuala Lumpur Stock Exchange
KMT	Kuomintang (*Guomindang*)
KOTRA	Korean Trade Promotion Corporation
MAS	Monetary Authority of Singapore
MCA	Malay Chinese Association
MCI	Ministry of Commerce and Industry
MENDAKI	Council for the Education of Muslim Children
MIA	Malayan Indian Association
MITI	Ministry of Trade and Industry
MNEs	multinational enterprises
MOF	Ministry of Finance
MPR	*Majelis Permusyawaratan Rakyat*
NAFTA	North American Free Trade Area
NAM	Non-Aligned Movement
NDP	National Development Policy
NDRP	New Democratic Republican Party
NEP	New Economic Policy
NESDB	National Economic and Social Development Board
NIEs	Newly Industrialized Economies
NKP	New Korea Party
NPKC	National Peace Keeping Council
NTUC	National Trade Union Congress
NWC	National Wages Council
ODA	overseas development aid
OECD	Organization for Economic Co-operation and Development
OPEC	Organization of Petroleum Exporting Countries
PAP	People's Action Party
PAS	*Partai Agama Se-Malaysia*
PBS	*Parti Bersatu Sabah*
PDI	*Partai Demokrasi Indonesia*
PDP	Palang Dharma Party
PECC	Pacific Economic Cooperation Council
PIA	Promotions of Investment Act
PKI	*Partai Kommunis Indonesia*
PLA	People's Liberation Army

PNB	*Permodalan Nasional Behad*
PNI	*Partai Nasional Indonesia*
PPP	*Partai Persatuan Pembangunan*
PRC	People's Republic of China
PRPK	People's Revolutionary Party of Kampuchea
RDP	Reunification Democratic Party
ROC	Republic of China (Taiwan)
ROK	Republic of Korea
SAR	Special Administrative Region
SCAP	Supreme Commander for the Allied Powers
SDP	Social Democratic Party
SEATO	South-East Asia Treaty Organization
SEP	Strategic Economic Plan
SEZs	Special Economic Zones
SIMEX	Singapore International Monetary Exchange
SLORC	State Law and Order Council
SMEs	small and medium-sized enterprises
SOEs	state-owned enterprises
SPSI	*Serikat Perburuhan Seluruh Indonesia*
TAC	Treaty of Amity and Cooperation
TRA	Taiwan Relations Act
UMNO	United Malays National Organization
UNCLOS	United Nations Convention governing the Law of the Sea
USTR	United States Trade Representative
WTO	World Trade Organization
ZOPFAN	Zone of Peace, Freedom and Neutrality

Note on Chinese Terms

For the most part Hanyu–Pinyin notation is used for Chinese terms in the text, although in certain places the Wade–Giles system is used, notably when discussing Taiwan, as that is the preferred usage on the island.

Introduction

In the wake of the disintegration of the Soviet Empire there has emerged a growing academic interest in both the economic and constitutional democratic evolution of contemporary Pacific Asia. Preoccupied by the Cold War, in the last decade of the twentieth century Europe and the United States suddenly faced a new economic and political challenge from a dynamic, prosperous and increasingly economically influential Pacific Asian littoral stretching from Japan in the North to archipelagic Indonesia in the South. The relatively recent identification of what the World Bank in 1993 termed an 'East Asian Miracle' in the High-Performing Asian Economies (HPAEs) of South Korea, Hong Kong, Taiwan, Thailand, Malaysia, Singapore and Indonesia has occasioned a debate over the economic and political lessons to be drawn from the dramatic transformation of Pacific Asia. This discussion involves a consideration of the political preconditions for economic development, the role of government in setting macroeconomic targets and picking industrial winners, and the prospects both for regional trading and for political arrangements in the post-communist and post-GATT (General Agreement on Tariffs and Trade) world order.

We can broadly identify two contrasting grand theoretical explanations of the economic and political development of Pacific Asia. On the one hand, Francis Fukuyama (1992, 1995a, 1995b) maintains that with the collapse of communism in Eastern Europe and its metamorphosis into nationalism in the People's Republic of China we have reached the end of an era of ideology and that variations on a liberal democratic theme, occasionally modified by local managerial practice, will increasingly become the global norm (Fukuyama 1992: 338). Somewhat more circumspectly, Samuel Huntington (1991, 1993b) identified a 'third wave' of democratization crashing upon East Asian shores, and although it may subsequently retreat, it will leave behind something more than a 'melancholy, long withdrawing roar'. This 1990s resuscitation of a modernization theory initially formulated by American liberals in the midst of the Cold War (Binder et al. 1971; Rostow 1971) maintains that the global trend is inexorably democratic. Indeed, institutions like Freedom House confirm this with empirical data to show just how far democracy has proceeded, whilst liberal journals like *The Economist*, *The Far Eastern Economic Review* and *The Asian Wall Street Journal* regularly report upon the spontaneous and benign conjunction of liberal democratic pluralism, freedom and economic growth. By contrast, a number of East Asian commentators and politicians are either reluctant to go with the flow of this particular historical tide, or find that it conceals a suspicious 'new found mission in the West to use the imposed (democratic) category as an international merit test' (Chan 1993: 6–7). In part this is a matter of self-regard. Confining post-colonial East Asians in an ideological straitjacket of western fashion seems to an increasingly self-conscious East Asian political elite to be either patronising or, worse, a ploy 'to bring about instability, economic decline and poverty' (Mahathir Mohamad, *Straits Times*, 31 August 1993).

In order to qualify this liberal democratic universalism, a number of East Asian commentators (Chan 1993; Mahbubani 1994; Ogata 1993; Mahathir and Ishihara 1995), supported by Harvard management theorists (Vogel and Lodge 1987; Vogel 1991), have advanced an alternative East Asian model of political development. They maintain, in fact, that the successful East Asian economies have modernized equitably and without social instability precisely because traditional, high cultural, political and moral values informed the Asian development process. Thus, politicians as various as Singapore's Lee Kuan Yew, Malaysia's Mahathir Mohamad, Indonesia's Suharto and South Korea's Roh Tae Woo have either resisted the universality of western concepts of democracy, right and law, or suggested that there are different, non-liberal, but equally valid 'Asian' understandings of these terms.

This pan-Asian ethic, it is asserted, is equally as effective in securing stable government and sustainable growth as its western counterpart. This ethic, often misleadingly characterized as Confucian or Neo-Confucian, is then advanced to explain the stability, order and dynamism of the Pacific littoral that contrasts dramatically with the 'dying economies' and civil disobedience that have come to characterize the Anglo-American world.

This debate has not been helped by a certain amount of conceptual incoherence. Contemporary East Asian political thought somewhat ambiguously dismisses western notions of democracy, whilst at the same time claiming that Asian values also meet certain democratic criteria. Ironically, those who claim to have discovered a distinctively Asian model of democracy draw upon a modernization literature whose capitalist democratic conclusions (Dunn 1991: 27) they evidently wish to reject (Chan 1993:

15–17; Mahbubani 1994). Even more confusingly, those who had recently announced the end of ideology now somewhat contradictorily maintain that late modernity might actually entertain either a clash between western, Islamic and Confucian 'civilizations' or alternatively support a 'Confucian'-style democracy (Fukuyama 1995a: 3–7; Huntington 1993a: 22). The debate is further obscured by the fact that in the United Kingdom and the United States those disillusioned by a decade of Thatcherite individualism and Reaganomics increasingly look eastward in their search for a model of socially responsible communitarian capitalism (Hutton 1995).

In an attempt to clarify what cross-cultural misunderstanding and political inadvertence obscures, this book addresses a series of related problems in the postwar development of Pacific Asia. How have the evolving political cultures of the HPAEs shaped political and constitutional development in contemporary South Korea, Taiwan, Hong Kong, Singapore, Indonesia, Malaysia and Thailand? How have these economies sustained growth since the 1950s, and to what extent can we refer to an Asian model of economic development? What implication does rapid postwar economic development have for democratization and civil society in Pacific Asia? And finally how did regional political and economic development relate to the character of the Cold War in Pacific Asia and what are the prospects for future development in the emerging new world order?

Chapter 1 begins with a brief exploration of the character of 'western' democracy and contrasts this with classical East Asian understandings of moral government. Having established the very different character of Pacific Asian understandings of rule and obligation, we then examine the way these high cultural understandings were modified in the light of a variety of colonial experiences and the ambivalent role they came to play in the military-backed or single-party dominant states that emerged in postwar Pacific Asia. An examination of the postwar political development of the HPAEs reveals certain commonalities of approach to the rule of law and constitutional practice and a continuing concern with order, hierarchy and balance. Hong Kong, in this context of regional political development is clearly anomalous.

Chapter 2 examines the extent to which the HPAEs, after 1950, followed like 'flying geese' a Japanese model of bureaucratically planned development. Tracing the changing relationship between business and government in both Taiwan and South Korea demonstrates the importance of technocratic planners in picking industrial winners. This experience is contrasted both with the economic development pursued by the city states of Singapore and Hong Kong and with the later foreign direct investment (FDI)-led growth of Indonesia, Malaysia and Thailand in Southeast Asia. This chapter also considers the overseas Chinese business community's bamboo network for generating development both in Southeast Asia and increasingly in Southern China. The chapter concludes by considering the extent to which trade and development in the Asia Pacific has become increasingly integrated together with the prospects for future Asia Pacific Economic Cooperation (APEC) in the light of growing American concern over restricted access to the domestic markets of the HPAEs.

Having established the curious mix of political culture and technocratic planning that has modernized the HPAEs over the past thirty years, chapter 3 considers the character of the new middle class in the booming urban centres of Pacific Asia: Jakarta, Bangkok, Kuala Lumpur, Singapore, Hong Kong, Taipei and Seoul. This new, urban class is the most obvious social product of successful and rapid development. Chapter 3 therefore analyses the character of this new class and its evolving relationship with the managerial technocracies that constitute the ruling elites of the HPAEs.

Finally, chapter 4 examines the changing international relations environment that has significantly impinged both upon the internal character of the HPAEs and their strategic economic development. Opposition to the threat of communist insurgency and the umbrella of security afforded by an alliance structure that linked the HPAEs economically and strategically to Washington critically affected both political development and export-led growth in Pacific Asia between 1950 and 1990. This chapter therefore examines the evolution of Pacific Asian security in the Cold War and the unresolved security issues that remain in Pacific Asia after the Cold War ended in Europe. It concludes with a somewhat sanguine analysis of the prospects for securing a balanced structure of trade and security in the Asia Pacific in view of mounting American concern over its burgeoning trade deficit with Pacific Asia, the regional problem posed by an increasingly irredentist China, and the absence of any coherent regional structure for dealing with issues of trade and security.

1

Political Culture and Political Development in Pacific Asia: The Evolution of the Developmental State

The passing of the Cold War has left in its aftermath a new academic industry devoted to democracy, civil society and democratization. The animating concern of much of this work is the prospect for democracy in an era of 'global interconnections' (Held 1993: 37). Applied to East Asia, much of the democratization literature either follows the modernization route, a Marxist 'bourgeois liberalization line' (Hewison et al. 1993; Potter 1993), or some version of the comparative historical methodology pioneered by Barrington Moore and developed by Schmitter and O'Donnell (Moore 1966; Skocpol 1973; O'Donnell et al. 1986). The preoccupation of these different methodological perspectives is the process of change and their relative indifference to the question 'why democracy?', or, more precisely, 'why the kind of democracy that comes with constitutional restraints on government, the rule of law and the protection of property rights that is often collapsed into the term "liberal" or "pluralist"?'

It is, in fact, important to unpack the distinction between 'liberal' and 'democratic' before we can clarify the nature of political or, more precisely, constitutional development in East and Southeast Asia. As David Beetham has indicated, 'the portmanteau construct liberal democracy' (Beetham 1993: 56) is paradoxical. The liberal project that has historically attempted to establish a rational basis for rule in the Anglo-American world provides not only the necessary foundation for, but also entails significant contractual restraints upon, a democratically legitimated constitutional order. As Ernest Gellner has argued, 'representative institutions which symbolize the equality of citizens' are clearly important, but what is essential to this order is 'the absence of either ideological or institutional monopoly' (Gellner 1994: 188). The political or constitutional understanding that has been collapsed into modern, liberal theories of democracy somewhat promiscuously mixes liberal values with a governmental practice, democracy, which, it is then asserted, is the only appropriate means of ruling a complex modern state (Fukuyama 1992, 1995a). In fact, as we shall see, liberal or constitutional democracy actually reveals one possible answer to the foundational question of traditional political thought: whether rule should be by good laws or good men. Consequently, before we explore the emerging Pacific Asian answer to the question of what legitimates government, we need to give some intitial attention both to the character of liberal democracy and to the contingent identity it makes possible.

The value concealed by the comparative political approach to democratization is that of freedom, and this freedom consists in what writers like Crick (1971), Arendt (1971), Oakeshott (1981) or Rorty (1989) would describe as an activity or practice of specifically designated actors or citizens in a particular and artificially created space or public realm. Hannah Arendt evinced that in the classical understanding of freedom, the virtue of citizens consisted in living together under conditions of isonomy (equal rules), or, more precisely, of choosing the rules that reason dictated virtuous citizens should follow. 'The polis was supposed to be an isonomy not a democracy' (Arendt 1971: 30). The understanding that free citizens should be governed not by other men but by the laws that they had themselves chosen through a process of deliberative persuasion was central to the evolution of a civic condition. Freedom therefore required a public or political space where free citizens could assemble and debate the condition of ruling and being ruled.

A political condition, then, is a constitutional or rule-governed order and its virtue consists in equal citizens actively participating in the arrangements through which they are governed. Extended in a representative democratic direction, in the course of the nineteenth century, democracy as a form of rule becomes procedural and communicatory, affording a spontaneous extended order of impersonal rules and administration (Hayek 1960: 160; Vanberg 1994: 77).

A particularly neglected feature of the structure of modern liberal democracies consists in their agreement on the procedural conditions for argumentative speech (Habermas 1976, 1987; Minogue 1987). Indeed, 'states having this character have traditionally been distinguished as free, or political, since they are characterised by self determination and the process of determination is by public talk' (Minogue 1987: 57). Such a communicatory arrangement as it developed in the political tradition of the West became 'a unique process of co-operation between fellow citizens in discovering the best thing to do, by way of competition in argument' (p. 61) Consequently, a free press is vital to the survival of a liberal democratic practice, supplying argumentative citizens with the material for making judgements about events.

Given the conditional nature of these rhetorical arrangements, these disenchanted liberals inhabit a world of plural values and are necessarilly tolerant (Berlin 1975; Rorty 1989). Such an arrangement further assumes a capacity to follow and revise self-chosen life projects. In the modern democratic condition this has led to the demand that we give 'people the freedom to develop their personality in their own way, however repugnant to ourselves and even to our moral sense' (Taylor 1992: 12).

The structure of constitutional rules that limit government intervention also establishes the condition of liberty to self-explore and self-enact (Buchanan 1975: ch. 1). Such a constitutional order facilitates not only the growth and development of an atomized 'modular man' (Gellner 1994: 129ff), but also a plural or civil society. As J.S. Mill described it, 'it is not by wearing down into uniformity all that is individual in themselves, but by cultivating it and calling it forth, within the limits imposed by the rights and interests of others, that human beings become a noble and beautiful object of contemplation' (Mill 1970: 192).

The private pursuit of freedom, choice and autonomy as if by an invisible hand also promotes political and economic progress. The individualism of the nineteenth and twentieth centuries thus not only facilitated progressive developments in social, educational and political arrangements, it also promoted wealth through trade. Consequently, liberals in the Anglo-American world have vigorously promoted the view that free trade and the market benefit all members of a liberal democracy. From this perspective, then, central to the liberal democratic project is the individual and his or her disenchanted pursuit of self-chosen projects. Such self-exploration requires a rule-governed arrangement that facilitates both toleration and self-projection and the articulation of diverse claims or interests. Such capacity for responsible self-exploration assumes an equal capacity on the part of others and it therefore requires a form of democracy.

However, the type of democratic practice such a language of political self-understanding facilitated was always somewhat ambivalent. Thus those who proposed a representative as opposed to a participatory form of democracy did so from mixed motives. On the one hand, as Dunn (1991) shows, it seemed to offer an efficient governmental means to the solution of the problems created by mass urbanization and industrialization in nineteenth-century England and the United States. However, those liberals who proposed such an arrangement remained deeply perturbed by the prospect of majority rule and its 'tyrannical' implications. As Mill worried, when the individual was lost in the crowd, public opinion ruled the world and 'the only power deserving the name was that of the masses' (Mill 1970: 195). In America the masses might be the 'whole white population, in England chiefly the middle class. But they are always a mass, that is to say collective mediocrity.' The suspicion of the masses that informed the late nineteenth-century writings of Arnold, de Tocqueville, Mill and Bagehot led them to press for representative government (Kahan 1992). This liberal fear enabled a subsequent generation of American capitalist democratic theorists to reduce democratic participation to elite competition (Schumpeter 1943: ch. xxii) or a polyarchic pluralism in which no single interest could permanently prevail (Dahl 1971).

From a very different perspective in the course of the twentieth century a number of European and American critics of western liberal democratic practice drew attention not only to the failings of an individualist ethic to facilitate the equal development of minorities within the modern *polis* (Kymlicka 1995: ch. 2), but also the dangerously self-regarding implications of liberal individualism. Thus, from a neo-Marxist perspective, Herbert Marcuse (1969) drew attention to the repressive tolerance of modern western democracy, whilst Christopher Lasch identified a self-indulgent 'culture of narcissism' (Lasch 1985: ch. 2), and Philip Rieff described modernity, or at least California, in terms of a hospital theatre in which the active citizen has degenerated into an invalid (Rieff 1987: ch. 8).

From an economic perspective, too, the role of the individualistic entrepreneur freely mobilizing capital to exploit new market opportunities has been the subject of increasing criticism. The market deregulation that formed a central tenet of Thatcherism and Reaganomics collapsed in inner-city decay, high levels of unemployment and economic dislocation. Consequently, the neoliberal economic programme has, it is claimed, weakened a sense of community and invisible handedly created a permanently ghettoized underclass (Etzioni 1994; Hutton 1995).

Thus the legacy of political or liberal constitutional democracy is a curious one. Centrally, its identity privileges the role of the 'ego secure' individual and his or her capacity to make rational choices between alternative life plans (Almond and Verba 1963; Lipset 1963). In order to facilitate personal and social progress, liberalism classically maintained the need for the self-chosen rule of law and, as a consequence, a capacity to articulate the need for particular rules in a contingent historical situation. In a modern mass condition representative institutions facilitate this democratic character. Yet, given the essentially political nature of its self-understanding, this project is necessarily ambivalent and value-plural. Some lament its decline into narcissistic irresponsibility whilst others celebrate its sceptical and clear-eyed disenchantment. The point remains, however, that it is a form of self-understanding that has grown out of the West's self-exploration and may or may not be transferable to equally modernized polities with an alternative cultural baggage and very different notions of the self's *mode d'assujetisement* (Foucault 1984: 356) to rule.

This ambivalent liberal democratic identity, then, introduces an ethical stake into the otherwise bland discussion of how or whether to instrumentalize democracy. Before we consider the process of political development in postwar Pacific Asia, it is necessary first to consider the traditional understandings of identity that have historically shaped political consciousness and have had profound implications for contemporary political practice in the region. It is to this ambivalent legacy that we next turn.

Classical Pacific Asian understandings of political identity

Significantly, the Aristotelian understanding of politics or constitutionalism emerged in opposition to what the Greeks and subsequently early modern theorists of the territorial state considered an Oriental or Asiatic mode of rule described pejoratively as both immoral and despotic. In the genealogy of western commentary upon the East from Aristotle to Marx and Mill in the nineteenth century and Wittfogel (1969) and Weber (1951) in the twentieth, East Asian rule has been considered tyrannical, decadent and corrupt (Springborg 1992). Such a characterization evolved in part in order to distinguish a virtuous rule of law from a corrupting rule of man.

However, some Athenians, most notably Socrates, saw the potential value in the rule of the good man instead of good laws. In this he stood outside what evolved into a western European rule of law tradition, but *within* the dominant Asian traditions of governance. For in East Asian political discourse the question of what is good government has been traditionally answered not with good law but good men. As Lee Kuan Yew, Singapore's Senior Minister, maintains, East Asians possess a different 'map up here in the mind' (*The Economist*, 29 June 1991).

Initially, the traditional eastern preoccupation with the rule of virtuous men and what that implied for an East Asian understanding of authority, obligation and moral identity emanated from a complex blending of and reflection upon Hindu, Buddhist, Islamic, Confucian and Neoconfucian ethical practice. It is not without significance, moreover, that the abstract formulation of what an East Asian practice of rule might entail in terms of procedures of self-enactment, self-disclosure and an ethical vocabulary occurred primarily in the course of the early modern period at the moment when Portuguese, Dutch, French and British merchant adventurers and missionaries began to establish a continuous engagement with East Asia (Reid 1993a, 1993b). It is in the context of this first 'global crisis' that Pacific Asians looked to their own historical resources and elaborated a basic grammar of self-understanding and self-disclosure together with a political theory and practice that contrasted dramatically with what the Qing Emperor Qianlong considered to be the activity of western barbarians (Peyrefitte 1993: 83). How, we shall next consider, did these traditions affect East and Southeast Asian understandings of rule, and, more pertinently, what elements in these traditions have survived to shape the modernizing political cultures of the Newly Industrialized Economies (NIEs) of contemporary East and Southeast Asia?

The legacy of political Confucianism in East Asia

The dominant political and economic orthodoxy, promulgated in academic and journalistic accounts of contemporary South Korea, Hong Kong, Taiwan and Singapore, uncritically assumes that the apparently shared Confucian or Neoconfucian cultures of these NIEs play a central role in generating both economic dynamism and social and political order. It is our intention here to examine this high cultural legacy, particularly those features that have been adapted to the needs of contemporary rule in East and Southeast Asia, and to assess their developmental implications. In this context it is important to establish that, like any political tradition, Confucianism is not without its ambiguities. Indeed, more than most traditions, Confucianism's aphoristic character has lent itself to interpretations that differ widely in their view of human nature, the role of education, the nature and character of authority and the character of popular obligation. Amongst contemporary interpreters it has been variously considered the basis for an Asian liberalism (de Bary 1981), irredeemably autocratic (Levenson 1965; Elvin 1986), an essentially religious doctrine (Fingarette 1972), an apolitical but benign moral and educational programme (Tu 1984; Cheng 1991), and sometimes 'opportunistically oriented to career goals' (Tu 1984: 133). As it evolved, 'Confucianism' came to connote 'the history of Chinese political thought', and in China and the Koreas 'was appropriated by the regime in both a narrow and a broad sense' (Cotton 1991: 120). What, then, is the content of this theory and what kind of political practice did it support in pre-colonial Pacific Asia?

Confucianism as a language of moral association is essentially conservative (Metzger 1977; Munro 1977). Its emblematic exponents stress the transmission of a wisdom located in the past, handed down and refined or adapted by subsequent hands. Both Confucius and subsequent Han, Sung, Ming and Qing Neoconfucian reformers shared an essentially conservative vision of a past golden age of virtue and attempted to apply this vision to reform the present.

The Confucian world view further assumed a universe linked through the operation of *dao* – the way. The *dao* that informs heaven, earth and man affords an ultimately mystical, and clearly problematic, composition of otherwise incompatible opposing forces: *yin* and *yang*; masculine and feminine; positive and negative. Moreover, to conform to *dao* is evidently the aim of both the superior man (*jinzi*) and of virtuous government in general. In order to guide this project, the Confucian further contends that such a perfectly ordered arrangement of virtuous rule and universal harmony had once existed in the golden age of Yao and Shun. Records handed down from that time memorialized a past utopia. Transmitted through Confucius' oracular understanding, this traditional wisdom offered the seductive possibility of its re-creation in the present.

Subsequent writers in the Neoconfucian tradition, notably Mencius and Zhu Xi, emphasized the importance of principle (*li*) to which men and institutions should ideally correspond. In fact, this principle offered a model to which the individual in his social relations and government in its management of the people should ideally conform. Consequently, Neoconfucians maintained that when the way is present in the state, uniformity and harmony naturally prevail.

In order to instrumentalize harmonious balance, Neoconfucians, following Zhu Xi (Chu and Lu 1967), paid attention both to the relationship between the inner realm of mind (*nei*) and the outer realm of society (*wai*) and to an education in appropriate codes of behaviour. For the Confucian, therefore, from Zhu Xi to Tu Wei-ming (1984), the central concern of the state, as of the enlightened individual, is didactic. Pedagogic tutelage established the way. Thus, the Confucian classic *The Great Learning* depicts a direct relationship between the character of the ruler and the quality of rule, because, 'their persons being cultivated, their families were regulated. Their families being regulated, their states were rightly governed' (Legge 1893: 131). Even in the late nineteenth century, Confucian critics of the Korean ruler, Taewongun's, autocratic attempt to modernize maintained that, 'if the king's mind is as clear as pure water, his desires will be purified and disappear', thus enabling heaven's principles to flow, government to be instrumentalized and 'the way . . . established without doubt' (Palliser 1991: 191).

From this tutelary perspective virtue could be inculcated, the people transformed and the success of the project measured. In fact, the Confucian state had three quantifiable functions: the increase of the population; the development of the economy, understood in agricultural not mercantile terms; and the promotion of education. Consequently a formula for virtuous rule could be deduced, 'the ruler should first concern himself with his own virtue. Possessing virtue he will win the people. Possessing the people he will win the realm. Possessing the realm he will command revenue. Possessing revenues he will have resources for all demands' (Legge 1893: 131).

It was the inculcation of virtue, rather than the rule of law, therefore, that transformed the moral and economic condition of the people. Guidance by virtue, however, required the government to maintain correct social relationships. Essentially, Confucianism posited five basic relationships: between Prince and Minister; father and son; husband and wife; older and younger brother; and friends. Properly ordered, they offered the corresponding moral possibilities of loyalty and respect, kindness and filial piety, mutual respect and separate duties, brotherly love and consideration, and truthfulness and trust. Moral exemplars like the Duke of Wei or Confucius offered the model and a virtuous elite of scholar bureaucrats (*jinzi* or *yangban* in Korea) monitored or rectified these relationships to ensure that name and reality coincided. Thus the ruler constantly examined the practice of the five relationships and scrupulously attended to both his own and his kingdom's cultivation in order to maintain true social harmony and political balance.

The corollary required that subjects learn the politically correct behaviour. Broadly, there existed four 'people': scholars, farmers, soldiers and merchants. Together with the 'five relationships' and the three 'bonds' or 'mainstays' between ruler and ruled, father and son, husband and wife, they expressed the totality of moral engagements.

This meticulous concern with relationship, in turn, reflects a characteristic East Asian self-understanding which vividly contrasts with European thinking on this subject (Needham 1978: 78). Harmony and balance was the Confucian goal. Therefore, egoistic, rationally self-interested, competitive individualism was anathematized. When each person followed precisely prescribed roles there existed no place for equal participation by equal citizens or constitutional limits on virtuous rule. In this understanding the self solidified not as an autonomous agent, but in a network of larger relations. Thus, as the Ming Neoconfucian near contemporary of Descartes and Hobbes, Wang Yang Ming, explained,

> in the mind of the sage, heaven, earth and the ten thousand things form one body . . . if one's task suited one's ability one spent all of one's life doing heavy work without regarding it as arduous . . . a single spirit flowed through everyone, a common purpose and feeling permeated everyone, and there was no distinction between other people and oneself, no gap between things and the self. (Metzger 1977: 81; see also Wang in Chan 1973: 667)

Freedom, from this perspective, does not involve active political participation, but a state of rest (*wu wei*). Significantly, Neoconfucians as well as Daoists and Buddhists conveyed this in powerful images of emptiness and quietude. Thus for Wang Yang Ming true freedom is balance where 'equilibrium is nothing but the principle of nature . . . one recognizes it when he has got rid of selfish human desires. It is like a bright mirror. It is entirely clear without a speck of dust attached to it' (Wang 1963: 52) – an image that contrasts strikingly with the western understanding of the self-interested self-owner of classical liberalism (Berlin 1975: xxxix).

Political virtue, therefore, manifested itself in the correct performance of duties, governed by a relational code that established hierarchy and harmony. As Joseph Needham observes, 'to invoke one's rights was looked on askance. . . . The great art was to give way on certain points and so accumulate an invisible fund of merit whereby one can later obtain advantages in other directions. . . . Only when something has happened and been examined can responsibility be assigned' (Needham 1978: 284).

Power thus could be acquired and ritualized. It accrued in symbolic performances where inferior subtly deferred to superior. Such power was both paternalistic and interestingly non-instrumental. For what really mattered in interpersonal conduct was *guanxi*, or connections, a relationship conducted in terms of face-saving and face-giving (Pye 1985: 293–5; 1988: ch. 2).

This East Asian social logic consequently failed to value either the articulation of an alternative viewpoint, or the need to consult interests, separate public and private or maintain inalienable rights. Balance hierarchically maintained denied the possibility of a doctrine of equal right or natural equality. For if one man exceeded his proper station, 'there will be disturbance throughout society'. Thus, when Duke Qing of Qi asked Confucius about government, Confucius replied, 'there is government when the prince is prince, and the minister is minister; when the father is father and the son is son' (Hsu 1935: 223).

Bureaucratic in method and paternalistic in form, power is not, however, unconstrained. The *tienzi* (Lord of Heaven) exercises Heaven's mandate in order both to rectify the people and promote their welfare. In order to achieve this, he cultivates both himself as a model for his people and a scholar bureaucracy committed to their maintenance.

Nevertheless, this view of rule by good men through correctly ordered relationship presented one outstanding difficulty. Unlike European dynastic rule, the mandate of Heaven did not reside in a particular lineage. As Mencius demonstrated, Yao, the founding Emperor of virtuous rule, had his mandate transferred not to his biological heir, but to the most qualified, Shun. More disturbingly, Heaven does not speak, 'but reveals itself through acts and deeds' (Mencius 1970: 143).

How, then, do you ensure the continuation of the virtuous condition after the death of the sage ruler? Neoconfucianism is surprisingly vague on the problem of succession. In practice, however, the dichotomy between the ideal and the reality of Ming or Qing rule led to a pragmatic or political Confucianism (Elman 1987; Hoston 1994: ch. 4) that increasingly resorted to punishment not only to rectify, but also to strengthen the ruler.

This pragmatic adaptation to political circumstances problematically elided into an amoral, legalizing centralism. In the actual theory and practice of the early modern Ming, Qing or the Korean Yi dynasty (1392–1905), there was a growing recourse to administrative law (*fa*) that derived from both Daoist and legalist criticism of Confucianism and a concern to order and classify the common people more rigorously. From the legalist viewpoint, 'the government itself . . . desires' the universal application of laws in order to 'safeguard its own power' and assumes that rule will be efficient if subjects know precisely what severe punishment non-observance entails (Duyvendak 1928: 81). In other words, administrative law, implemented by a Confucianized bureaucracy, did not limit government constitutionally, but rather enhanced its operational competence. In Yi dynasty Korea, the law and the judiciary in fact became one 'of the chief instruments of autocratic dominance' (Henderson 1968: 242). Administrative law in East Asia provided the precise model to which the subject conformed. As Han Fei Zi remarked, 'the defining of everybody's duties is the road that leads to orderly government, whilst the failure to define responsibilities accurately is the road that leads to disorder' (Han 1964: 115).

In order to monitor performance, the ruler supplemented administrative law with technique. This required the maintenance of an impersonal, governmental machine. The ruler established the machinery and then permitted it to run by itself, reposing in non-action, whilst above and below his ministers trembled and obeyed. 'From your place of darkness,' Han Fei Zi advised, 'take hold of the handles of government carefully and grip them tightly' (p. 17). The wise ruler, therefore, 'creates laws, but a foolish man is controlled by them; a man of talent reforms rites, but a worthless man is enslaved by them' (Duyvendak 1928: 98)

Between the Confucian ethical project for instrumentalizing virtue and the legalist desire for the strong state there appears no common ground. Yet not the least remarkable feature of East Asian political understanding is its capacity to accommodate opposites. Hence, from as early as the Han dynasty synthesis of legalistic and Confucian political thinking performed by Tung Chung-shu (Chan 1973: 271–8), a bureaucracy theoretically imbued with a Confucian ethical code, implemented a Daoist–legalist view of imperial power. Such a remarkable accommodation of antithetic understandings can only be explained by the syncretic character of both Confucian and Daoist understandings of *dao*, the Way, which ultimately reconciles all apparent opposition.

Moreover, both legalist and Confucian agreed upon the political need for constant rectification. Both required a strict correspondence between names and things. Moreover, Confucian political rationalism led to a cynicism in political practice that supported order at the expense of virtue, a practice that facilitated the legalist desire to perfect a bureaucratic machine. Pragmatically recognizing that the conventions of polite behaviour could never reach the common people, political Confucianism came to discriminate between the virtue of the self-cultivated superior man and the punishments appropriate for the ignorant masses.

This political Confucianism favoured an increasingly autocratic style of rule in the Ming and Qing dynasties. Certainly, by the Qing period (1644–1911) the Confucian bureaucracy seemed increasingly compromised by its need for imperial support. The autocratic Emperor in his remote forbidden city inhabited a realm beyond the reach of criticism, meanwhile the Confucian bureaucracy, instead of instrumentalizing the reign of virtue, paradoxically became its political target when that project failed. Somewhat differently, in Korea, the Confucian *yangban* bureaucracy remained in the ascendant, despite the Taewongun ruler's attempt in the 1860s to reform it. Nevertheless, despite local variations, by the late nineteenth century, political Confucianism offered a seductive vision of order, balance and harmony founded on the precise performance of roles measured, assessed and monitored by a virtuous bureaucracy. Externally set standards governing prosperity, peace and public welfare in turn assessed and legitimated this bureaucratic practice.

Before we consider what elements of this understanding survived in the modernized and modernizing states of East Asia, we shall discuss the alternative notions of rule and political identity in *Nanyang*, the lands to the South of China that sometimes paid tribute to the Emperor of all under heaven but, unlike Korea, Japan and Vietnam, never fell directly under the influence of Chinese political thought.

Political syncretism in Southeast Asia

The Southeast Asian cultures of Malaysia, Indonesia and Thailand were largely untroubled by the Confucian or legalist political traditions of East Asia. Here a different vocabulary of rule and obligation affected the evolution of political identity. Historically, Buddhist and Hindu conceptions of power created a view of rule in which divine authority was concentrated in the body, or more precisely the phallus, of the ruler. The kingdoms of what Coedes (1971) termed 'farther India' were profoundly influenced by Buddhist and Hindu ideas that considered temporal rule the reflection of a divine cosmology. The Sririjaya, Sailiendra, Funan, Majapahit, Ayudhya and Mataram empires of Southeast Asia were conceived, as Heine-Geldern observes, 'to be an image of the heavenly world of stars and gods' (Heine-Geldern 1956: 172).

The political–theocratic practice of the Siamese Ayudhya Empire (1569–1767) (precursor of the Bangkok-based Chakri dynasty [1782–] that after 1939 metamorphosed into Thailand) blended court brahmanism with a distinctive Theravada Buddhism (Wyatt 1984: chs 3 and 4; Ishii 1993: 187; Neher 1994: 27). The brahminically influenced Buddhist King, ruling in accordance with the ten kingly virtues outlined in the Sukhothai *Traiphuum Phra Ruang* of King Lithai (1346–74), was both a righteous, Buddha-like *mahacakkavattiraja* liberated from the three worlds of phenomenal existence (Jackson 1991: 196–9) and possessed the Hindu attributes of a God King, or *devaraja*. This amalgam produced a world-revolving, 'wheel-turning, universal monarch'.

Religious syncretism thus legitimated Siamese absolutism. Moreover, although a distinction existed in Buddhist thought between the priesthood (*sangha*) and the temporal order (*anachak*), it never occasioned the clash between spiritual and temporal values that marked the dynastic evolution of early modern Europe. In fact, through royal patronage, religion became a tool of the centralizing state (Reid 1993a: 90). The evolution of an interpretively malleable and state-regulated Buddhism ethically reinforced the hierarchical concerns of the early modern Siamese monarchy. In particular the concept of *karma*, or merit, reinforced a preoccupation with status by maintaining that spiritual enlightenment and wealth or power derived from 'merit . . . acquired in present or previous lives' (Girling 1981: 36). The monarch, moreover, constituted a repository of merit linking the kingdom to the cosmos and possessed 'both in his person and in his office a relationship to the invisible world by which his body and his actions were made sacred' (Wyatt 1989: 60). The additional belief that impermanence characterized the material world whilst enlightenment consisted in detachment from the wheel of *karma* further reinforced political passivity. Enhancement of Buddhist values came consequently to be a prerequisite both for Ayudhya and the successor Chakri dynasty rulers of Siam, and a defining feature of Siamese identity.

Monarchically promulgated law, notably during the reign of King Borommatrailokanat (1448–88), further established both administrative control over manpower resources and a more precise definition of status. These exhaustive laws graded every possible permutation of rank 'specifying everyone's relative position' (Wyatt 1984: 73), assigned to everyone 'a number of units of *sakdi na* [field power]' (p. 73) and apportioned punishment according to rank. The self thus came to be understood in terms of clearly defined social relations. The paramount concern of Ayudhyan rule, therefore, was 'to regulate natural human inequality for the sake of the proper functioning of the social order' (p. 73).

The evolution of a distinctively Thai culture that inculcates respect and the karmic understanding of merit and status derived from past perform-ance even in past lives vividly contrasts with the liberal ideal of autonomous self-realization and individual right. Indeed, the contemporary Thai term for 'right' (*sitthi*) continues to carry with it the traditional view of freedom and right 'as privileges of the ruler' (Thanet 1995: 3). From a Buddhist perspective true freedom represents an ascetic and inward release from material desire and considers the classical liberal view of freedom, as a self-interested individual pursuit, anathema (Berlin 1975: xxxxix; Thanet 1995: 3). Rather than individual freedom, Thai self-understanding emphasized the joys of social adaptability and dependence that endowed superiors with *metta*, a patronizing kindness facilitating *karuna*, the ability to lead others in constructive ways. Consequently, power was nurturing, affording the inferior *kamlungjie*, or the capacity to act. In gratitude, the inferior responds with *krengjie*, or awe. Those outside this 'connectual structure' (Jin 1995: 271) were considered dangerously anti-social. Indeed, to be free in an active sense, or *thuan*, was to be without patrons, an undesirable, raw, wild and untamed condition.

This monarcho–Buddhist attempt to abstract from traditional practice and local tradition an externally validated, textually authenticated, universal and widely promulgated authority further promoted bureaucratic admin-istration (Ishii 1993: 189; Reid 1993a: 16). Ayudhyan kings, nevertheless, failed to secure 'overarching loyalties to monarch and state that could tran-scend the personal ties around which cliques and factions formed' (Wyatt 1984: 97). Although the monarch possessed a theoretical omnipotence, subjects being mere 'dust beneath the royal feet', in practice everything depended upon the loyalty and competence of palace advisers and the mon-arch's personal capacity to control the periphery against an often aggressive Burma to the West, Vietnamese penetration from the East and separatist tendencies in the South and North.

Moreover, because *karma* legitimated the King, Ayudhya failed to estab-lish a rule of primogeniture. Consequently, 'kings lacked the power to name their own successors, and blood was a less effective claim to the throne than strength' (p. 107). Succession crises, consequently, typified Ayudhyan absolutism. Paradoxically, as the monarchy projected its power, it became increasingly unstable, for 'the crown was more worth fighting for than ever before' (p. 107). Consequently, every royal succession 'turned into a political crisis' (p. 107). The combination of an inadequate king, an evolving manpower crisis and bureaucratic deadlock followed by a Burmese invasion in 1765 led to the sacking of Ayudhya and the collapse of the Empire in 1767 (p. 137).

A similar disjunction between the absolute authority of the ruler and the uncertainty of transition affected the ruling arrangements surrounding

Ayudhya. Unlike the early modern rulers of Siam and Burma, the kings of Java found Hindu political theology more suitable to their cosmological requirements. They considered themselves incarnations of Siva and they participated in Siva's divine authority whilst the subject's obedience 'implied religious rapport or *bhakti*' (Wolters 1982: 11). The fourteenth-century *Nagarakatagama* thus depicted the Majapahit rulers as Sivaite incarnations and the king's *lingga* or phallus was worshipped at temple sites like Prambanan. This phallocratic power radiated from the ruler's capital like a mandala. In practice the mandala constituted an unstable and mutable geographical area without fixed boundaries (p. 17). In fact, it depended not upon territorial boundaries, but upon the network of loyalties mobilized by the ruler's prowess. Mandalas expanded and contracted. Exceptionally, when an exemplary 'man of prowess' ruled, the mandala might extend over considerable areas. Thus the Majapahit Mandala (1222–1447) comprised Java, much of Sumatra and other Indonesian islands. Indeed, the Majapahit poet Prapanca claimed that his ruler 'protected' most of mainland Southeast Asia (Coedes 1971: ch. xiv; Wolters 1982: 22–8).

The Javanese view of history further reinforced the oscillating mandala of authority. Traditionally, the Javanese, like the Chinese and Siamese, conceived history in cyclical terms. Javanese historical thinking depicted a cycle of ages moving from a golden age, *Jaman Mas*, through successively less happy epochs. Ultimately, the Javanese world view was, 'one of cosmological oscillation between periods of concentration of power and periods of its diffusion' (Anderson 1990: 34). Such an understanding of power, moreover, explains two notable features of Javanese political psychology: its underlying pessimism and its susceptibility to messianic appeal (p. 35).

It also explains the seminal importance attached in Southeast Asia to the man of prowess. The leadership of 'big men' 'would depend on their being attributed with an abnormal amount of soul stuff' which explained their performance (Wolters 1982: 6). The ability to absorb, concentrate and project power characterized the man of prowess. This also entailed 'the ability to concentrate opposites' (Anderson 1990: 28). Indeed the ruler was 'at once masculine and feminine, containing both elements within himself and holding them in a tense electric balance' (p. 29). The ability to contain opposites and absorb adversaries manifested itself in the ruler's *wahyu* (divine radiance). The public visage of the ruler 'glowed' and offered a visual display of an inner, creative and ultimately sexual potency. Such prowess further enabled the ruler syncretically to combine understandings drawn from Javanese, Islamic and subsequently western thought without contradiction.

Yet Javanese syncretism, like its Ayudhyan equivalent, offered little in the way of guidance when it came to the transference of power. Given the traditional view of divine authority, power resided in certain signs and the possession of certain magical regalia rather than in a royal blood. Thus 'the deification of the king, while raising him to an almost unbelievably exalted position', did not stabilize government (Heine-Geldern 1956: 175). Indeed, the theory of divine incarnation and even more so that of rebirth and of *karma*, offered a ready subterfuge for potential usurpers. The problem was further exacerbated by the uncertainty of the rules of succession: 'sometimes the King himself chose his successor. Sometimes the ministers appointed a prince as king' (p. 175). Consequently, 'the empires of Southeast Asia from the very beginning were torn by frequent rebellion, often resulting in the overthrow of kings or even dynasties' (p. 175).

Rule as a form of divine ritual had further ramifications for Southeast Asian moral and political identity. The emergence of men of prowess assumed relationships of dependency. The structure of traditional Malay/Indonesian society was uncompromisingly hierarchic. A fundamental cleavage existed between the peasantry and the *priyayi* elite (Smail 1989: 87). *Priyayi* status expressed itself in a refined language (*krama*) spoken by the Javanese elite that differed from the coarse dialect spoken by the lower orders. A proper command of *krama* was an outward and visible sign, along with a smooth appearance, of an inward spiritual accomplishment. A *priyayi* was *halus*, 'refined, able to control his emotions, attuned to God's will' (p. 87), whilst the peasantry were *kasar*, 'little more aware than animals' (p. 87).

A further feature of this concern for *halus* was a separation of the inner self, the *batin*, from the outer aspects of life. To order the inner life was a work of practice. Four principles animated *priyayi* etiquette: 'the proper form for the proper rank; indirection; dissimulation: and the avoidance of any act suggesting disorder or lack of self-control' (Geertz 1960: 243). Such control preserved the self and came to value pretence, or *etak-etak*, in interpersonal conduct. This socially approved form of 'proper lying' required little justification (p. 246). In terms of political etiquette, *etak-etak* was particularly 'valued as a way of concealing one's own wishes in deference to one's opposite' (p. 246).

Such practices had important implications for Javanese government. In an intensely hierarchical society, elaborately coded rituals of deference governed courtly and regional politics. Crowning this paternalistic hierarchy, the man of prowess exemplified the *priyayi* ideal. These *priyayi* ideals then came to inform political practice in an elaborate process of decision-making, or *mufakat*. Decisions required extensive consultation and deliberation (*musyawarah*) yet avoided contention through the practice of the *priyayi* virtues of deception and self-concealment. This Javanese self-understanding and the practice of dissimulation actually facilitated *gotong royong*, a procedure in which community mutual assistance and discussion led to harmony and consensus. Thus the traditional Malayo-Indonesian language of politics elaborated both an autocratic and hierarchical view of rule, but one constrained by practices of self-regulation that evolved through time. Central to this political practice is a dynamic syncretism that reconciles, through the mystical technique of the man of prowess, apparently contradictory ideas and policies. This syncretic understanding had important implications for the subsequent reception of Islam into the Malay world.

The accommodation of Islam in Southeast Asia

A remarkable feature of the Malay world of Southeast Asia from the fifteenth to the nineteenth century was its capacity to blend Islam with essentially Hindu and Buddhistic political traditions. This was partly a reflection of Islam's highly adaptive character and partly because Islam arrived in Southeast Asia not by conquest but through a developing pattern of Southeast Asian trade (Reid 1993a: ch. 3) The more Islamized sultanates of the Malay peninsula, Kedah, Kelantan, Terengganu and Malacca, demonstrated this process of accommodation. The Malaccan sultanate (1444–1641) inherited the older Sririjayan mandala that enveloped parts of Sumatra, the Malay peninsula and the Riau archipelago. Surviving accounts of the installation of Islamic rulers illustrate the facility with which Islam reinforced traditional, sacral and magical attributes of rule (Wolters 1982: 24–5). Thus 'a ruler's ascent to the throne was marked first by ritual lustration, signifying exaltation from the ranks of his kinsmen and the creation of a new and larger personality' (Smail 1989: 78). He was then equipped with the royal regalia (*kebesaran*) which both signified and held the supernatural qualities of kingship (Steinberg 1989: 78). Finally, a senior official of the court mosque uttered the Koranic text, 'Lo! we have set thee as a viceroy on the earth', to mark the ruler's position as defender and arbiter of the faith. Even in the late nineteenth century the staunchly Islamic, but syncretically aware, ruler of Kedah carefully guarded the royal regalia and musical instruments which held his supernatural power (Gullick 1991: 29).

In Java, Islam spread more problematically (Anderson 1990: 69). As the religion of traders it established a hold initially in *pasisir* urban, commercial communities on the Javanese and Sumatran coasts. It had, moreover, already been 'patrimonialized' sufficiently to fit the prevailing Javanese world view. Thus, rulers 'assumed Islamic titles, kept Islamic officials in their entourage, and added Islam to the panoply of their attributes' (p. 69). Indeed, by the early seventeenth century, the Mataram dynasty of Jogjakarta in its syncretic adaptation of Islam oscillated between Javanese and Islamic titles for rule (Smail 1989: 84). A further characteristic of this indigenous flexibility was the modification of Islamic *shariah* to customary *adat* law. Indeed, a salient factor in the Islamization of Southeast Asia was the fact that 'Muslim law' never enjoyed 'the same sanction in Malaya and Indonesia as in other Muslim countries' (Hall 1991: 234).

However, this reception of Islam raised a number of political difficulties. The more purely Islamized urban, trading communities gradually drew apart from the agrarian interior and introduced 'an abiding tension into Javanese culture' (Smail 1989: 84). This tension grew more acute in the nineteenth century when a reforming Islam questioned not only colonial rule, but also traditional, hierarchical and legal understandings. Islam also presented an internal management problem for the developing states of Siam/Thailand, whose southern boundary came to include substantial Islamic minorities, but whose official religion and in time national identity rejected the blandishments of the Prophet.

The metamorphoses of tradition in post-colonial political development

We have so far outlined traditional East and Southeast Asian political understandings that have implications for the emerging political cultures of Pacific Asia. What aspects of these understandings survive, therefore, and how have they mediated the transition to modernity in the East and Southeast Asian HPAEs?

The legacy is obviously a difficult one. Ultimately, traditional patterns of rule failed. Thus in East Asia, and particularly in Hong Kong, Taiwan and South Korea, the Confucian HPAEs we are concerned with, the traditional scholar elite's failure to adjust to the emergence of global capitalism in the late nineteenth century had catastrophic consequences. The Opium War and the demands of British merchants, like Jardine Matheson, for access to the impenetrable Chinese market had as early as the Treaty of Nanjing 1841 forced the Celestial Empire to concede the island of Hong Kong to British rule. In the case of Taiwan, the failure of the Confucian mandarinate to adjust to the challenges posed internally by the Taiping Rebellion (1864–5) and externally by mounting foreign pressure to open further the Chinese market led to the weakening of the Imperial Mandate and the formal cession of the island to Japan in 1895.

In Korea, the hermit kingdom's *yangban* bureaucracy similarly failed to come to grips with both the internal challenge of peasant rebellion by the *Tonghak* (1894–5) and the external challenge of late nineteenth-century colonial rivalry. This failure ultimately led to the collapse of the Yi dynasty and formal annexation by Japan in 1910. Ultimately, the colonial experiment

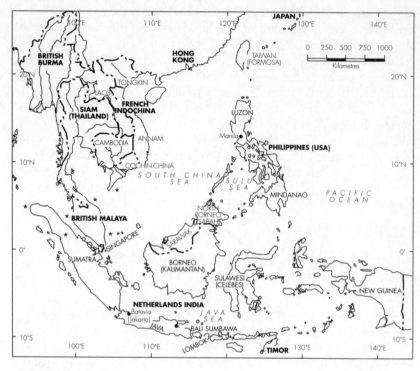

MAP 1.1 Colonial Southeast Asia before 1939
Source: Tarling 1992: 80 (slightly adapted)

left an ambivalent legacy of efficient, bureaucratic management of the people as an exploitable and mobilizable resource, together with an inchoate desire for national self-renewal characterized in China by the May 4th movement and in Korea by that of 1 March 1919.

Somewhat differently, but in keeping with its historical blending of seemingly incompatible understandings, Southeast Asia enjoyed a mixture of colonial and semi-colonial experiences. Indeed, the Chakri dynasty of Siam by a felicitous amalgam of accident and political design managed to escape colonial annexation altogether. The Malay world was less fortunate and succumbed to an arbitrary division into Dutch and British spheres of interest by the Treaty of London 1824 (see map 1.1). Nevertheless, as the European colonial regimes sought to accommodate customary arrangements, traditional elites continued to exercise a vestigial authority. The traditional rulers' facile adaptation to colonial rule negatively affected their standing with the Islamic revivalism and modernizing nationalism that attracted growing popular support in Southeast Asia at the beginning of the twentieth century.

This negative perception of both colonialism and tradition throughout Pacific Asia by the early decades of the twentieth century also facilitated the reception of Marxism-Leninism and the proliferation of a brand of East and Southeast Asian communism that threatened not only the European and American colonial powers, but also the indigenous elites they had successfully manipulated. Nationalist, communist and revived Islamic doctrines introduced a hitherto unknown mass activism into traditional political understanding and its already problematic accommodation with European power either directly, in the form of colonialism, or indirectly, through unfair treaties and trading concessions that graphically illustrated the technological, military and economic superiority of the West. Mass organization further introduced millenial ideas of liberation through collective action that clearly threatened not only colonial rule, but also traditional practices whether of a Neoconfucian or of a Hindu–Buddhist provenance. The new ideologies introduced into East and Southeast Asian politics a new identity and a democratic principle.

However, the reforming rulers of Siam and the revolutionary nationalists in Java, Malaya, China and Korea interpreted democracy in a non-liberal manner, constructing the people not as autonomous, diverse individuals, but as an active mass, organized to liberate both themselves and their inchoate nations from colonial oppression. In their attempt to create new Chinese, Thai and Indonesian identities appropriate to the demands of modernity, moreover, these doctrines were essentially progressive and viewed not only the yoke of imperialism but also the hierarchical aspects of traditional culture as repressive impediments to the creation of a liberated post-colonial utopia. In fact a significant theme of twentieth-century East Asian political discourse concerns the extent to which tradition impeded a 'positive creed' and 'active belief' in building new national communities (Sukarno 1966: 336–7) from otherwise problematic 'trays of loose sand' (Chiang 1943: 46).

The essentially ideological and forward-looking character of revolutionary nationalism and communism, therefore, powerfully undermined the possibility of traditional or conservative revivals in both East and Southeast Asia. Moreover, at the same time, the new Asian consciousness, whilst democratic and activist, was also powerfully anti-liberal, a doctrine that both communist and nationalist leaders associated with decadence and western colonial exploitation. Indeed, as in Malaysia, the new identity necessitated a new political vocabulary to cover concepts like 'state', 'nation' and 'politics' (Milner 1994: chs 2–3; Roff 1994: 247).

Moreover, after 1942 the collapse of European colonial rule in Southeast Asia and the brief imposition of a Japanese regional hegemony further strengthened regional nationalism. The Japan-led Greater East Asian Co-Prosperity Sphere (1942–5), although far more brutally exploitative than its

European predecessor, nevertheless undermined the belief in any natural caucasian superiority and right to rule.

Furthermore, the unexpected nuclear solution to the liberation of East and Southeast Asia in 1945 left in its fallout a political vacuum that the reimposition of European rule after 1945 dramatically failed to fill. In Pacific Asia, the aftermath of 1945 ultimately entailed a stand-off between two ideological versions of the new Asian identity built upon either a revolutionary nationalist or a Marxist-Leninist–Maoist base. The evolving polarization of these two identities during the Cold War, moreover, effectively dominated the conduct of Pacific Asian politics internally and externally until 1990, and continues to influence the debate on the possibility for democratization in East and Southeast Asia in the 1990s (Hoston 1994: ch. 10).

In the rest of this chapter we shall examine how traditional ideas received a conditional reinvention by newly established nationalist regimes in East and Southeast Asia, new regimes that nevertheless also wished to claim popular consent for their liberating rule and their modernization plans. It is to the paradoxical application of tradition to development in the East and Southeast Asian HPAES of South Korea, Taiwan, Singapore, Thailand, Malaysia and Indonesia that we next turn (see map 1.2).

Political identity and constitutional development in Thailand, Indonesia and Malaysia

Thailand   A combination of contingency and pragmatism enabled the kingdom of Siam to evade the European colonization that befell its neighbours. Remarkably, the sacking of Ayudhya by the Burmese in 1769 provided the necessary impetus for the successor Chakri dynasty to reconstruct the kingdom. Establishing the new capital at Bangkok along astrologically approved lines, King Rama I (1782–1809) and his successors revitalized tradition in a pragmatic attempt to evade European colonization. Thus Rama I promulgated a definitive legal code, the Three Seals Law, which served the state for the next century. Subsequently, Mongkut (Rama IV, 1851–68) critically adapted Buddhist theory and practice to the requirements of Thai unity. By the end of the century the royal reforms had tightened the rules governing succession and established an institutionalized Buddhism that effectively integrated the kingdom through the promulgation of a uniform practice (Wyatt 1984: 216). The reign of Chulalongkorn (Rama V, 1868–1910), by contrast, witnessed a determined pursuit of modernization. The King created modern ministries, and launched a massive programme of reorganization and reform comparable to that undertaken by his contemporaries in Meiji Japan. By 1910, Chulalongkorn had centralized political control. The

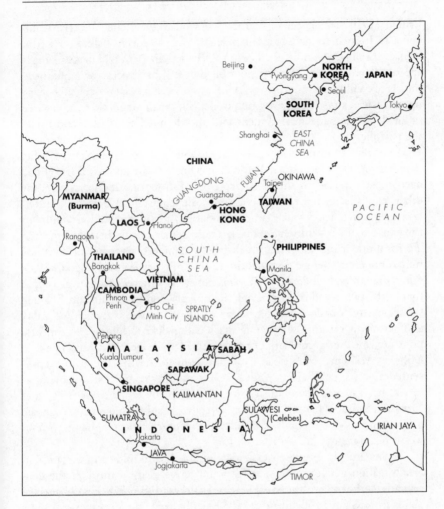

MAP 1.2 Pacific Asia

schools, the monkhood and the bureaucracy actively reinforced the notion that all Siamese were subjects of a single king and members of a distinct body politic. This nationhood was expressed in patrimonial terms. All the peoples of Siam were now clients of one patron, the King.

Yet for all its success in maintaining Siamese autonomy, the Chakri dynasty's achievement was an ambivalent one. Beginning with the Bowring Treaty (1855), which granted British extra-territoriality and abolished royal monopolies, and culminating in the 'unfair' treaties with France (1893) and

Britain (1910) which ceded Siamese-controlled Laos and Western Cambodia to French Indochina and suzerainty over the Malay states of Perlis, Kedah, Trengganu and Kelentan to the British, the Chakri kings anxiously appeased the western colonial powers. Indeed, the process of modernization represented an uneven response to western pressure, relied heavily upon western advice, and even followed a European model that emphasized rational bureaucratic management and the dominance of the centre over the periphery.

Moreover, exposure to western ideas engendered a problematic elite nationalism. On the one hand, the elite who, by education and travel had been most exposed to the West, resented European superiority. On the other, exposure to the scale of the European achievement both drew attention to the deficiencies of Siamese modernization and stimulated calls for the panacea of constitutional reform. These demands culminated in the first Third World coup in 1932, which briefly launched a period of constitutional monarchy before degenerating into a military dictatorship. In 1935, King Prajadhipak abdicated and the monarchy entered a political eclipse that lasted two decades. After 1938, the military, led by Lieutenant Colonel, subsequently Marshal, Phibun, came to dominate the National Assembly and set about creating a dynamic mass nationalism. Phibun, the son of a poor peasant, but a graduate of the increasingly influential Chulachamklao Military Academy established by Rama V to modernize the army, represented a new type of Asian leader. Like a number of his Asian contemporaries, he was impressed by the mass activism of Hitler's Germany and Mussolini's Italy. Closer to home, Japan's successful colonial expansion offered the modern Thai the seductive prospect of development without westernization.

To this end, Phibun's government sought to build not a new state, but a new nation actively mobilized to a collective destiny through the charismatic authority of 'the great leader' (Girling 1981: 59). The change of name from Siam to Thailand in 1939 symbolized this new consciousness (Wyatt 1984: 253; Samudavinija 1991: 69; Terwiel 1991: ch. 5). To legitimate Phibun's autocratic rule, the regime devoted increasing attention to the question of nation-building. In particular Phibun gave prominence to the regime's continuity with a historical Thailand, threatened not only by western colonial predation, but also by new anti-Thai forces, especially communism, increasingly associated in the public mind with the Chinese, the 'Jews' of the new Thailand (Wyatt 1984: 54; Samudavinija 1991: 73). This new mass nationalism selectively appealed to a Thai tradition of Buddhist merit, deference, loyalty and dependence. Yet it also required the negation of those otiose practices that hindered the emergence of the new Thai spirit. Consequently, a series of Cultural Mandates between 1939 and 1942 'aimed at uplifting the national spirit and moral code of the nation and instilling progressive tendencies and a newness in Thai life' (Wyatt 1984: 255). Predictably, this required saluting the flag, singing the anthem and eschewing imported goods; somewhat contradictorily the mandates also enjoined Thais to lead 'modern' lives and 'wear hats' (p. 255). This nationalist rationalism further promoted a uniform Thai language and an irridentism that demanded the return of traditional Thai lands lost to France and Britain by unequal nineteenth-century treaties.

Thai enthusiasm for a pan-Asian nationalism under nominal Japanese tutelage evaporated with the collapse of the Greater East Asian Co-Prosperity Sphere in 1945. Phibun resigned and the ruling elite pragmatically forestalled British and French demands for reparations by forging close relations with the United States (Kissinger 1994b: 452). External events, particularly the victory of Mao's communist forces in China and the deepening alliance with the United States, facilitated the rehabilitation of the military and the previously disgraced Phibun in 1948. The military subsequently came to play a key role in the bureaucratic polity that developed postwar Thailand.

However, political stability remained a problem and Thai political development has oscillated uneasily between a military-bureaucratic authoritarianism and an insecure semi-democracy. In fact, the military coup came to represent a distinctively Thai way of solving political deadlock and bureaucratic inertia that clearly resembles the succession struggles of the Ayudhya period. By 1992, Thailand had experienced seventeen coups in sixty years. The Thai army, like its counterpart in South Korea and Indonesia, assumes responsibility for the integrity of the nation, and this involves both the extirpation of 'foreign' communism, and the promotion of economic development. The periodic recourse to the coup illustrated the army's capacity to maintain strong, hierarchical and personal patron–client relationships while inculcating social cohesion. Along with the military went an increasingly omnicompetent bureaucracy that presided in the course of the 1950s and 1960s over a patrimonial and prebendal style of capitalist development.

This was most evidently the work of another strong leader, Marshal Sarit Thanarat, who succeeded Phibun after a bloodless coup in 1957 (Wyatt 1984: 274–5). In Sarit's understanding, constitutional democracy was inappropriate for a developing Thailand. Instead, he erected a nationalist ideology which syncretically blended traditional paternalism with development. Sarit systematically rehabilitated the monarchy as the symbolic focus of Thai loyalty. King Bhumipol (1946–) thus legitimated a military-bureaucratic government paternalistically devoted to developing the country in the interest of the common good. The mass promotion of traditional high cultural values of status and karmic determinism reinforced a political culture informed by dependence (Girling 1981: 154; Pye 1985: 109). Gentle paternalism was the Thai way. Indeed, Thanat Khoman, one of a new breed of scholar bureaucrats in Pacific Asia, maintained, 'if we look back at our national history, we can see that this country works better and prospers under an authority around which all elements of the nation can rally' (Girling 1981: 112; Wyatt 1984: 280).

This, notwithstanding economic recession and escalating communist insurgency in Northeast Thailand, prompted Sarit's military successors, Generals Thanom and Praphas, first to introduce a limited constitution in 1968 and then to stage a coup against it in 1971. Subsequent, student demonstrations in Bangkok in October 1973 evoked growing middle-class sympathy. When the King distanced himself from the coup group, Thanom and Praphas fled into exile.

The events of 1973 seemed to have inaugurated a new era of constitutional democracy. This, however, was not to be the case. The democratically elected legislatures of 1974–6 proved both indecisive and unwieldy. In particular the *Nawaphon* (New Force) movement mobilized support for a revived Thai nationalism. This culminated in the brutal suppression of student demonstrations at Thammasat University, followed by a military coup in 1976 that sought to resurrect the Thai nation around the slogan first coined by Rama VI of 'nation, religion, and king'.

The brief experiment with constitutionalism and its turbulent aftermath gave way once more to the autocratic principle, this time in the form of General Prem Tinsulanonda (1980–8), who emerged as the leader of a cohesive military political group with royal backing in the course of the late 1970s. A new constitution that weighted power in favour of a nominated, and military-dominated, senate in a bicameral legislature afforded Prem's regime a veneer of respectability. Under Prem's tutelage, elections held in August 1988 returned the first civilian Prime Minister in twelve years. Chatichai Choonhavan's Chart Thai (Thai Nation) party led a five-party, nationalist coalition closely connected to the military. Yet despite the fact that Chatichai's government constituted no threat to the bureaucracy and presided over an unprecedented economic boom that promised to transform former Indochinese 'battlefields into a marketplace' (Tan 1992: 292), it nevertheless provoked another military coup in February 1991. The openly corrupt dealings between 'unusually rich' politicians and the Sino-Thai business conglomerates ostensibly legitimated Thailand's seventeenth coup since 1932. The new Junta, led by Army Commander Suchinda Kraprayoon, and composed of classmates from the elite Chulachamklao Military Academy, formed a National Peace Keeping Council (NPKC) and subsequently appointed Anand Panyarachun of the Saha Union conglomerate as caretaker Prime Minister in March 1991.

Anand's interim technocratic administration (1991–2) contrasted dramatically with the overt corruption of the Chatichai period and the covert corruption of the bureaucratic polity, providing Thailand with its cleanest and most efficient government of the postwar period (*The Nation*, 25 October 1991). However, the continuing need to legitimate the intervention of the NPKC required both a new constitution and new elections held in March 1992. These resulted in the leader of the pro-military Samakkhi Tham party, Narong Wongwan, forming a coalition government. Revelations that Narong was on a US Drug Enforcement Agency blacklist and a corrupt provincial 'godfather', or *jao pho*, undermined the credibility both of the new government and of its military backers. General Suchinda's subsequent decision to replace him and govern himself as an unelected Prime Minster prompted mass demonstrations against arbitrary rule. The army brutally suppressed the demonstrations in Bangkok on 12 May 1992. Once more, the King intervened, and at his instigation Suchinda retired from politics and the technocrat Anand returned to lead a caretaker government before new elections were held in September 1993 under a revised constitution that required the Prime Minster to be an elected member of government.

The September 1993 elections resulted in a new coalition consisting of five parties, which, like the Palang Dharma Party (PDP) and the Democrats, had most vigorously opposed military rule. However, acrimonious clashes between the coalition partners quickly undermined Chuan Leekpai's government of pro-democracy 'angels'. Consequently, the constitution, in which veto power continued to reside in an unelected senate of 270 mainly military members, received only cosmetic adjustments. Eventually, the coalition disintegrated over a land scandal in Phuket and a general election held in June 1995 saw a new coalition of seven parties, dominated this time by Banharn Silpa-archa's Chart Thai party. Chart Thai had earned the appellation 'devil' in 1993 because of its close links both with the military and with provincial *jao pho*. Indeed, Banharn himself was largely responsible for the 'money politics' that characterized the election campaign, especially in the provinces, where the average vote cost $30. The Chart Thai party spent $1 billion on the election. Equally surprising was the coalitional behaviour of the smaller parties that joined Banharn's government. Whilst the Democrats now constituted the main opposition, the formerly angelic PDP joined Banharn's government on pragmatic grounds until rumours of a bank scandal in August 1996 persuaded its technocratic leader, Thaksin Shinawatra, to abandon the coalition. In fact, the unhappy coalition lasted only thirteen months before allegations of mismanagement and corruption and a vote of no confidence led to Banharn's resignation and the dissolution of parliament in October 1996.

These often bewildering shifts from autocracy to quasi-democracy reflect the historical difficulty that Thailand has encountered in institutionalizing political change. It also demonstrates the enduring difficulty in accommodating an attenuated version of traditional political practice to western understandings of democratic accountability. Thus, although a tradition of autocracy and deference facilitated the evolution of a bureaucratic polity in the 1960s, by the 1980s it was evident that the military and political bureaucracy had become both too corrupt and too faction-ridden to command popular approbation. Meanwhile, the postwar period has also witnessed thirteen constitutions that have so far failed to reconcile democratic form to military-bureaucratic substance primarily because of the ineffectual coalitional character of Thai party politics and its susceptibility to corruption and 'money politics' (*The Nation*, 29 November 1995).

Seventeen coups and thirteen and a half constitutions since 1932 indicate, then, the continuing fragility of Thai institutions. In theory, *Ratthammanun* (the Thai for constitution) involves *thamma* (*karma*) or ethical value, but in practice successive constitutions, rather than framing a set of general rules, have merely justified the most recent coup (Neher 1994: 28). The inability of political parties to establish constitutional guidelines further reflects the difficulty in establishing contractual law in a society historically permeated by acute sensitivity towards hierarchical differentiation. Interviewed in 1994, former Democrat Prime Minister Chuan Leekpai observed, 'the law is clearly used in a discriminating manner' (*Far Eastern Economic Review*, 1 December 1994).

Significantly, the enduring attraction of Buddhist syncretism and its insistence on merit and deference reinforced by a traditional monarchy largely reinvented after 1958 remain the enduring values underpinning Thailand's flexible but fragile political culture. Indeed, the monarch's personal intervention on a number of occasions since 1958, notably in 1973 and 1992, has enabled Thailand to negotiate leadership transition without undue bloodshed. Whether these traditional understandings will sustain Thailand after the King's death remains, however, to be seen.

Pancasila *democracy and Indonesia's New Order*   It was through a burgeoning resistance to colonial rule in the early twentieth century, and the desire to define an independent identity, that a revivalist Islam achieved popular support and sought to reform traditional Islamic practice. Out of this concern emerged the first organized mass movements in Indonesia. Primarily concerned with self-renewal, movements like *Sarekat Islam* for the first time mobilized the peasants and urban workers on a mass basis. This new mass organization also introduced an increasingly problematic cleavage in Southeast Asia between the purer Islamic vision of the *santri* and the syncretic, traditional practices of the *abangan*.

When Sarekat Islam collapsed in 1923 it provided a powerful stimulus not only to the emergence of an Indonesian communist party (*Partai Kommunis Indonesia* – PKI), but also for an indigenous nationalist movement, Sukarno's *Partai Nasional Indonesia* (PNI) (Smail 1989: 307; Lapidus 1991: 67). It was here that the notion of an *Indonesia Raya* emerged as an arrangement that potentially embraced the whole Malay world, or, as the Youth Congress of 1928 put it, 'one nation – Indonesia, one people – Indonesian and one language – Indonesian'. The concept 'Indonesia' in fact represented both a 'leap of the imagination' (Smail 1989: 308) and a work of language. Indeed, the crucial vehicle for twentieth-century nationalism 'was the transmutation of the Malay of the islands into the national language' (p. 309). The attempt to forge a new national identity in the 1920s and 1930s clearly involved both mass democratic participation and a radical break with a hierarchical self-understanding linguistically preserved in high Javanese (Wolters 1982: 111; Koentjaraningrat 1990: 67–76).

The armed struggle to remove the Dutch colonial power from the Indonesian archipelago between 1945 and 1949 and the role played by the military (*Angkatan Bersenjata Republik Indonesia* – ABRI) in securing independence also had important implications for the evolving political identity of modern Indonesia (Suryadinata 1989). Indeed, as a consequence of the democratic second Independence constitution of 1950 the four streams, or *aliran*, that reflected different aspects of national consciousness, notably Islamic, nationalist, communist and ABRI, became increasingly manifest in Indonesian political life. Moreover, because there existed no Indonesian tradition of political pluralism, growing conflict between the different *aliran* generated political insecurity.

The multipartism and political contestation that emerged between 1950 and 1957 illustrated the lack of a shared understanding and alienated the army by excluding it from government (Suryadinata 1990: 23). The instability of party politics evident in national elections held in 1955 led both ABRI and founding father, first President, Sukarno to reassess the value of constitutional democratic practice. In 1957 the President abrogated the 1950 constitution and restored the more conservative and presidential 1945 constitution in order to both balance the competing *aliran* and restore strong leadership and national unity.

The 1945 constitution provided for a quinquennial parliament and a People's Consultative Assembly (*Majelis Permusyawaratan Rakyat* – MPR), both composed of directly elected and military-nominated members. Since 1966 the MPR has met every five years to elect the President. To further the cause of unity Sukarno promoted *pancasila*, an ideology 'dug up from the soil of our motherland' (Legge 1972: 318). *Pancasila* requires all Indonesians to subscribe to principles of unity, humanity, belief in an all-embracing God, social justice and a democracy henceforth informed by traditional understandings of guidance, cooperation and consultation (Omar 1993: 43).

With the obliteration of the communist PKI *aliran* in the coup and counter-coup of 1965, and the depoliticization of Islam in the course of the 1970s, Indonesian political development assumed a corporatist character (Anderson and McVey 1971; Suryadinata 1990: 18–20). Moreover, in the aftermath of the bloody transition from Sukarno to General Suharto (1965–6), the army came to occupy an increasingly prominent political role. In the New Order (1966–) the army assumed a dual responsibility (*dwifungsi*) both for defence and for national integrity (Suryadinata 1990: 26), whilst President Suharto assumed the role of paternal guardian of the republic. Under the slogan 'unity through diversity', the New Order regime developed the state ideology *pancasila* to manage both government, bureaucracy and opposition. Thus under the New Order interpretation of the 1945 constitution the MPR elects the President every five years by unanimous agreement upon a single candidate. The fact that Suharto and ABRI take responsibility for choosing half the 1000 MPR delegates clearly facilitates unanimity (Schwarz 1994: 271). Under this constitution, Suharto embarked upon his sixth term as President in 1991.

Moreover, to promote New Order consensus in parliament, ABRI General Ali Moertopo established a military-bureaucratic party consisting of linked functional groups (*Golongan Karya, Golkar*). With the financial and political support of ABRI and the bureaucracy, of which it is an extension, *Golkar* has consistently secured large majorities in all parliamentary elections held since 1971. To ensure that the opposition functions according to *pancasila* principles, the government further required a multiplicity of competing parties to amalgamate into two groups promoting non-ideological programmes (Suryadinata 1990: 18). Consequently, after 1973, electoral opposition assumed either of the state-licensed forms represented by the Islamic United Development Party (*Partai Persatuan Pembangunan* – PPP) or the smaller Indonesian Democrat Party (*Partai Demkrasi Indonesia* – PDI). It became particularly evident in the course of New Order rule, moreover, that hierarchical practices, abandoned in the course of the independence struggle and the brief era of multipartism, were assuming increasing importance. Reinvented tradition provided stability and offered a prophylactic against the ever-present internal and external threat posed by the anathematized communists. Even with the evident dissipation of any putative communist threat by the early 1990s, the New Order has been notably reluctant to modify its interpretation of the constitution. Consequently, when the PDI had the temerity to elect a new leader, Megawati Sukarnoputri, the daughter of the founding father, in 1993 without first seeking approval, the government eventually intervened. At a PDI party congress orchestrated by the government, held in Surabaya in June 1996, Megawati was ousted and replaced by the more pliable figure of Suryadi. The subsequent exclusion of Megawati and her supporters from the list of PDI candidates for elections to the MPR in 1997, together with the arrest of the activist student leader Budiman Sujatmiko for alleged subversion of *pancasila* principles, illustrates the New Order's continuing concern with political stability (*The Economist*, 21 September 1996).

The fact, moreover, that Suharto magically reconciled the differences that threatened to undermine the infant Indonesian Republic in 1966 made him peculiarly placed to exploit further traditional understandings of rule. In Lucian Pye's view, Suharto is a 'Javanese mystic' who has 'come much closer to embodying the essence of Javanese culture' (Pye 1985: 115). Suharto's tutelage has particularly fostered the revival of paternalistic dependency. Suharto himself has been officially described since 1983 as '*bapak pembangunan* – the father of development' (Vatikiotis 1993: 2). Patrimonialism ramifies the bureaucracy and draws upon the symbolism valued in the wider culture. Significantly, Suharto projects himself as Semar, 'one of the most revered figures in the Javanese *wayang* [shadow play]' (Bresnan 1993: 49). These reinvented traditions affect both intra-bureaucratic communication and that between rulers and people, encoding political performance in an elaborate shadow play. The political culture, therefore, places increasing emphasis upon balance, consensus building and cooperation. The New Order elite view blunt language and clear expression of views pejoratively, and feudalistic political terms have increasingly replaced democratic equivalents, providing a vocabulary that fits with the 'emphasis on politeness in political and formal relationships' (Vatikiotis 1993: 112).

This revival of traditional practices has clearly facilitated a corporate managerialism that has both provided political stability and, since the 1980s, achieved impressive economic growth. This has led some commentators (Chalmers 1991) to assume the emergence of an incipient pressure to democratize. Yet what remains the problem for the New Order, just as it was for the old one, as well as for the pre-modern rulers of Mataram and Majapahit, is who succeeds the man of prowess when his *wahyu* begins to wane. Our analysis of future Indonesian political development in chapter 3 addresses the relationship between economic growth, the succession issue and democratization.

The evolution of one-party rule in Malaysia   Malaysia enjoyed a much briefer colonial experience: the British federated the peninsular Malay states only in 1895 and maintained the form if not the substance of traditional Sultanic rule. This, together with the relatively untroubled negotiation of independence for the Federated Malay States in 1958, has facilitated the application of attenuated traditional understandings to political conduct in contemporary Malaysia. Here again the experience of instability, notably communist insurgency during the Malayan Emergency (1948–58) and communalist, inter-racial riots in 1969, undermined an early intimation of a post-independence, multiparty, political democracy. Instead the political development of modern Malaysia has favoured the political marginalization of the large Chinese and smaller Indian minority races in Malaysia and the imposition of an affirmative action, *bumiputera* (sons of the soil) policy after 1971 designed to facilitate greater Malay participation in social and economic life. In this context, the constitution of 1957 has been steadily modified to suit the needs of the leadership of the United Malays National Organization (UMNO), which has dominated government since Independence in the Malay interest. UMNO came into being in 1946 as the vehicle for a new democratic Malay national consciousness (Omar 1993: ch. 2; Roff 1994: 246–7) and successfully campaigned to defeat a British proposal for a centralized Malayan Union in 1947. UMNO contested such a union on the grounds that it would vest too much power in the urban centres where large Chinese and Indian immigrant populations predominated.

The complicated machinery of checks and balances that emerged in the federal constitution of 1957 reflected the wishes of both the indigenous Malays and their traditional rulers in the peninsula states of Johor, Kedah, Kelantan, Negeri Sembilan, Perak, Perlis, Pahang, Selangor and Terengganu to negate the possibility of both political centralization and marginalization in the new multi-ethnic state. Consequently, the constitution provided for a monarchy of king in parliament that bore an obvious resemblance to the Westminster model. The nine hereditary Sultans of the Malay peninsula chose one of their number in order of preference to be monarch or *Yang Di-Pertuan Agong*, for five years. Meanwhile parliament consisted of two houses: a lower house of representatives (*Dewan Rakyat*) elected by universal suffrage; and an upper house (*Dewan Negara*) representing state assemblies and special interests. Additionally each peninsular state and, when they joined the Malaysian Federation in 1963, Sabah and Sarawak, elected their own assemblies for state government and retained either a Sultan or governor as state executive.

However, one-party dominance since 1963 has significantly eroded a constitution designed to facilitate multipartism, the rule of law and federalism. In the course of the 1960s, UMNO ruled in an unequal multi-ethnic alliance with the Malay Chinese Association (MCA) and Malayan Indian Association (MIA) as junior partners. At the same time, the largely Chinese Democratic Action Party (DAP) and Malay Islamic Party (*Parti Agama Se-Malaysia* – PAS) constituted an increasingly vibrant opposition at both national and state elections. The erosion of the UMNO vote and the loss of control of state assemblies in Penang, Perak and Terengganu in the 1969 elections, together with the perceived economic disparity between ethnic Malays and urban Chinese, sparked intercommunal riots in May 1969. The May 13th riots caused both the resignation of the aristocratic and liberal founding father of Malaysia, Tunku Abdul Rahman, and the imposition of a state of emergency. Subsequently, UMNO altered the constitution, 'removing issues considered sensitive from public discourse' (Mahmood 1990: 34) and gerrymandering electoral districts in favour of ethnic Malay constituencies. Thus whilst in 1969, the UMNO-led alliance won 48.6 per cent of the vote and 63.5 per cent of parliamentary seats, by 1978 UMNO, together with its ethnic and regional affiliates in its new National Front (*Barisan Nasional* – BN) coalition, won 57.1 per cent of the vote but received 82.5 per cent of parliamentary seats (Mahmood 1990: 32). Events since 1969 evince that while an UMNO elite practises political accommodation, they are also willing to alter the constitution and manipulate electoral boundaries to preserve their authority (Mauzy 1983: 145).

In order to extend oligarchical control over central and local government and, through its post-1969 New Economic Policy (NEP), the economy, UMNO has had increasing ideological recourse to traditional values selectively chosen to reinforce its political dominance. This tendency has been particularly apparent during Mahathir Mohamad's tenure as Prime Minister and Party President (1981–). This period has been characterized by strident attacks on western values and an increasing emphasis on paternalistic guidance at the expense of political pluralism – a guidance facilitated by press controls and the periodic recourse to the draconic Internal Security Act initially introduced during the Malayan Emergency but periodically invoked since then to forestall opposition. In 1987, security forces launched operation *lalang*, arresting 109 people, including the leader of the DAP, Lim Kit Siang, and members of PAS. In 1991, the charismatic leader of the indigenous Kadazhan *Parti Bersatu Sabah* (PBS), Joseph Pairin Kitingan, was detained for two years and subsequently charged with corruption on his release in December 1993.

The combination of the erosion of constitutional checks and the recourse to emergency legislation has facilitated an official reassertion of traditional ideas in order to create a balanced and harmonious, Malay-dominated Malaysia. However, Mahathir's desire to create an economically dynamic Malaysia through an untraditional mobilization of the Malay masses has significantly modified recourse to tradition. As his 1970 excursion into political philosophy, *The Malay Dilemma*, indicates, Mahathir's 'ultra'-nationalism requires strong leadership and an UMNO-dominated, centralized state. Eugenic ideas preoccupy the medically trained doctor. His diagnosis maintains that environmental and hereditary factors have bred in the Malays a feckless '*tidapathy*'.

This 'lassitude' made possible exploitation first by the British and, since Independence, by the 'unscrupulous' Chinese, who constitute a problematically large proportion of the population (Mahatir 1989: ch. 3; 1993a: ch. 7). To cure Malay weakness, therefore, Mahathir prescribed more rigorous government intervention. After 1981, he intensified the New Economic Policy begun in 1971 that afforded Malay businessmen special treatment and reserved governmental and educational places for indigenous, or *bumiputera*, Malays. This Malaysian version of 'affirmative action' has formed the cornerstone of Mahathir's political thought and received its apotheosis in the thirty-year plan, Vision 2020, to create a fully modernized Malaysia (Mahatir 1993b).

To realize utopia, however, demands the severing of some traditional attachments, both customary and constitutional, that hinder Malay progress whilst reinforcing those that facilitate a centralized authority. In 1983, Mahathir succeeded in removing the *Yang Di-Pertuan Agong*'s power of veto over parliamentary bills and in 1986 he succeeded in curtailing the constitutional independence of the judiciary (Metzger 1994: ch. 8). At the same time, in order to forge a progressive, but Malaysian, identity, the UMNO leadership selectively asserted its historical Islamic roots in the Malacca sultanate. Yet although Islam is the official religion, its practice is not permitted to inhibit development. As in Indonesia, the Malaysian bureaucratic elite has great difficulty in syncretizing the Islamic fundamentalist interest represented by PAS in Kelentan with its developmental goals. Evident contradictions in Mahathir's vision are, however, effectively suppressed by a conventional mixture of intimidation and corruption. The muzzling of critical debate in parliament and the strict licensing of the press have effectively curtailed criticism of Mahathir's increasingly autocratic rule. By the early 1990s 'parliament, the judiciary, and the royalty have been forced to surrender their powers gradually to the UMNO executive . . . to which everything else in the country is subservient' (Chandra Muzaffar, in *Far Eastern Economic Review*, 11 February 1993: 28).

In modern Malaysia, then, the UMNO elite selectively deploys tradition to promote centralization and economic development. The effect of blending tradition with development has created an increasingly technocratized and urbanized Malaysia. Malay *kampungs* (villages) preserve vestiges of customary practice and the government encourages a moderate Islam, yet continually revises tradition in order to create a flexible identity paradoxically equipped to mobilize the people towards a future golden age.

Clearly these traditional practices and the way they have been modified for purposes of economic development and social control have important implications for political democracy in Malay-speaking Southeast Asia. As all debate in modernized Southeast Asia occurs within a context of consensus seeking, *musyawarah*, where protagonists seek to maintain face, nothing can be said that might agitate others. The result is a contemporary practice informed by the Javanese art of indirectness, calculated to ensure that one neither provokes another nor reveals one's own feelings.

An elite penchant for ideological certainty further limits the possibility of communicatory politics. Thus the most powerful ideological currents in Indonesia and Malaysia until the 1980s, communism, nationalism and Islam (both reformist and orthodox), all represent modes of explaining an increasingly complex and confusing world. The adherents of each of these *aliran* believe they have acquired a comprehensive picture of the universe and its workings, a belief reinforced by their hermetic quality (Anderson 1990: 57). Adherents sharply distinguish themselves from non-adherents, a social practice that lends itself to bureaucratic management oiled by a patrimonial 'money politics'.

Consequently a traditional understanding of power and its vehicle, the man of prowess, continues to reconcile apparent contradictions in modernized Southeast Asia. Things have a natural tendency to fall apart and it is the particular genius of the ruler, Suharto or Mahathir, or, less successfully in Thailand, Sarit or Prem, to hold them together. The problem that the traditional rule of good men never resolved, however, was how to ensure continuity. As we shall see in chapter 3, the cleavages emerging in Indonesia between middle-class technocrats and ABRI functionaries or in Malaysia between a thrusting urban 'vision team' and an ageing leader do not necessarily intimate increased political communication or 'democratization', but the traditional problem of managing transition as the respective *wahyus* of Mahathir and Suharto begins to wane.

The reinvention of tradition: the Confucianized political cultures of contemporary South Korea, Taiwan and Singapore

Political Confucianism in nineteenth- and early twentieth-century China, Korea and Vietnam failed the challenge posed by 'western' technology and the need to modernize (Levenson 1965: 3; Hoston 1994: ch. 4). Despite a brief, late nineteenth-century attempt at self-strengthening, the Confucianized cultures of East Asia, with the exception of Japan, demonstrated no creative conservative response to the challenge posed by western modernity or Marxism-Leninism–Maoism (Wright 1957; Elvin 1986). This failure left China spiritually and intellectually resourceless. After 1911, the Celestial Empire collapsed under the weight of unfair treaties with European powers and the United States. China subsequently disintegrated into warlordism, and became prey to Japanese imperialism after 1934. Only after the internecine conflict between Chiang Kai-shek's Nationalist *Guomindang* (Kuomintang – KMT) and Mao's Chinese communist forces was resolved in Mao's favour in 1949 did some semblance of order return to the People's Republic of China (PRC). Analogously, in Korea the failure of late nineteenth-century Confucian rule to meet the Japanese challenge spawned, it is claimed, an inchoate nationalism that drew increasing inspiration from western sources, most significantly the Christian churches (Henderson 1968: 80–6; Cumings 1989, vol. 1: ch. 1) that grew in popularity in the course of the twentieth century.

In the course of the last decade, however, a number of Asian scholars have come to reject the Confucian decay thesis. They argue that the successful modernization of a number of East Asian economies in the last thirty years owes a significant debt to the survival of Neoconfucian values (Tu 1989; Cheng 1991; Lodge 1991). Students of the East Asian economic miracle claim that the Confucian ethical practice of relationship, balance and harmony facilitated 'a consensual – as opposed to a contractual – relationship between managers and managed'. This communitarian ideology, moreover, engenders both competitiveness and order (Vogel and Lodge 1987; Vogel 1991: ch. 5).

This reversal of Max Weber's thesis (1951) that Confucianism prevented East Asia developing the requisite ethic to modernize has had important implications for the explanation of political and economic development in capitalist East Asia with Chinese roots, notably in South Korea, Taiwan, Singapore and, to a lesser degree, Hong Kong (Redding 1993: chs 1–3). Contemporary Neoconfucian scholars like Tu Wei-ming (1989) and Chung-ying Cheng (1991), bathing in the unaccustomed luxury of the new compatibility between Confucianism and entrepreneurial flair, have tried to draw a distinction between a failed Confucian political project and its still flourishing ethical legacy. In this view, Neoconfucian ethics, far from failing the challenge of modernity, inform the stability, rise in educational standards and economic vitality of contemporary East Asia – an argument to some extent corroborated in the 'lessons' drawn from the East Asian experience by the World Bank (Leipziger and Thomas 1993: 24–8; see also chapter 2).

The only point of agreement between these rival accounts of the role of Confucian values in the developmental process is that ethical Confucians like Tu and Cheng agree with the proponents of Confucian decay that a Confucian political project cannot be revived (Elman 1987). This is somewhat curious given the fact that Confucianism centrally maintained the ethical inseparability of the social and the political. Given that a Confucian ethic has either sustained itself into the twentieth century or been revived for ideological purposes, what aspects of it inform the contemporary political cultures of South Korea, Taiwan and South Korea?

Evidently, for a classical Neoconfucian, certain key features of the project are irretrievable. The idea of re-creating a golden age and the hierarchical ordering and self-cultivation it entailed is no longer viable in contemporary Seoul, Taipei or Singapore. Contemporary Confucianism has, then, lost a crucial conservative element in its vision. Lost, too, is an economic ideal. No contemporary East Asian would seriously subscribe to the classic Daoist or Confucian economic programme that either despises or forbids entrepreneurial activity. This is not a little ironic, given the apparent centrality accorded by management theorists to the Confucian roots of East Asian economic dynamism.

By contrast, political Confucianism traditionally, and, we shall argue, in the contemporary NIEs political and technocratic development displayed a concern with order, balance and harmony. If the world is ordered according to a principle, then the way will inexorably be established. This understanding initially seemed irrelevant to the Nationalist KMT tentatively establishing their rule in Taiwan after their humiliating expulsion from the mainland in 1949 by Mao's communist forces, or Syngman Rhee attempting to stave off the imminent collapse of South Korea between 1950 and 1953 or Lee Kuan Yew riding the tiger of political instability in Singapore after 1963. These first-generation rulers of newly formed East Asian states vindicated their rule in terms of 'nation-building' rather than traditional values. Indeed, political leaders in both South Korea and Singapore initially accepted political pluralism and multiparty democracy as a reflection of the national will they represented. Only latterly did the spectre of communism and the need for unity attenuate radically the possibility of political difference.

Political culture and political development in South Korea, 1948–1992   In 1945, Korea, which for the previous forty years had been first dominated and then colonized by Japan, 'escaped that embrace only to be split in two in the immediate aftermath of the Pacific War' (Cumings 1989, vol. 1: xxi). Divided at the thirty-eighth parallel between a Moscow-protected North and an American-protected South, Korea's immediate postwar history constituted a defining moment for America's postwar entanglement in Pacific Asia (see chapter 4). By 1948, the deepening Cold War led the United States to establish in the South the first Korean Republic (ROK) with a democratic, presidential constitution that bore more than a passing resemblance to the American constitution. The circumstances of the Korean War (1950–3) and the subsequent division of the peninsula into a communist North and an American-protected South undermined the infant democracy. The period 1953–60 south of the 38th parallel witnessed increasingly autocractic rule by first President Syngman Rhee, whilst in the North, the Great Leader Kim Il Jung established a self-reliant socialist state (Baik

1973: 18). Significantly Rhee's rule resembled the bureaucratic centralism of the late Yi dynasty (Henderson 1968: 214). Rhee, in appropriately Neoconfucian terms, maintained that a good political system required good men, and that good men required correct thought. To this end, Rhee's Minister of Education and chief ideologist An Ho-Sang widely disseminated the principle of *ilminjui* throughout the education system. This 'one people principle' maintained that the Korean nation was a family and Rhee both its patriarch and 'messiah' (Cumings 1989, vol. 2: 211). Those who rejected *ilminjui* were subject to arbitrary arrest and 'guidance', which often took the form of torture.

Rhee's regime laid the foundations of an authoritarianism made more plausible by the omnipresent threat posed by the communist North. After student demonstrations in 1960, Rhee was replaced by a brief constitutional experiment (1960–1) which ended in a military coup. Increasing bureaucratization and military rule punctuated by often violent resistance characterized domestic politics between 1960 and 1987. The 1961 coup announced a military presence in Korean politics that lasted twenty-seven years, initially under General and subsequently President Park Chung Hee (1961–79). In order to give a cloak of legitimacy to military rule, the Park regime, through a compelling mixture of constitutional manipulation, press control, periodic arrest of opposition leaders and the evolution of a highly effective security machinery under the auspices of the Korean Central Intelligence Agency (KCIA), succeeded in winning controlled elections held in 1963, 1967 and 1971. Moreover, under the terms of the Yushin constitution (1972) and the Revitalizing Reforms, Park made himself eligible for life-time presidency (Kim 1993: 43).

The assassination of President Park, ironically by the chief of the KCIA, inaugurated another brief cycle of constitutional rule between 1979 and 1980. Again a military coup, this time led by General Chun Doo Hwan, put an end to the prospect of liberalization. Any doubts about Chun's intentions were allayed when student protesters demonstrating against the declaration of martial law in May 1980 received a visit from Chun's Special Forces. The aftermath of the Kwanju Incident left an estimated two hundred students dead (p. 43). A carefully selected National Conference for Unification met in September 1980 and elected Chun President. In order to legitimate his mandate, Chun set about establishing a constitutional façade.

In 1981, Chun introduced a constitution approved by the curious device of a referendum held under martial law that forbade debate on any of its proposals. The new constitution was only slightly less restrictive than the 1972 version, but it did require the President to be indirectly elected by an electoral college and stand for one seven-year term only. The constitution also provided for a partly elected and partly military-nominated National

Assembly. Before elections to the National Assembly in March 1981, the government, in classic corporatist style, licensed a number of political parties. These included a government party, the Democratic Justice Party (DJP), and seventeen opposition parties. The strategy sought to divide the opposition into easily defeatable segments. Despite electoral gerrymandering, the DJP received only 35 per cent of the popular vote, which nevertheless translated into 55 per cent of the seats. Elections held in 1985 repeated this pattern. Confronted by large-scale student demonstrations in 1985, Chun promised democratic reform.

However, when the two most prominent civilian opposition party leaders, Kim Dae Jung and Kim Young Sam, proposed to form a united opposition party, the Chun government responded with increased repression. In particular Chun stifled dissent prior to the 1986 Olympic Games and reneged upon his promise of constitutional reform, nominating, instead, his army colleague, General Roh Tae Woo, to succeed him as President. These arbitrary actions sparked large-scale popular unrest in June 1987 and prompted General Roh on 29 June to announce sweeping proposals for constitutional reforms, which were quickly adopted by the 'lame-duck Chun administration' (p. 42).

The new constitution provided for a President directly elected for one five-year term only, together with a directly elected National Assembly. After April 1988, the 299-seat National Assembly adopted a single-member constituency system. Presidential elections held in February 1988, remarkably, saw Roh defeat his two civilian rivals, Kim Dae Jung and Kim Young Sam. Subsequent National Assembly elections also witnessed Roh's DJP securing a majority.

Roh's presidency continued the programme of political reform. The government attempted to reduce nepotism and corruption, establish greater judicial independence and remove the armed forces from the political arena. Moreover, in an attempt to break the cycle of conflict and institutionalize democracy, Roh's ruling DJP announced in January 1990 its decision to merge with the largest opposition party, Kim Young Sam's Reunification Democratic Party (RDP), and Kim Jong Pil's smaller New Democratic Republican Party (NDRP) in order to form an unbeatable coalition, the Democratic Liberal Party (DLP), evidently modelled upon Japan's 'mammoth ruling party' (p. 46). Subsequently, President Roh designated Kim Young Sam to succeed him. Presidential elections held in December 1992 resulted in victory for Kim Young Sam, who became Korea's first civilian President since 1961.

Although Kim's autocratic style alienated Kim Jong Pil and undermined the DLP coalition in the National Assembly, general elections held in April 1996 enabled Kim's New Korea Party (NKP) to secure control of the legislative. Since 1992, Kim's administration has introduced reforms to render government more transparent, the judiciary more independent and exposed the murky links between big business and politics.

Nevertheless, a well-established pattern of violent student and worker demonstration and police repression continued alongside these more positive institutional signs. The government continues, and in 1996 extended restrictions on media reporting, press and television ownership and curtailed opposition through a mixture of legal restraint and unofficial bribery. Ideological crime, which involves the canvasing of left of centre socialist or Marxist-inspired thought, remains a criminal act under legislation introduced during the Korean War.

Moreover, revelations in the course of 1995 of former President Roh's manipulation of both business and politics through a massive $650 million slush fund have cast a pall over the democratization process between 1988 and 1992. Roh's fund, collected from the leading Korean industrial conglomerates, not only enabled him to buy off political opponents like Kim Dae Jung, through a 2 billion won bribe, but also oiled the political merger of 1990 that led to President Kim's election in 1992 (*Far Eastern Economic Review*, 30 November 1995).

Authoritarian rule facilitating technocratic development has, then, characterized South Korea's postwar development. Although a succession of restrictive constitutions and strictly regulated elections in the period 1960–88 veiled the naked use of force with a fig leaf of respectability, it was the incumbent regime's capacity to engineer economic growth and distribute economic benefits without consultation that ultimately legitimated rule prior to 1992. Furthermore, the shift to greater accountability since 1988 has not affected the President's capacity to act in an arbitrary manner. Thus, recent revelations of corruption in the 1980s have not been allowed to sully the reputation of Kim Young Sam. Meanwhile the sentence of life imprisonment passed against former President Chun for his treasonable role in the 1979 coup and the 1980 Kwanju massacre, and the sentence of seventeen years' imprisonment for Roh for corrupting Korean politics, reflect the vindictive tradition of Yi dynasty autocracy rather than the triumph of the rule of law.

The continuing political arbitrariness and the uncertainty that informs the recent democratic transition reflect an attenuated Confucianism that continues to inform both institutional and economic development. This dates from Syngman Rhee's attempt to present himself as the legitimate vehicle of the Korean nation (Suh 1983: 160–1) through the promotion of an ideological 'pastiche of Korean Confucianism, Western fascism, democratic slogans [and] Chinese Nationalist pretentiousness' (Cumings 1989, vol. 2: 209).

A Confucian concern with hierarchy facilitated socio-economic management by a new technocratic elite that inherited the mantle of the Yi dynasty *yangban*. Analogously, the Confucian view that Korea should be ruled by superior men engendered a continuing suspicion of the rule of law and gave credence to the attempts of successive Presidents to frame constitutions appropriate to their perception of Korea's needs. In 1987, President Roh Tae Woo introduced Koreans to their sixth constitution since 1948. This rule of virtuous men facilitating economic development, moreover, increasingly required the active participation of the people, mobilized towards developmental targets. During President Park's regime, therefore, the *Samil Dongnip Undong* movement sought to inculcate 'a national spirit . . . more fundamental than the national spirit of modern nationalism' (Suh 1983: 160). This required imbuing in 'the Korean populace the Confucian value of *cheng hyo* (loyalty to the state, filial piety and harmony)' (Chowdhury and Islam 1993: 32).

However, the reinvention of this Confucian identity for the purposes of regime stability has not been without problems, especially in terms of the transition from Yao to Shun or in South Korea's case from Park to Chun and Roh to Kim. The enduringly Confucian moral conception of leadership leads, 'on the one hand to a strong emphasis on obedience and conformity and on the other hand, to irreconcilable political conflict' (Kim 1990: 67). The self righteously moral ruler demands conformity and views opposition as unconscionable, *e converso*, any challenge to leadership has to be posed in non-negotiable moral terms. This transforms Korean politics into an endless 'morality play' (p. 67), illustrated in the recent disgrace of former Presidents Chun and Roh.

Consequently, where opposition has emerged, and since 1988 been constitutionally endorsed, politics as argumentative talk is rendered otiose by the practice of *ch'ijo*, which considers an inflexible stance on matters of principle a supreme virtue. Reinforced by personal, factional and regional ties (*inmaek*), it leads 'power players to overestimate their own strength and underestimate that of their rivals' (Han 1989: 285). Clearly, such self-understanding premised on a moral certitude combined with the need for conformity and hierarchy renders future democratization problematic.

Taiwan's troubled political development, 1949–1995   A similar Confucian self-righteousness shaped political development in Taiwan. Whilst Korea is the most culturally and racially homogeneous country in Asia, if not the world, Taiwan was initially divided in 1949 between the mainlanders, who arrived like an occupying force after their defeat by Mao's communists, and the native Taiwanese, who between 1895 and 1945 formed part of a modernizing Japanese empire (Pye 1985: 228–9). The immediate aftermath of the defeat of Chiang Kai-shek's Nationalist forces (KMT) on the Chinese mainland and the retreat to Taiwan had important implications for the island's political development. Fresh from defeat, Nationalist rule considered success in Taiwan a 'sacred mission' (Tsang 1993: 48). Initially, this required the brutal repression of indigenous Taiwanese political aspirations. The Nationalist Army's massacre of 28,000 indigenes in February 1947 graphically illustrated the 'hard authoritarianism' of the missionaries from the mainland (Winckler 1984: 481).

The Nationalist doctrine and autocratic practice that the defeated KMT brought with them to Taiwan had grown out of an ambivalent response to classical Confucianism. Sun Yat-sen's doctrine (1981), which formed the ideological core of the KMT movement, emphasized the 'three principles of the people' (*San Min Chu I*), namely, anti-imperialist nationalism, democracy and socialism, rather than Confucian virtue. Following Sun's theory, the KMT's 1947 constitution for the Republic of China, which, given the changes on the mainland, applied only to Taiwan after 1949, specified a National Assembly as the embodiment of popular sovereignty, a President indirectly elected by the Assembly and a further division of power between five councils: the Executive, Legislative, Control (of government performance), Judicial and Examination Yuan.

However, as Sun Yat-sen had provided for an undefined period of 'tutelage' to consolidate the nation, Sun's successor as leader of the Chinese Nationalist movement, Generalissimo Chiang Kai-shek, concentrated power in the executive and the leader. (Chiang 1943). As early as 1934, Chiang began modifying the democratic elements in Sun's philosophy and developing an organic ideology, drawing not only from Sun's views on nationalism and socialism, but also increasingly upon 'his own views of the central tenets of traditional Confucianism, especially with regard to the formation of a loyal and moral human character' (Spence 1991: 414). This mixture Chiang then leavened with mass activism derived from his admiration for German and Italian fascism (pp. 414–15).

This vision of a renewed nation inspired by a traditional respect for order and hierarchy, but informed by an active and unifying zeal to modernize, had failed on the mainland. This notwithstanding, Chiang applied his leadership principles with a few adjustments to the social and economic organization of Taiwan (Clark 1989: 121). The successful adaptation of this ideology to Taiwan contrasts vividly with its failure on the mainland. In part this can be explained by the small size of the island and the KMT's evolving machinery of political control. One important and highly successful modification to mainland practice involved the KMT in an American-inspired rural reconstruction programme that transferred land to peasant farmers between 1950 and 1953 (Vogel 1991: 19). This, together with the creation of a Taiwanese entrepreneurial class, gave indigenous Taiwanese an economic stake in development, whilst political and economic guidance remained in the hands of the KMT. The fact that economic advance was 'relatively equally distributed' (Vogel 1991: 40) as Taiwan's economy grew dramatically in the 1960s increasingly legitimated the government's claim to guide and rectify in the economic interest of the common people.

The uncertain international conditions that affected Taiwan's emergence as an independent entity during the first Cold War further conduced to an evolving authoritarianism. Thus, the fact that KMT representatives elected to the Legislative Yuan and the National Assembly in 1947 continued to represent mainland constituencies indefinitely because of the continuing state of emergency on the mainland enhanced tutelary rule (Kuo and Myers 1988: 123). At the same time, Chiang used the threat of invasion from the mainland, which remained a possibility throughout the 1950s, to amend the 1947 constitution in an autocratic direction. In 1948 Temporary Provisions to the constitution granted the President emergency powers. In May 1949, the Executive Yuan imposed martial law on Taiwan and the offshore islands, giving the government power to arrest and try in military courts those who posed a threat to social and political order (Chao and Myers 1994: 17). The quasi-Leninist structure of the KMT further promoted parallelism between party and state and enabled party organs to control the military and administration at village, county and township level. The evolving structure of internal and external security effectively constituted a machinery of total control (Cheng 1989: 477). Even in 1988, the *Asian Wall Street Journal* observed that 'all major decisions are first made by the KMT's 31 member Central Standing Committee . . . [and] the cabinet rubber stamps decisions handed down by the KMT leaders' (6 July).

Nevertheless, despite its evident success in mobilizing the masses towards export-led growth between 1950 and 1977, the KMT was the subject of mounting internal and external criticism, particularly in the United States, for its persecution of political opponents. In particular, the death of founding father Chiang Kai-shek in 1977 and the succession of his son, Chiang Ching-kuo (1978–87), to the presidency, together with the growing need to incorporate indigenous Taiwanese into the party state as the mainlander generation died out, and the growing international isolation of Taiwan after the loss of United Nations membership in 1971, presaged a softening of party controls. In other words, an accumulation of domestic and external crises prompted a reevaluation of the tutelary strategy.

The government had in fact intimated a tolerance for limited opposition by permitting restricted competition for local government office in the early 1950s. In 1972, the party state allowed competitive elections for a limited number of seats in the Legislative Yuan and the National Assembly, and a number of native Taiwanese, like future President Lee Teng-hui, were recruited into the higher echelons of the party. In this changing environment a number of young indigenous activists began to refer to themselves as *tangwai*, or outside the ruling party (Chao and Myers 1994: 218). The KMT, however, was, as yet, not prepared to tolerate multipartism. The security services closely monitored *tangwai* activity and subjected members to censorship, arrest and imprisonment, culminating in the Kaohsiung Incident in 1979, when the reformist group associated with the *Formosa* magazine were given long prison sentences under the Temporary Provisions legislation.

Nevertheless regular, triennial, competitive elections for vacant seats in both the Legislative Yuan and the National Assembly as well as at the local level became increasingly commonplace after 1980. Indeed, through a judicious mixture of media control, financial inducements and the occasional recourse to the Temporary Provisions, Chiang Ching-kuo incrementally engineered a 'quiet revolution' in democratic accountability and laid the foundation for official recognition of a united Taiwanese opposition party (the Democratic Progressive Party – DPP) in 1986 and the repeal of the Emergency decree and martial law in 1987 (Clark 1989: 136–9). The KMT has continued this strategy of party-led democratization during Lee Teng-hui's presidency (1988–). As the first indigenous President, Lee was able successfully to blend support for the KMT's continuing mission to bring enlightened national development to the mainland, whilst giving some credence to the separatist, independence claims promoted, somewhat irresolutely, by the opposition DPP. Indeed, the mainstream faction within the KMT that Lee represents successfully coopted the more popular opposition reform strategies in order to maintain and in fact extend its authority (pp. 140–1). Public reconciliation with the opposition in April 1990 paved the way both for an official recognition of and public apology for the massacre of 1947 and further constitutional amendment between 1992 and 1995.

Thus, with DPP backing, the KMT-managed Council of Grand Justices ruled that the mainland representatives who had sat uninterrupted since 1949 relinquish their seats in the National Assembly by December 1991. In April 1991, the KMT convened an extraordinary session of the National Assembly which terminated the Temporary Provisions (1949) and added ten articles to the constitution, dissolving mainland constituencies and requiring national elections to replace all senior national representatives. This facilitated Taiwan's first major national election to the second National Assembly in early 1992. The same year also witnessed island-wide elections for the 161-seat Legislative Yuan. In both elections the KMT won a comfortable majority, securing 247 delegates and 71.2 per cent of the votes cast for the 314-seat National Assembly. Subsequent changes to the constitution in the course of 1993 and 1994 required regular quadrennial elections to both the Legislative Yuan and National Assembly. More significantly, in

May 1994, the National Assembly legislated that, at the end of Lee Teng-hui's incumbency, the President would be directly elected for a six-year term.

Although the KMT mainstream faction successfully engineered this constitutional transformation, it occurred against a backdrop of mounting criticism externally from the PRC and internally within the ranks of the KMT itself. In particular, the non-mainstream faction of the KMT, including former Premier Hau Pei-tsun, objected to the pace of reform and the growing sense of Taiwanese autonomy it conveyed. In August 1993, Hau and faction members close to him broke away to form the New Party. Nevertheless, the first direct presidential elections in March 1996 returned Lee Teng-hui to the presidency with 54 per cent of the popular vote, his nearest rival, Peng Ming-min of the DPP, receiving a mere 21 per cent (*Far Eastern Economic Review*, 4 April 1996).

Elite-driven democratization has enabled the KMT, paradoxically, to consolidate its mandate to rule. Remarkably, despite constitutional change and the institutionalization of opposition, there has been no 'turnover of power' (Huntington 1993b: 39) and the KMT has, it would seem, successfully embraced constitutional reform in order to promote a continuing Confucian concern with consensus and stability.

Article 11 of the KMT charter requires the preservation of Chinese culture. The sedulous preservation and promotion of an officially mediated understanding of Chinese culture and Confucian values, together with a language policy that promotes Mandarinization at the expense of native Taiwanese culture, has had important ramifications for Taiwan's political development. The KMT has successfully maintained a stable social and political order by promoting an elaborate ideology compounded of an attenuated Confucianism, blended with a developing sense of national purpose through a cohesive and highly effective party apparatus organized on democratic centralist lines and reinforced by an all-pervasive but not always visible security apparatus. As one Taiwanese political scientist explains, through the party's 'exclusive control over such socialization agents as schools and mass media, the mainlander elite constructed an ideologically indoctrinated popular coalition where all members of society believed that the KMT state embodied the interest of all classes' (Chu 1994: 100) The official promotion through public education of a respect for filial piety and hierarchical order reinforces the notion that the party has the moral authority to rule. The KMT drew upon this reservoir of moral authority to promote representative institutions and continue its authority constitutionally.

At the same time it has exercised control and influence through a ubiquitous network of business, financial and local government ties. These connections (*guanxi*) have in fact made the KMT the richest ruling party in the world, with well-established financial and media arms (*Far Eastern Economic Review*, 11 August 1994). In other words, the KMT's continuing ability to act as political party, financier and employer, together with its ability to dictate the pace of change and the character of debate, made the adoption of democratic forms after 1988 less risky than it might initially appear. Moreover, the fact that the ruling party functions in a political culture where 'tolerance for different opinions' is not widely developed (Kuo and Myers 1988: 122) crucially affects the character of this evolving Confucian democracy. Significantly, political debate in the National Assembly and Legislative Yuan often degenerates into un-Confucian brawling, and encourages a highly intolerant party politics. In these circumstances uncritical adherence to the KMT, oiled by judicious vote buying, *guanxi* and peculation, has increasingly characterized the evolving political culture as a means of avoiding the uncertainty of the democratic process. Thus Lee Teng-hui reflected the incoherence of this confused Confucian democratic experiment when he characterized any opposition attempt 'to change the mandate of heaven' as a threat to 'violate the constitution and destroy the country' (*Straits Times*, 13 November 1994).

Singapore – the evolution of the administrative state   The independent city state of Singapore, 77.7 per cent of whose population is of Chinese extraction (Lau 1992: 2), was undoubtedy influenced by the nationalist thinking of both Sun Yat-sen and Chiang Kai-shek. Nevertheless, the single-party dominant state evolved a somewhat different ideological practice after its colonial ties with Britain were dissolved in 1963. Interestingly, Singapore's recent spectacular economic growth originated in humiliating political circumstances. During the Malayan Emergency the Rendal Commission (1954) gave Singapore Crown Colony status, and in 1963 Lee Kuan Yew, the leader of the governing People's Action Party (PAP), negotiated the city state's entry into the recently formed Malaysian Federation. In 1965, however, Singapore was unceremoniously expelled from the Federation largely because Lee Kuan Yew refused to confine PAP activity to the city state. The anxiety generated internally by the threat of communist and communist front activity symbolized in the Hock Lee Bus Company riots (1955), and externally by the fact that the resourceless, ethnically Chinese city resided uncertainly in a South China 'sea of Malay peoples' (Turnbull 1992: ch. 8; Hill and Lian 1995: 63), together with its unwanted autonomy, profoundly coloured the PAP's political strategy and Singapore's evolving political culture.

Regularly re-elected into power on eight occasions since 1959, the PAP has curtailed opposition because *raison d'état* dictates the need to preserve unity and avoid communalist ethnic tension. The struggle for power with the proto-communist *Barisan Socialis* in the early 1960s, together with

Singapore's ejection from the inchoate Malaysian Federation in 1965, left the PAP firmly opposed to mass, popular, participatory, 'democratic politics in both principle and in fact' (Chew 1995: 943).

To justify one-party 'hegemony' (Lee 1990: 16) and to curb unwarranted opposition, the PAP initially promoted an official ideology of pragmatic survivalism. This ideology, combined with the periodic invocation of the spectre of communism and communalism, which was amplified by far-reaching controls on the press and electronic media, enabled the party's first-generation leaders like R.J. Rajaratnam and Devan Nair to promote the view that the PAP was rationally building a uniquely multicultural nation state blending the best of East and West (Seow 1994: 5–10; Chua 1995: ch. 1; Hill and Lian 1995: 32). In order to construct the new nation, the government gradually modified the common law practice and constitution inherited from the former colonial power. The government abolished trial by jury in 1968, restricted the discretionary powers of judges in 1973 and abolished appeals to the Privy Council in London in 1995. In the process the party established effective control over the judiciary (Asia Watch Report 1989; Seow 1994: 173–95; Tremewan 1994: 213). Singaporeans subsequently 'learnt that the only effective means to elicit a response from the government was the use of officially established political channels' (Chan 1991: 170). The tough measures taken against socialist and communist opponents in the 1960s 'stymied the growth of all opposition' (p. 170) and Singaporeans underwent 'steady depoliticization' (p. 170). Indeed, the uninterrupted rule of the PAP since independence has facilitated the emergence of an apolitical, administrative state (p. 170) dominated by the PAP and its founding father and current Senior Minister Lee Kuan Yew.

Nevertheless, this one 'party dominant system' (Chan 1993: 16) has successfully modernized Singapore through an evolving practice of technocratic management. It has also severely curtailed the space for critical comment, let alone political opposition. As former deputy premier Goh Keng Swee cynically observed in 1988, the most important prerequisite for Singapore's success was 'an efficient secret police' (Chew 1995: 942). Over its thirty-five year tenure, the PAP has eroded the distinction between government and party and applied 'severe legal and political measures to combat the emergence and growth of a credible opposition political organization' (Lee 1996: 59). In practice the PAP has 'fine-tuned' the 1963 constitution in the interest of what party technocrats rationalize as efficient and proactive political management. In 1991, the PAP introduced a law institutionalizing Religious Harmony and legislating the separation of religion from politics (Quah 1994: 98). In the same year, the PAP amended the unicameral 'Westminster model' parliament (Chan 1993: 16) by introducing a directly elected President whose primary responsibility consists in maintaining Singapore's fiscal probity in the event of a 'freak' election result turning the PAP out of office.

There is little likelihood of such an outcome. After J.P. Jeyeratnam, a prominent PAP critic, was returned for the Anson constituency in a 1981 by-election, the party state went to considerable lengths both to curtail freedom of speech in parliament and to alter constituency boundaries to prevent further unforeseen results. In 1988, the Group Representation Constituencies (GRCs) amendment to the Constitution and Elections Act amalgamated 39 single-member constituencies into 13 GRCs. To contest a GRC required a slate of three candidates, all of whom were returned if their party received a plurality of the votes cast. The scheme blended the 10 most marginal PAP seats in the 1984 elections with 10 safe PAP seats. Thus, although the PAP vote at general elections fell from 75.5 per cent in 1980 to 61.76 per cent in 1988, the party nevertheless retained all 80 seats in parliament after the GRC-amended 1988 election. The prospect of a further erosion in the PAP vote in elections held in January 1997 inspired the Electoral Boundaries Review Committee to divide Singapore into 15 new GRCs of between 3 and 6 members and 9 single-member constituencies. The consequences were highly effective, with the PAP improving its share of the vote and winning 81 of the 83 seats in the new parliament (*Straits Times Weekly*, 7 December 1996; *Straits Times Interactive*, 3 January 1997).

Furthermore, judicial control, the extension of the Internal Security Act after 1989 and a liberal interpretation of defamation has enabled the party state to bankrupt opposition leaders who appear electorally attractive (Chee 1994). In May 1987 the Internal Security Department arrested sixteen young Singaporeans in 'connection with a clandestine communist network' (Seow 1994: 67). In the 1988 general election, their lawyer, former Attorney General Francis Seow, was returned as an MP. Accused of corruption, he fled the country (Seow 1994: ch. 12; Tremewan 1994: 213ff.). In the same year, parliament disbarred Jeyeratnam for his 'treasonable' allegation that the PAP had interfered with judicial independence, and his implied defamation of Prime Minister Lee Kuan Yew cost him $260,000. Analogously, in 1992, when the electorally attractive university lecturer Chee Soon Juan stood as an opposition Social Democratic Party (SDP) candidate in Prime Minister Goh Chok Tong's Marine Parade GRC, he subsequently lost the by-election, his job and was fined $260,000 for allegedly defaming his Head of Department and PAP MP Professor Vasoo (*Straits Times*, 18 April 1993; Chee 1994). More recently, opposition candidate Tang Liang Hong had his assets sequestered and faced 12 charges of libel for remarks made in the 1997 elections.

Meanwhile, Minister for Home Affairs, and former Law Professor, Jayakumar considers the Emergency Powers dating from the Communist

Insurgency central to the management of domestic crime. Consequently, over 1,000 Singaporeans suspected of vice-related activities languish in indefinite 'preventive detention' under these provisions (*Straits Times*, 7 August 1992). As the Association of the Bar of New York discovered in 1991, the PAP in Singapore and UMNO in Malaysia have systematically intimidated dissenters and limited the independence of the judiciary, 'resulting in the decline of the rule of law' (Frank et al. 1991: 16).

Coterminous with the evolution of judicial, political and media control, the administrative state has also attempted to implement an inclusionary, rather than exclusionary, corporatist strategy of popular management 'to bond Singaporeans to Singapore' (Goh Chok Tong, *Straits Times Weekly*, 20 April 1996). As early as 1968, the Employment Act established a government-licensed trade union council (National Trade Union Congress, NTUC). In the course of the 1980s, government extended the licensing of approved interest groups to ethnic and religious organizations like MENDAKI (Council for the Education of Muslim Children), whilst a government-approved feeback unit encouraged 'grassroot' opinion. This policy of state-licensed feedback culminated in the appointment of up to six nominated MPs after 1989 to provide 'articulate dissent' (Chan 1993: 15) and a broader cross-section of views in the PAP-dominated unicameral legislature.

However, the extension of consultative mechanisms does not involve tolerance for unlicensed opposition or a deregulated pluralism. The 1991 general election and its aftermath demonstrated the limits of inclusionary corporatism. In November 1990, founding father Lee Kuan Yew officially 'stepped down' as Prime Minister to allow a new second-generation team of carefully groomed technocrats led by new Prime Minister Goh Chok Tong and Lee's son Deputy Prime Minister Lee Hsien Loong. Lee, however, remained in the cabinet as a pater familias or Senior Minister. In January 1991, the new team announced a blueprint for Singapore's 'Next Lap' of development (Government of Singapore 1991). This required, in the view of party ideologist and Minister for the Arts B.G. Yeo, a judicious pruning of the 'banyan tree' state in order to widen 'the circle of participation' to promote 'civic society' (Yeo, *Straits Times*, 21 June 1991). At the same time, Goh Chok Tong promoted a 'caring and consultative style' of leadership that contrasted with the autocratic manner of the Senior Minister. However, elections in August 1991 saw the unanticipated return of four opposition MPs and a reduction of the PAP vote to 61 per cent. The policy of openness, Goh regretted in September 1991, had cost the party dearly and would have to be reviewed (*Straits Times*, 2 September 1991). The period since 1991 has, therefore, witnessed a tightening of media controls and an escalating use of the judiciary to curtail criticism and real or imagined libel of the party leadership. The change in style has been associated with the return to political prominence of Lee Kuan Yew, who interestingly describes Goh Chok Tong as 'my Prime Minister' (*Straits Times*, 23 November 1993).

The PAP increasingly maintains, moreover, that its continuing right to guide and admonish the people derives from a carefully nurtured Confucianism that differs significantly from the pragmatic ideology of the early 1970s. Indeed, as the threat of communist insurgency and communal tension that initially legitimated the oligarchical dominance of the PAP diminished in the late 1970s, the PAP had increasing recourse to what it defines as national, shared or Asian values. The inculcation of these values, moreover, occurred at a time when the technocratic efficiency of the administrative state had realized a standard of living second only to Japan in East Asia. To forestall a perceived but, as yet, unrealized call for greater political freedom, the PAP technocracy has assiduously reinvented traditional values and inculcated them into a multicultural population of Chinese, Indians and Malays. Central to this policy has been a critique of individual autonomy, an emphasis on community before self, and consensus and harmony rather than contestation (Quah 1994: 91–2). In order to inculcate such values the PAP has at various times devised educational programmes in Confucian ethics. More effective, however, are the regular mass mobilization campaigns analogous to those first devised by Chiang Kai-shek in Taiwan to inculcate courtesy, cooperation, responsible breeding and civic hygiene.

Indeed, in the political thinking of the island's founding father and current Senior Minister, Lee Kuan Yew, the recently developed Asian dragon cannot afford to allow its increasingly affluent citizens to create their own identity. Instead, the government does it for them. Just as the PAP intervened in all aspects of the economy to generate impressive growth in the 1970s and 1980s, a variety of units and programmes now seek to organize every aspect of the Singaporean psyche. Moreover, Lee Kuan Yew is constantly on hand to offer correct guidance and paternal rectification. Thus in Singapore citizenship consists in the digitally precise performance of an alloted role in an unfolding master plan. Such political managerialism clearly has implications for any future democratization of the city state.

Hong Kong – the regional anomaly

Unlike the other regional high-performing economies, Britain has administered Hong Kong as a colony since 1841, apart from a brief rupture between 1942 and 1945. The Hong Kong Charter of 1843 established the island as a Crown colony. Britain extracted additional territories and dependencies through what the Chinese government termed 'unequal treaties' in 1860 and 1898. These were also administered under the letters patent of the Crown. The governor of the island, appointed by the Secretary of State at

Westminster, constituted and presided over a nominated Legislative (Legco) and an Executive Council. Since 1844, the Governor in conjunction with his executive and legislative has made law. Until 1991, the only limitation on this legislative power forbade the Governor assenting to any bill relating to 10 specified subjects without prior approval of the Secretary of State at Westminster (Miners 1991: 57).

In 1850, two *unofficial* members were admitted to the Legislative Council and were joined in 1884 by the first Chinese unofficial. By 1939, the constitution of Hong Kong provided for an Executive Council of seven official members (including the Governor) and three unofficial members, and a Legislative Council of ten official members and eight unofficials (Tsang 1988: 2–3). After 1966, the unofficial members increased to eight and subsequently varied in number between eight and eleven. In 1991, eight of the ten Executive unofficials were Chinese and six unofficials were also members of the Legislative Council (Miners 1991: 74). The position of the Executive Council in the government of Hong Kong corresponds to that of the cabinet in the government of the United Kingdom. However, the governor is more than a Prime Minister and can veto legislation approved by the Legislative and Executive. Between 1844 and 1985 the Legislative was directly appointed by the Governor. A government White Paper published in 1984 provided for twenty-four of the seats to the fifty seven seat Legislative Council to be indirectly elected, twelve by district boards and twelve elected from nine functional constituencies comprised by commerce, finance, industry, labour, social services and various professions.

The movement towards limited democratic representation in the Hong Kong legislature after 1984 directly related to the fact that Britain's lease on the New Territories expires in 1997. In 1982, the British government had entered into negotiations with Beijing, and in 1984 concluded a Joint Declaration on the administration of Hong Kong after 1997. The two governments directly concluded the Declaration without consulting the views of the 6.7 million residents of Hong Kong. Hong Kong, it was agreed, would after 1997 become a Special Administrative Region (SAR) within the PRC, enjoying a high degree of autonomy and theoretically retaining its own system of law and administration (Miners 1991: 10). The two governments also agreed to establish a Joint Liaison Group to implement the Joint Declaration. After the ratification of the treaty in 1985, China established a committee to draft the Basic Law constitution to govern the SAR after 1997.

The Basic Law (1988) stressed the resumption of China's sovereignty over Hong Kong, 'not the consent of the people to a particular form of government' (Scott 1993: 67), and requires legislation 'to prohibit any act of treason, secession, sedition, subversion against the Central People's Government' (Lee and Bray 1995: 367). The Basic Law did, however, pledge to keep Hong Kong unchanged for fifty years under 'the one-country two-systems formula' that ostensibly gives Hong Kong a high degree of economic, legal and adminstrative autonomy.

The events of June 1989 'when the tanks of the People's Liberation Army massacred the student protesters in Tiananmen Square' severely compromised the undemocratic, but nevertheless relatively successful, diplomatic negotiation of the post-1997 takeover of Hong Kong (Miners 1991: 11). The events of 1989 profoundly affected popular perception of the PRC and exacerbated tensions between Hong Kong, Westminster and Beijing. In May 1989 an estimated one million Hong Kongers protested against the imposition of Martial Law in China (Scott 1993: 68). Diplomatic relations between Beijing and Westminster were suspended for four months and the aftermath of Tiananmen left a legacy of suspicion. After 1989, and particularly since 1991, successive governors of Hong Kong have widened the electoral franchise and extended legal protections through a Bill of Rights Ordinance (1991). Elections to the Legislative Council in 1991 saw elected members outnumber appointees by 39 to 21. Moreover, under the democratizing influence of Hong Kong's last Governor, Chris Patten, all members of Hong Kong's legislative council were directly elected either by functional or geographic constituencies in elections held in 1995.

Beijing has greeted the democratization undertaken by the Governor since 1991, and vocally supported by Martin Lee's United Democrats, who enjoy widespread popular support, with a mixture of resentment and rejection. Viewing post-1989 reform as an insidious western ploy to undermine the emergence of greater China, the PRC will dissolve the Legislative Council in 1997 and replace it with a 60-member provisional legislature chosen by a 400-member Selection Committee. In December 1996, the Selection Committee chose conservative businessman Tung Chee-hwa as Chief Executive of post-hand over Hong Kong (*The Economist*, 14 December 1996). Moreover, as the Basic Law makes no provision for a Bill of Rights, this, too, will evidently be abrogated in 1997. The legal ramifications of the deal struck between Westminster and Beijing in 1995 over the composition of the Court of Final Appeal to replace the British appellate court for Hong Kong are even more disturbing for the continuation of the rule of law after 1997. This critical agreement established that the appeal court bench should henceforth comprise four local and one overseas judge, an arrangement that by no means ensures the future independence of the judiciary. Although the decision has smoothed the path to transition, it may also have undermined the legal guarantee of contract, central to Hong Kong's credibility as a financial centre for the region (*Far Eastern Economic Review*, 26 January 1995: 49).

A decade and a half of economic growth and political activity has, thus, invisible-handedly promoted the spontaneous evolution of a wide variety of local interest groups and a vibrant civil society. Interestingly, the width and variety of associational groups contrasts noticeably with the previous one hundred and forty years of Hong Kong's development. Indeed, before 1984, the Hong Kong Chinese community generally displayed a high degree of political indifference. This was due in part to the early effectiveness of the colonial state in restricting legal entitlements, proscribing trade unions and political groups and accommodating the Chinese merchant class, and in part to the efficiency of Hong Kong's civil service, the pattern of immigrant settlement from the mainland after 1949 and the passive Confucian culture they brought with them. Significantly a survey of public opinion in 1986 still found 73 per cent of respondents agreeing with the statement that 'Government should treat the people like a father treats his children' (Miners 1991: 36).

Events since 1985, however, have facilitated growing popular identification with the rule of law and the civil space created by the colonial regime, and manifest in a vibrant media and the rapid growth of popular support for Martin Lee's liberal United Democrats Party. This civil society stands in marked contrast to the other HPAEs considered here and is unlikely to survive the return of Hong Kong to mainland control in 1997.

The reinvention of tradition and the problem of development

Obviously, the HPAEs are culturally highly diverse. Nevertheless, with the exception of anomalous Hong Kong, we can broadly identify a number of what might be termed shared values that significantly shape political and economic development. Moreover, the enduring attraction of paternalism, dependency, balance and harmony clearly poses difficulties for future democratization, as we shall examine further in chapter 3. 'Consensus', as modernized Asian politicians describe the traditional pursuit of balance, does not require a pluralistic consultation of a multiplicity of interests, far less submission to popular taste. Politically, East Asian political thought of a Confucian provenance asserted the need for hierarchy and expertise. Rule was always the responsibility of a virtuous elite or a man of prowess. In a Confucian tradition it was the self-cultivated *jinzi* who rectified the people, whilst in Southeast Asia, with its blend of Hindu, Islamic and Buddhist political–theocratic understandings, indirect consultation enabled rule to proceed by apparent agreement, or *gotong royong*. In its modern version, the professional expert replaces the *jinzi* and technocratically adjusts the people to their required role. Harmony is still valued and achieved, not by a proliferation of interests, but by each member precisely fulfilling an ordained relationship, or, in Southeast Asia, by subtly deferring to the requirements of respectful consensus building (*musyawarah maafekat*).

Managerial science, however, syncretizes tradition to suit the needs of instrumental reason and technocratic rule. As we have observed, political Confucianism and Southeast Asian political theocracy are hierarchical and demonstrate a paternalistic concern for the welfare of the people. They countenance neither a popular right of resistance, participation, nor any inalienable individual right. There is no room here for politics as an essentially pluralistic activity, or for the notion that government reflects a popular will. This Asian map of the mind, moreover, explains the consistent failure of western commentators and governments to grasp an East Asian attitude to law and its embodiment in a constitution. Traditionally, Confucians had little regard for laws and considered them detrimental to the promulgation of virtue. Chinese legalism, by contrast, enthusiastically embraced a notion of law that entailed a precisely defined code of conduct applied to all subjects. Similarly, in Thailand the *sakdi na* system reinforced a cosmically determined hierarchy. Subsequently, in Southeast Asia, nationalist movements reinforced traditional understandings of dependency and consensus and forged a new identity at the expense of 'colonial' understandings of the rule of law.

The traditional Pacific Asian understandings of law, therefore, have little in common with Anglo-American jurisprudential thought and practice. *Fa* cannot accommodate legal right or what Hayek terms the spontaneous extended order of the constitution of liberty (Hayek 1960: 150–60). It provides instead for a precise regulation of duties through mechanically administered rules. East Asian law neither reflects a transcendental natural law, nor proposes a contract with mutual obligations enforceable by an independent judiciary. Consequently constitutions can be rectified by the virtuous, a fact that explains the endless modification of constitutions in East and Southeast Asia. Law, except in Hong Kong until 1997, is essentially administrative and responds to the requirements of the technocratic planning of the latest growth plan and social cohesion. This is evident in the use of martial law in Taiwan, the new constitutions that appear with nearly every change of President in South Korea, the similar pattern that obtains in Thailand with its thirteen and a half constitutions since 1932, and the regular constitutional amendments that occur in Malaysia and Singapore. Indeed, the purpose of East and Southeast Asian managerial rule is essentially apolitical or anti-communicatory. Central to this technical and rationalistic interpretation of law in East Asia is the traditional preoccupation with the rectification of names. Rectification provides the technique for adjusting law to the new developmental reality. In the contemporary practice of the East Asian multifunction *polis* this is now termed 'fine-tuning' and 'proactive' pragmatism.

Meanwhile, the modernized understanding of virtuous benevolence requires that virtuous rulers and an elite technocracy pragmatically guide and adjust policy to economic targets. Consequently, the modern, like the traditional, elite responds to externally validated criteria. Neoconfucianism traditionally justified virtuous government because it created prosperity as well as harmony, whilst the golden age created by the man of prowess in Southeast Asia was also a time of order, wealth and harmony. A residual paternalistic concern with benevolence or the welfare of the masses has been intensified by the fact that the post-independence rulers of the HPAEs claim both to represent a national history, and to overcome the past failing of tradition by moulding a new and progressive Asian identity.

Such concern appears democratic, but clearly it is not a liberal understanding of democracy. Only the skilled technocrat can plan 'the next lap' of development. The people need to know their new responsibilities and they may 'feedback' their views. They also need to be reminded in mass campaigns of their new identity as morally reborn vehicles of a curiously ill-defined national mission. Consequently, reinvented Confucian, Buddhist or modified Islamic practice facilitate collective mobilization toward developmental targets and provide the technocratic planners of state-led development with an invaluable source of legitimacy. But this national culture is no longer invariant custom. Instead tradition, centrally disseminated, metamorphoses into a set of ritual practices governed by rules, which inculcate 'certain values and norms of behavior by repetition' (Hobsbawm 1983: 2). Furthermore, these norms do not attempt to revive a past golden age but rather, as one Singapore National Day song expresses it, guide the building of a 'better tomorrow'.

Tradition, thus, still informs rule in the modern Pacific Asian state. However, under the influence of powerful twentieth-century ideological understandings, these attenuated traditions serve the paradoxical purpose of furthering progress. This drive to realize an ill-defined new Asian identity requires continual mass mobilization towards short-term moral, social and economic objectives. This syncretic combination of managerial planning, progress and tradition reinforces a moralistic view of rule in which the dependency and security offered by the techno-paternalist elite resolve the anxiety created by the constant need to compete for export-led growth. The problem of how to manage generational change, however, remains. The concern for order and the emphasis on dependency and self-concealment present clear difficulties for an impersonal constitutional order or communicatory democracy. To the extent that Pacific Asian states like South Korea and Thailand have abandoned military rule, they have, as in Malaysia and Taiwan, replaced military-bureaucratic ties with those to party and faction oiled by money politics. Links to the ruling elite or attachment to faction constitute the new ties of dependence. It is this development and its implications for an Asian method of managing economic, social and internal and external political change that we address in subsequent chapters.

2
The State They're In: The Political Economy of Pacific Asia

Recent interest in the politics and society of Pacific Asia clearly relates to the nature of East Asian economic development. Since at least the early 1960s the Pacific Asian economies discussed in this study have witnessed prodigious annual rates of growth (see table 2.1). After a brief recession in the mid-1980s this growth has continued, sometimes at double-digit rates, into the 1990s (see table 2.2), and the World Bank (1993a) accords this the status of an East Asian miracle. The question that arises for students of international political economy and developmental economics is how this growth was achieved and whether it is sustainable. Furthermore, if it can be sustained, are there lessons to be drawn from the Asian model that could both promote development elsewhere in Asia and reform what a growing number of Asian politicians and social scientists regard as the dying economies of the West. Such large questions with potentially critical policy implications have generated an often heated debate about the character of economic development in Pacific Asia. In order to clarify this debate we will briefly examine these competing interpretations before examining the character of economic development in what the World Bank currently terms the High-Performing Asian Economies (HPAEs).

Prior to the 1980s the key debate in developmental economics concerned the relative merits of import substitution or a relatively open trading order with limited government intervention for securing growth and modernization. Import-substituting industrialization (ISI), especially as it was practised in South America after 1945 (Jacobs 1984: ch. 4), initially entailed using earnings from primary-product exports and foreign borrowing to finance the import of selected producer goods (Cardoso and Faletto 1979; Haggard

TABLE 2.1 GDP growth rates, 1980–1990 (average annual growth, per cent)

Country	1980	1981	1982	1983	1984	1985	1986	1987	1988	1989	1990
HK	9.5	9.4	3.0	6.5	9.5	-0.1	11.1	13.8	7.3	8.6	2.5
Sing.	9.0	9.6	6.9	8.2	8.3	-1.6	1.8	9.4	11.0	9.2	8.5
ROK	-3.3	6.9	7.4	12.1	9.2	6.9	12.3	11.6	11.3	6.4	9.3
ROC	9.7	6.2	3.6	8.4	10.6	5.0	11.6	12.3	7.3	7.7	5.2
Indon.	7.9	7.4	-0.4	8.8	6.8	2.6	5.8	4.9	5.8	7.5	7.2
Mal.	7.4	6.9	6.0	6.4	7.8	-1.1	1.2	5.4	8.9	8.7	9.8
Thai.	4.7	6.3	4.0	7.2	7.2	3.2	5.1	9.6	13.4	12.2	10.3

Sources: Andrews 1991: 149; Tan 1992: 115; World Bank 1992: 22; Klintworth 1994: 110; Fishburn 1994; Pacific Economic Cooperation Council 1994b; *Far Eastern Economic Review*, 14 March 1996: 64–5

TABLE 2.2 GDP growth rates, 1991–1995 (average annual growth, per cent)

Country	1991	1992	1993	1994	1995
HK	5.5	5.2	5.3	5.2	5.0
Sing.	7.7	5.6	9.9	7.0	8.3
ROK	8.7	4.7	5.6	7.4	9.2
ROC	7.4	6.1	5.9	6.2	9.2
Indon.	6.2	5.5	6.3	6.4	7.2
Mal.	8.6	8.0	8.5	8.3	9.2
Thai.	8.2	7.4	7.9	8.2	8.6

Sources: As table 2.1

1990: 24). These imports formed the basis for government-subsidized local manufacturing. Such a strategy favoured restrictive measures such as tariff barriers or import quotas to restrict the volume of imports. In time 'domestic products . . . substitute for the imported goods through increased [domestic] production' (Watanabe 1992: 70). The size of the domestic market further constituted a key variable in explaining the duration of ISI. The alternative to ISI favoured, it would seem, some variety of free trade, where the industrializing country pursued its comparative advantage in such areas as high domestic savings and a cheap, plentiful, but educated and technically literate labour force to promote growth. The failure of a variety of South American economies after apparently favourable beginnings in the course of the 1960s and 1970s and the impressive post war growth of Japan, Taiwan, South Korea, Hong Kong and Singapore through a potent mixture of an educated, adaptable and relatively cheap labour force, and high domestic savings rates that enabled manufacturing industries to establish a competitive advantage in overseas markets, appeared by the early 1980s to have resolved this debate in favour of the open trading regime and neoliberal economic theory. The proponents of global market liberalization as the engine of world economic growth received a further boost with market-friendly reforms in China in 1978, particularly the creation of economic free trading zones in Guangdong and Fujian, the collapse of the *dirigiste* Soviet Empire after 1989 and the rapid adoption of market liberalization policies by newly independent Eastern European democracies like Hungary, Czechoslovakia (later the Czech Republic) and Poland. The successful conclusion of the Uruguay round of GATT in 1995 and the establishment of a World Trade Organization (WTO), moreover, seemed to presage a new post-Cold War economic order premised on the universally beneficial, invisible-handed consequences of increasingly global free trade.

Nevertheless, despite the balance of economic evidence in favour of market-friendly over government-managed development, the high-performing economies of East and Southeast Asia by no means meet the requirements of the classic *laisser-faire* model of economic growth. In particular a series of studies in the course of the 1980s by Chalmers Johnson (1982), Alice Amsden (1989), Stephen Haggard (1990), Robert Wade (1990) and Gordon White and Robert Wade (1988) drew attention to the highly interventionist nature of the newly industrialized states in both their industrial and financial policy.

Following Johnson's classic analysis of market intervention and regulation by the Japanese Ministry of Trade and Industry (MITI), a new model of state-sponsored, export-led growth emerged. From this viewpoint, a notably autonomous and highly interventionist state technocracy identified and promoted key manufacturing and industrial sectors of the economy. Somewhat differently, Robert Wade (1990; 1992) identified in South Korea and Taiwan a technocratic strategy for proactively governing the market. This strategy combined high levels of government-directed investment in key industries with exposure of these industries to international competition. Moreover, 'using incentives, controls and mechanisms to spread risk, these policies enabled the government to guide – or govern – market processes of resource allocation so as to produce different production and investment outcomes than would have occurred with . . . free market . . . policies' (Wade 1990: 26). Effective guidance, consequently, required 'strong' states characterized by a high degree of autonomy from special interest group, particularly trade union, pressure, coupled with the managerial capacity to set and meet industrial targets.

The proponents of the export-led growth thesis further share the view that the embedded liberalism of the international trading order established by the United States and the United Kingdom at Bretton Woods in 1944 contributed substantially to the subsequent success of the Pacific Asian economies. The post-1944 trading order rejected the economic nationalism of the 1930s and sought to establish a multilateral trading order, which nevertheless countenanced domestic interventionism. Consequently GATT affirmed the principle of non-discrimination and tariff reduction, but nevertheless tolerated exemptions and restrictions to protect the domestic balance of payments and a variety of social policies (Ruggie 1993: 16; Helleiner 1994: 164). Drawn into this multilateral order by their Cold War alliance with the United States after 1945, Japan and, subsequently, Taiwan and South Korea, and more recently Thailand and Malaysia and to a lesser extent Indonesia, took advantage of the post-Bretton Woods environment to facilitate growth by exporting first labour-intensive and subsequently high value-added electronic and manufactured goods throughout the developed world in general and to the US market in particular by targeting and subsidizing certain industries and restricting imports (Thurow 1996: ch. 3).

A number of neoclassical market theorists have challenged this revisionist account of Pacific Asian growth, maintaining essentially that although both Northeast and Southeast Asian development displayed certain market-governing features, the trend, nevertheless, as these economies matured, was inexorably towards deregulation and greater market openness (Chowdhury and Islam 1993). In order to explore this debate and its ramifications for the Pacific Asian trading order, we shall briefly examine the Japanese model of the developmental state and consider the extent to which it has influenced both its Northeast Asian former colonies of South Korea and Taiwan as well as economic development in the two port cities of Pacific Asia, Hong Kong and Singapore. Subsequently, we shall consider the development of what Kunio Yoshihara (1988) terms the 'ersatz capitalism' in the later developing Southeast Asian economies of Indonesia, Thailand and Malaysia, and the role of overseas Chinese entrepreneurs in the Southeast Asian economy. In this context, we shall explore the significant differences that appear between the more Confucianized 'strong' states like South Korea and Taiwan and the weaker Southeast Asian economies with their less competent technocracies and their conspicuous dependence upon FDI. Finally we shall assess the nature of the new Pacific Asian trading order and its sustainability in the context of emerging tensions over the terms of trade in Pacific Asia.

The Japanese model

Modern industries attained their present development primarily through free competition. However, various evils of [the capitalist order] are becoming apparent. Holding to absolute freedom will not rescue the industrial world from its present disturbances. Industry needs a plan of comprehensive development and a measure of control. (Yohino Shinji 1935, cited in Johnson 1982: 108)

It was in the 1960s 'that the Japanese economy began attracting international attention' (Yoshihara 1994: vii) because of its rapid postwar recovery and successful industrialization. By the late 1980s, as Japanese industrial production, manufacturing technology and consequently gross domestic product (GDP) overtook that of most western industrialized nations, Japan had become a model not only for other late developing economies, but even for reforming western managerial and industrial practice. In the view of most Japanese commentators, western management theorists and a growing band of western political economists, 'Japan offers to developing countries a different developmental model from that of the west' (p. viii). Whilst historically industrialization in the United States and the United Kingdom occurred in the context of individual entrepreneurial enterprise, Japan's late modernization significantly subjugated individual interest for the sake of the group. As Chalmers Johnson observes, Japan's planned development from the Meiji Restoration (1868) onward derived not from Anglo-American notions of economic individualism, but from the school of mercantilist political economy associated with Friedrich List (1983) and sometimes labelled 'economic nationalism' (Johnson 1982: 17; Semmel 1993: 63). Government direction of the economy was already foreshadowed in the Meiji era development of infrastructure and the textile industry, followed in the period 1912–36 by the rise of heavy industry (Yoshihara 1994: 8–11) and government-linked, family-led conglomerates (*zaibatsu*) such as Mitsubishi, Mitsui and Sumitomo.

The failure of the military-led expansion into China and Southeast Asia after 1937, the collapse of the Greater East Asian Co-Prosperity Sphere in 1945 and the subsequent American occupation of Japan between 1945 and 1951 occasioned certain important modifications to the emerging developmental state. Although the chief task of the Supreme Commander for the Allied Powers (SCAP) was the destruction of the military superstructure that had devastated Asia between 1934 and 1945, the American presence initiated a series of institutional and economic reforms. In the economic sector, SCAP dissolved the influential family-led *zaibatsu* and introduced land reforms that both dissolved the economic base of the landlords and gave security of tenure and the prospect of improved living conditions to peasant farmers. As Yoshihara observes, 'the dissolution of the *zaibatsu* and the land reforms spread economic power more evenly over the population, making it more difficult for a small group of people to dominate national politics' (Yoshihara 1994: 123). Labour reforms further offered workers the right to organize. Nevertheless, these reforms did not sufficiently 'deconcentrate' the Japanese economy. 'In perhaps the Occupation's most portentous failure, SCAP failed to reorient Japanese corporations . . . toward the direct finance, based on capital markets then prevailing in the United States' (Calder 1993: 43). It thus perpetuated the dependence of Japanese corporations upon Japanese banks and reinforced their reluctance to resort to the markets for their primary financing.

The Occupation further failed to undermine the authority of a plan rational state, where 'the government will give the greatest precedence to industrial policy, that is to a concern with the structure of domestic industry and with promoting the structure that enhances the nation's international competitiveness' (Johnson 1982: 19). Such a policy implies a strategic or goal-oriented view both of the developing economy and of trade. In the period after 1952 a number of bureaucratic sites for economic planning evolved to shape Japan's postwar development. Moreover, 'a political consensus in favour of rapid growth, ample opportunity to catch up with the west, a liberal trading regime that gave Japan access to overseas markets, a capital market insulated from international money markets, and access to dependable and cheap materials and energy – especially oil', all conduced to plan rationality (Matthews and Ravenhill 1994: 42).

Economic conditions altered for the worse after 1973. As early as 1964, membership of the Organization for Economic Cooperation and Development (OECD) and GATT had required the reduction of tariff and quota barriers that restricted overseas access to the Japanese domestic market. More disturbingly, the Organization of Petroleum Exporting Countries' (OPEC) oil embargo of October 1973 exposed Japan's resource dependence. In this new context, the planner's task changed from that of nursing infant heavy industries to creating industrial superstars. As Yoshihara explains, 'machinery and equipment replaced industrial materials as Japan's leading industrial sector in the mid-1970s' (Yoshihara 1994: 24). Significantly, automobiles rose from 7 to 18 per cent of total exports in this period. In the course of the 1980s, moreover, exports in colour television sets and video cassette recorders (VCRs) approached the export market share of automobiles, whilst by the late 1980s the semiconductor and computer industry had achieved global leadership (Mathews and Ravenhill 1994: 56).

The explanation of Japan's dramatic growth lies in its ability to stimulate export growth in a number of sectors rather than relying on several basic industries. In order to develop one industrial sector after another, successful technocratic guidance has been crucial (Yoshihara 1994: 78). Let us examine then a little more closely the way Japan's bureaucracy in general and MITI in particular engineered the Japanese miracle.

In his classic study of MITI, industrial policy and the growth of the developmental state, Chalmers Johnson (1982) traced a continuous evolution of industrial policy in Japan from the 1920s. Although MITI, founded in 1949, dates from the period of US occupation, its origins may be located in the wartime Ministry of Munitions and the prewar Ministry of Commerce and Industry. In the course of the 1950s, MITI, together with the Ministry of Finance (MOF), intervened directly to boost advanced steel-making technology. MITI not only facilitated infrastructural development favourable to the steel industry, it also extended preferential low-interest loans through the Japanese Development Bank (JDB). In other words, MITI influenced the direction and form of investment and effectively directed the principal Japanese producers to adopt the latest technologies. To protect this massive investment and ensure market stability, the government protected the domestic market from imports. The protected home market enabled industry 'to achieve impressive scale economies and to be well positioned to capture export markets, when, by the late 1960s, capacity began to outstrip domestic demand' (Matthews and Ravenhill 1994: 45). Moreover, the growing efficiency of Japanese industry, notably in process technology, offered scope for technological externalities, or the diffusion of technological expertise into adjacent manufacturing sectors.

Technocratic planning, rather than any obvious comparative advantage, further explains the growth of Japanese automobile, colour television, VCR and computer manufacturing. Thus, in 1951, the government designated automobile manufacture a strategic industry and arranged loans for the Nissan and Toyota marques (Matthews and Ravenhill 1994: 46). Simultaneously, the government, by manipulating protective tariffs and severely restricting foreign direct investment, sheltered industry from foreign competition. This extensive protection was none the less 'time-bound' and the threat of future competition spurred the industry to expand productive capacity and avoid excessive price competition. Toyota in particular embraced techniques of lean and flexible manufacturing, enhancing quality and producing a wider range of products. When domestic demand slackened from the early 1970s, these measures facilitated a decisive Japanese competitive advantage in foreign markets. In fact, the American market became 'the engine that drove the growth of the Japanese auto industry' (Dunn 1989: 165).

Similarly, Japanese dominance in the world television market was again helped by a combination of government policies, import tariffs and quotas, controls on direct foreign investment, tax incentives for exports and a government-financed research programme. Again, in the 1980s, the Japanese government identified the semiconductor and computer industries for special assistance. Not only did the government-aided Japan Electric Computer Company (JECC) spur the industry's development, but government policy restricted the access of IBM and Texas Instruments to the Japanese market (Fallows 1994: ch. 1). The focus on generic technologies with broad applications distributed amongst competing domestic firms constituted a crucial ingredient in the strategy for promoting these high value-added products. In this way industrial policy reduced the cost of risky and expensive research, whilst offering competing firms a common technological base and generating benefits to other sectors created by the rapid growth of the computer and semiconductor industries.

Central to Japan's corporate development, therefore, was a far-sighted industrial policy dictated by a small, elite cadre of technocrats selected from the best universities in Japan and located in strategically critical governmental agencies (primarily the MOF, Bank of Japan and MITI) with close links to business and government. Indeed, the evolution of Japan's business and political culture has promoted an iron triangle of bureaucracy, government and business. The Liberal Democratic Party (LDP), which governed Japan uninterruptedly from 1952 to 1992 and in a series of coalitional arrangements after 1993, particularly fostered technocratic guidance. As Johnson classically observed, the party reigned but the bureaucrats ruled. They did so because the formally democratic political system effectively limited the legal and judicial branches of government and deterred interest groups from distorting the priorities of the developmental state, whilst the bureaucracy possessed a large discretionary authority to guide the economy and sponsor market-conforming measures. The fact that Japan's 'most important postwar politicians . . . were all former senior bureaucrats' (Johnson 1982: 322) and the practice of *amakudari*, or descent from heaven, which enables senior civil servants to move to the boardrooms of large private organizations on retirement cemented this triangular relationship (Van Wolferen 1990: 45).

However, the iron triangle responsible for planned development is not entirely impervious to influence. As Daniel Okimoto observes, the evolving relationship between business and government has increasingly modified bureaucratic autonomy, creating in the process a 'network' (*keiretsu*) state. In such an arrangement, 'strength is derived from the convergence of public and private interests and the extensive network of ties binding the two sectors together' (Okimoto 1989: 145). Such networks not only permeate business and government relations, but business itself functions on the basis of established ties between distributors and manufacturers and between small- and large-scale producers, or between companies through cross-cutting share holdings.

These *keiretsu* arrangements form an integral part of Japanese corporate culture yet have remained curiously neglected. The characteristic structure of *keiretsu* gives them considerable scope for taking strategic initiatives. As Yoshihara points out, 'when there is a bank within the group, which is usually the case, the debt–equity ratio is high, which further reduces the importance of outside shareholders' (Yoshihara 1994: 144). Such inter-corporate holdings linked to associate banks significantly reduces the impact of share price fluctuation on manufacturers. At the same time, vertical *keiretsu* arrangements, most evident in the automobile industry, between an assembler, its suppliers and their subcontractors, promote both investment and efficiency. Although suppliers and assemblers maintain intercorporate holdings, they remain separate companies. Consequently, although business between them represents a market transaction, they nevertheless remain linked 'by long term ties, unlike those in the market place which are freely formed and terminated' (p. 144). Links with a *sogoshosha*, or general trading company which eases the entry of a Japanese company into an overseas market, further facilitates the *keiretsu*'s export effectiveness. These networks, together with the developmental policies promoted by MITI, have both modified the impact of open market competition on the small scale and traditional producer and successfully promoted Japanese trade in overseas markets, whilst at the same time preventing those without access to networks penetrating the domestic market.

Somewhat differently, Kent Calder's (1993) analysis of the strategic operation of Japanese capital in general, and the *keiretsu* exploitation of domestic and foreign markets in particular, questions both the efficiency of Japan's plan rationality and MITI's continuing capacity to manage the Japanese economy. The Ministry of Finance and MITI have frequently clashed over the level of governmental support for manufacturing industries, undermining the assumption of a bureaucratic consensus on industrial policy. Moreover, even an interventionist ministry like MITI was often more concerned with a macroeconomic policy of low inflation rather than with 'an explicit developmental perspective' (Calder 1993: 74). Significantly, global multinationals like Toyota and Sony received little government protection during the more vulnerable stages of their development. Consequently, although MITI managed the automobile and computer sectors through its authority to 'impose control to obtain strategic results', in a number of other areas 'private sector borrowers . . . have been highly dynamic in the credit allocation process' (p. 174). This strategic view of Japanese capitalism emphasizes the credit allocation role played by semi-private banks like the Industrial Bank of Japan. *Keiretsu* borrowing from the private sector creates 'circles of compensation' combining public and private actors with common interests in a particular public policy endeavour. In this assessment, 'rather than picking winners . . . in a flexible fashion across the political economy as a whole, the Japanese state has allocated benefits, including industrial credit, through these established circles, which have, in turn, provided diversified support to the bureaucracy' (p. 246). Moreover, systematic discrimination operates against outsiders. Thus, 'new members periodically enter the circles, but few leave . . . imparting a conservative, often clientelist bias to government industrial credit policy' (p. 246).

In fact, Japan's political economy increasingly resembles a case of 'corporate-led strategic capitalism' in which neither state nor market dominates. Moreover, the dual impact of clientelist pressure for government credit and external pressure from the United States and the WTO to open the Japanese domestic market has rendered this strategic, bureaucratically led policy increasingly difficult. Paradoxically, the very efficacy of corporate-led strategic capitalism in capturing overseas markets in the course of the 1980s has excerbated this difficulty.

By 1985, the trade surpluses achieved by Japan prompted growing OECD pressure for the yen to revalue (Yoshihara 1994: 25). Through the 1985 Plaza Agreement and the 1987 Louvre Accord, the industrialized nations attempted to establish concerted foreign exchange intervention and target bands for exchange rates between the leading currencies. The exchange rate of the yen, which traded at 250 to the US dollar in mid-1985, appreciated to 123 to the dollar by the end of 1987. Yet, between 1987 and 1991, the Japanese economy continued to grow at 5 per cent per annum as Japanese manufacturers relocated to Southeast Asia 'where labour costs were lower' (p. 25). At the same time, *endaka* (the high-value yen), combined with low Bank of Japan interest rates, occasioned a surge in bank loans, stock values and real estate and office property prices, especially in Tokyo. It also encouraged Japanese companies, fortified by *endaka,* to invest in speculative real estate, hotel and communications ventures in Europe, America and Australia. This created a liquidity bubble. As *The Economist* explained, 'companies invested as if capital cost nothing. Banks lent as if risk had been abolished. . . . Security firms tried to manipulate the financial markets. . . . All these assumptions were wrong, a fact that emerged in January 1990, when the Tokyo stock market began its almost 50 per cent fall' (14 March 1992: 17). Stung by the drop in property prices at home, Japanese companies restricted overseas investment, creating a shortage of yen worldwide to pay for Japanese exports, thus forcing exchange rates higher and further exacerbating surpluses in Japan's trade balance. Indeed between 1992 and 1995, Japan ran annual current account trade surpluses of over $100 billion.

The strong yen coupled with a stagnating property market and bad debt accruing from property speculation plunged Japan into recession after 1992. By 1995, despite a series of massive investment packages, and escalating threats from the office of the United States Trade Representative (USTR) to invoke Section 301 of the Trade Act (1974) to restrict Japanese trade (Ryan 1995: 337), Japan's surplus remained largely undented. The yen briefly appreciated in May 1995 to 80 to the dollar whilst Japanese land prices were estimated to be worth only 10 per cent of their 1991 peak (*Asian Wall Street Journal*, 21–22 July 1995). The recession not only prompted manufacturers to move offshore in increasing numbers, leaving in their wake growing unemployment, it also left Japanese banks and *jusen* (financial institutions) mired in bad debt. Five years after the real estate bubble burst, the Japanese property market was frozen in illiquidity. Suffering from an estimated 50 trillion yen ($670 billion) in non-performing loans, the immature and opaque Japanese financial sector looked decidedly weak (*Asian Wall Street Journal*, 21–22 July 1995). Ironically, the very success of protecting domestic markets whilst single-mindedly capturing overseas ones has, in combination with the revaluation of the yen after 1985, produced domestic recession and a deflation of assets.

The Japanese model is thus a somewhat ambivalent one. Developmental in its origins, the Japanese state gave a wide degree of autonomy to state bureaucrats to implement policy. Industrial policy changed over time as the economy matured. The very success of the strategy, however, exposed the bureaucracy to both political and business pressure so that consensus, which superficially appears monolithic, actually entails compromise decisions of an ultimately market-unfriendly nature. Moreover the increased access of multinational *keiretsu* to government, and the problematic debt portfolio of banks and *jusen*, further erode the bureaucratic ability to chart an independent course of action. Immersed, moreover, in a face-saving political culture, the bureaucracy cannot break with the paternalistic and corporatist practices necessary to release the Japanese economy from recession. To what extent, we might next consider, have the former Japanese colonies of South Korea and Taiwan followed or modified the Japanese model and assumed their appointed place in the flying geese pattern of harmonious, but ultimately problematic Pacific Asian growth?

The political economy of Northeast Asia

South Korea Incorporated

As the World Bank maintains, 'despite unfavourable initial conditions' that included colonization by Japan from 1910 to 1945 and civil war from 1950 to 1953, real GNP growth in South Korea (ROK) has 'tripled in every decade since 1962' (World Bank 1993b: ix). In the World Bank's opinion, the 'benefits of growth have been distributed widely' and occasioned a sharp reduction in the incidence of absolute poverty. This 'was only possible in an environment in which the state saw economic development as its primary responsibility' (p. ix). In the view of the World Bank, 'Korea managed . . . to "condense" a century of growth into three decades' (p. 1), a condensation achieved, moreover, by rigorous planning and export-oriented growth.

Before we endorse the World Bank's paean to planning, it is helpful initially to trace the impact of prewar Japanese colonialism and American postwar aid on the ROK economy. Although Japan's dominion of Korea 'brought both exploitation and modernization in a mixture that is hotly debated and can hardly be unscrambled' (Henderson 1968: 111; Cumings 1989, vol. 1: ch. 1), in the period 1922–44 colonization nevertheless developed Korea's mining industry and domestic infrastructure. Postwar American influence, and the external and internal threat of communism, further facilitated, in a traditionally autocratic culture, the control of the labour movement and the reform of agriculture. The government effectively broke radical trade union activity and successive regimes subsequently controlled labour through state-sponsored organizations (Park 1987: 911). American aid throughout the 1950s further facilitated a policy of import substitution which permitted the Rhee government to finance the import of selected producer goods and export primary products (Haggard 1990: 24, 54–6). From the end of the Korean War to 1975, when aid stopped, the United States supplied $13 billion in economic and military assistance (Steinberg 1993: 38). Aid also made possible the 1954 Land Reform, whereby the government appropriated land in exchange for five-year bonds and redistributed it to peasant farmers in the form of smallholdings (World Bank 1993b: 6). By the 1960s, rural landholding consisted primarily of 'small farming families owning their own land' (Moore 1988: 144). During President Park's regime (1961–79) the government continued to protect and intervene in agriculture. The *Saemaul Undong* (New Community) movement provided an ideological and organizational framework for rural development to achieve agricultural self-sufficiency (Pye 1985: 224; Moore 1988: 146). Indeed between 1962 and 1976, agriculture, forestry and fisheries received 25 per cent of all government investment (World Bank 1993b: 6). The government management and protection of agriculture in the period 1961–90 had the additional political merit of guaranteeing the Park, Chun and Roh regimes with a passive and dependent peasantry. Agricultural reform, together with US financial and food aid, upon which 1950s South Korea was 'almost totally dependent' (World Bank 1993b: 1), and favourable access to the American market after 1961, constituted the foundation of subsequent South Korean industrial development.

TABLE 2.3 GDP per capita, 1995

Country	US$
Hong Kong	22,840
Singapore	24,900
Republic of Korea	9,600
Republic of China (Taiwan)	12,600
Indonesia	940
Malaysia	3,520
Thailand	2,600

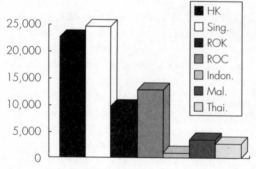

Sources: Fishburn 1994: 94–8; *Far Eastern Economic Review*, 28 December 1996: 124

This notwithstanding, South Korea in the early 1960s seemed a distinctly unpromising place for rapid modernization. Located at the periphery of the world economy (Wade 1992: 277), Korea's infrastructure ranked well below that of Turkey, Colombia or Taiwan (World Bank 1993b: 10). Yet from such unpromising beginnings the ROK's real GNP has tripled every decade since 1962. This, together with a military-style campaign to reduce population growth, produced significant per capita GDP income gains, rising from $110 in 1962 to $8,470 by 1993 (see table 2.3; Wade 1990: 35; *The Economist*, 3 June 1995: 4). Korea moved from ninety-ninth to forty-fourth in the World Bank ranking of national economic performance between 1962 and 1986 (Wade 1990: 34). It was, moreover, in the era of Park Chung Hee's authoritarian rule that the ROK moved decisively away from a policy of import substitution towards export-led growth, or, as Park put, it *suchul ipguk* (nation building through exports). With the Japanese model before him, and mindful of Korea's lack of resources, cheap labour and a population 'unusually greedy for. . . . education' (Wade 1992: 312), there was no obvious alternative.

Korea's primary economic priority in the 1960s was to expand manufactured exports (Song 1990: 120). The Park regime adopted a 'variant of authoritarian capitalism, in which enterprises were privately owned but the management was shared between the government and the owners' (World Bank 1993b: 1). The Economic Planning Board (EPB) established by Park, together with the Ministry of Commerce and Industry (MCI) and the Ministry of Finance (MOF), assumed central responsibility for planning industrial policy. In order to promote development, Park's government, in the course of the 1970s, contributed 33 per cent of government direct investment towards infrastructure. Government promoted imports of capital and intermediate goods required by exporters and provided macroeconomic stability by restricting currency trading, maintaining an undervalued won and managing the banking sector in a manner that allocated capital to fund industrial and export expansion (Rhee 1994: 66). Support for exporters included an export-friendly tax and trade regime, effective policies for technology acquisition and international marketing through agencies like the Korean Trade Promotion Corporation (KOTRA) and General Trading Companies (GTCs) that received preferential access to foreign exchange. As the GTCs controlled exports, the government could effectively control industry both through them and through control of the banking sector (Patrick and Park 1994: 330).

Throughout the 1960s and early 1970s, exports, not profitability, constituted the yardstick of industrial performance. Even during the oil-shock of 1973, the Park regime promoted growth rather than stability. Indeed, 'to qualify as a regular customer of the government for long term subsidized credit . . . Big firms and small firms, young firms and old firms had to export' (Amsden 1989: 18). Moreover, since the government favoured economies of scale in production, marketing and technology acquisition, it rewarded size with better access to credit (World Bank 1993b: 3). As the EPB performed the Korean equivalent of MITI but more so, it particularly favoured private, family-run conglomerates (*chaebol*) that resembled prewar Japanese *zaibatsu*. The emerging conglomerates offered an economy of scope, acting as marketing agents for small firms which proved 'particularly helpful in the early stages of economic development' (p. 35). On the other hand, as *chaebol* expanded in the 1970s, profitable units had to subsidize inefficient ones, locking resources into questionable uses and exposing the group to business fluctuations.

The internal management culture of the *chaebol* further promoted bureaucratic direction of the private sector. *Chaebol* are family-owned, corporate patriarchies. Founding families own 60 per cent of the equity in the leading thirty *chaebol* and favour a personalized and often obsessive management style. Thus, Kim Woo Chung, founder of the Daewoo *chaebol* in

1967, took his first day off only in 1990 to attend the funeral of his son. 'His employees were expected to work six days a week, twelve hours a day, until the mid-1980s' (*The Economist*, 3 June 1995: 5). Analogously, Choo Young Chung rose from an unskilled labourer in prewar Kangwondo province to found and oversee the Hyundai *chaebol* in an equally autocratic manner (Watanabe 1992: 115). This patriachal style extends to share ownership and a kinship-based corporate management. Thus, 'among the twenty one major firms under the Hyundai conglomerate, four firms . . . are dominated by Mr Chung's family with his shareholding amounting to more than 40 per cent of total shares, while more than 20 per cent of eleven firms shares are held by his family' (p. 114). A similar pattern of share ownership characterizes Lee Byung Chul's domination of the Samsung conglomerate. By the 1990s Korea's top four *chaebol*, Hyundai, Samsung, Daewoo and Lucky Goldstar, represented 22 per cent of the nation's assets and 57 per cent of exports. The 'top two Hyundai and Samsung together have sales equivalent to a quarter of South Korea's economy' (*The Economist*, 3 June 1995: 18).

It was the presidential decision in 1973 to reduce support for cheap, labour-intensive, export-oriented light industry in footwear and textiles and promote instead the Heavy and Chemical Industry Plan (HCIP) (World Bank 1993b: 18; Rhee 1994: 77) that proved highly conducive to this characteristic form of South Korean business conglomeration. The decision was dictated both by the economic downturn of the late 1960s and by the American decision to reduce its military commitment in Pacific Asia after 1972, necessitating, Park felt, the foundation of an indigenous armaments industry. The new industrial policy promoted export-oriented heavy and chemical industries to overcome the limits of the small domestic market, creating large-sized facilities favouring economies of scale and the further expansion of the *chaebol* (Rhee 1994: 68). HCIP focused on the 'strategic industries' of iron and steel, machinery, non-ferrous metals, electronics, shipbuilding, automobiles and petrochemicals. Apart from a cheap and generally compliant labour force, Korea possessed no evident comparative heavy industrial advantage. The programme classically evinced 'big leadership' by the state technocracy. Bolstered by the six promotional laws introduced during the second Five-Year Plan (1967–72), President Park's decree 'mobilized Korea's bureaucracy to achieve his goals' (World Bank 1993b: 20). Planning was so detailed that designated industries had to pass through four bureaucratically determined stages, proceeding from a minimum scale of active government planning, to an optimum scale where government support continued as the industry matured, before finally achieving a first-class scale of international competitiveness (World Bank 1993b: 20).

The Korean achievement in the steel, automobile, shipbuilding and electronics industry to some extent vindicated this state-sponsored industrial strategy. Thus, in 1974, the EPB outlined an industry-specific plan for automobiles covering a decade. The plan sought to achieve 90 per cent domestic content for small passenger cars and the transformation of the industry into a major exporter by the early 1980s. The government identified three primary producers: 'Hyundai, Kia, and GM Korea – later called Saehan and then Daewoo' (Wade 1990: 310). Planning required the primary producers to meet a domestic content schedule and cooperate in the production of standard parts. The MCI selected 'certain items and their assigned producers for special promotion, with a complete import ban once the item met the government's price and quality standards. Later the three producers were required to set export targets [and] . . . they were encouraged to set their export price below the cost of production' (p. 310). Domestic sales subsidized exports. Thus, 'the Hyundai Pony cost US$3,700 in 1979, sold domestically for $5,000 and sold abroad for $2,200. . . . The practice continues today' (p. 310). Import-substituting restrictions and tariffs on imported vehicles made possible price distorting strategies in the domestic market while exploiting opportunities in the American and European markets. Under intense pressure from the office of the USTR, the government 'announced an automobile liberalization schedule which permits small car imports to begin in 1988 for the first time in over twenty five years, but with a duty of 200 per cent to be lowered to 100 per cent after two years' (Wade 1990: 311). Nevertheless, even in 1994, automobile imports constituted less than 1 per cent of the domestic automobile market, whilst the Korean industry exported 52 per cent of the more than one million domestically produced units. Indeed, 'one of the most important reasons why the Korean auto industry may succeed in becoming a major world producer is the government's ability to restrict entry of new producers, and thereby protect economies of scale' (p. 311).

An analogous triumph of industrial planning accounted for the spectacular growth of Samsung as a world electronics giant. Again in 1974, the EPB, surveying the world for 'needed markets capital and technology' (Cumings 1994: 219), outlined an eight-year, Electronics Industry Development Plan. The plan identified three targets: research and development; advanced training; and technology imports via licensing and consultancies rather than by foreign direct investment. In 1976, the government established the Korean Institute of Electronics Technology (KIET) as a research institution. KIET mounted training programmes for Korean firms, sent engineers abroad to gain experience and took an active part in technology transfer negotiations. In 1980, it built Korea's first full-scale wafer fabrication facility (Wade 1990: 314). In addition, throughout the 1970s and 1980s the government targeted the industry for concessional credit, protected it, imposed domestic content requirements and used public procurement to steer demand towards

Korean-made products (Wade 1990: 313). In the 1980s, the government used its control over telecommunications to aid *chaebol* entry into semiconductor fabrication. In 1982, the government published the long-term Semiconductor Industry Promotion Plan (1982–6), giving the electronic *chaebol* (Samsung, Lucky Goldstar and Daewoo) greater autonomy. In 1989 Samsung secured a thirteen-year cross-licensing agreement with IBM that 'implies that IBM considers Samsung an important and independent developer of advanced semiconductor technology' (Wade 1990: 317). By the early 1990s Korea had become the third largest fabricator of large-capacity memory chips.

Similar impressive strides have been made in both shipbuilding and steel. Korean yards have come to dominate the world shipbuilding industry while the state-run Pohang steel company POSCO was, in the view of the World Bank, 'a bold and successful gamble' in building a 'state of the art integrated steel plant' (World Bank 1993b: 26). Indeed by 1990, Korean-style state capitalism had yielded a 'dynamically efficient industry . . . financing its own second generation expansion . . . and propelling Korea into a capital intensive stage of industrialization perhaps a decade earlier than expected' (p. 26).

Yet despite these achievements, HCIP was not an unalloyed success. The initial experience of government-led and *chaebol*-implemented heavy industrialization was 'one of considerable waste' (Steinberg 1993: 36). Between 1973 and 1981, the government mobilized domestic and foreign capital through enforced public savings and external borrowing to fund the HCI initiative. 'Korea', as the World Bank observes, is 'a nation of savers' (World Bank 1994: 12). Personal savings 'exploded' to 16 per cent of GNP in the 1980s. Although the savers' primary objective was housing and education, the Korean return on savings was, and remains, low. Government deployed domestic saving to defray the cost of HCI. Even so, domestic credit was insufficient to support the grandiose scale of HCI and the government consequently contracted a large foreign debt in the course of the 1970s. The EPB directed domestic and foreign credit towards HCI and away from export oriented light industries. In response to government inducements, *chaebol* invested in the power and heavy machinery industries, fuelling, in 1976, the 'Changwon Rush' into a heavy machinery complex established in the southern part of Korea.

Changwon, however, was beset by 'poor technical decisions . . . [and] low capacity utilization . . . by all accounts it was not a profitable investment' (World Bank 1993b: 23). By September 1979 the 'average operation ratio of sixty firms in the Changwon Machinery Industrial Complex, the key estate of the HCIs, was below 30 per cent' (Rhee 1994: 112). Thus, although 'approximately 70 per cent of policy loans went to the HCI sectors' (Rhee 1994: 81), by the late 1970s the heavy industrial companies faced a growing shortage of finance. Moreover, there was a low level of capacity utilization in some industries, such as machinery and fabricated metals, and an over-capacity in energy production. At the same time, state investment in light industry and small and medium-sized enterprises (SMEs) evaporated. In other words, certain sectors, notably finance, SMEs and heavy machinery, incurred heavy economic losses as a consequence of state planning. Indeed, by 1980, Park's bureaucratically engineered growth had generated a current account deficit that represented 9 per cent of GNP and a disturbing, and still unresolved, external debt burden estimated at 49 per cent of GNP (*The Economist*, 3 June1995: 17). This, together with the second OPEC oil-shock of 1979, saw GDP growth cut back to −2.9 per cent and inflation reaching 29 per cent per annum.

The assassination of President Park in October 1979, growing tension within the EPB and MCI over industrial policy and a breakdown in state corporatist control of labour further exacerbated the crisis. The period 1979–80, therefore, witnessed both 'the disorder of political institutions, of policy networks between the state and social groups and of the financial system' and 'the ineffective implementation of economic stabilization policy measures' (Rhee 1994: 146). It was in these difficult circumstances that the military coup staged by General Chun Doo Hwan in May 1980 re-established authoritarian controls. The coup also facilitated a radical reform of the economic bureaucracy and a re-evaluation of the relationship between government and big business. In order to legitimize its authority, Chun's regime embarked upon a programme of economic liberalization. In this context, the Social Purification Subcommittee's purge of bureaucrats and labour union leaders in 1980 established the preconditions for a more eco-nomically liberal EPB to adjust the HCIP and distance itself from the close and often corrupt ties with the *chaebol* established during Park's regime.

Two principles guided the post-1980 drive for industrial restructuring: rationalizing the overcapacity created by the drive to HCI; and reducing business concentration. The meeting held in August 1980 between the chairman of the Subcommittee on Industry and Resources and 'the top managers of the Hyundai Business Group and the Daewoo Business Group' graphically illustrates the process: 'there, the Hyundai Group chose the passenger car field, leaving the Daewoo Group to monopolise the power-generating equipment field' (Rhee 1994: 160). To achieve corporate compli-ance with administrative-guided reduction of business concentration, the government relied on 'credit allocation, tax investigation and even naked intimidation by the security agencies as instruments of policy enforcement' (Moon 1994: 148). Unsurprisingly, the more compliant conglomerates bene-fited from the reorganization, whilst those less cooperative, like Hyundai, suffered, or collapsed, like the Kukje *chaebol* in 1985. At the same time, in order to liberalize the financial sector and provide greater scope for SMEs, the EPB and President Chun's economic secretariat sponsored a comprehensive credit management system and the privatization of the state-owned commercial banks.

Chun's economic reforms significantly affected relations between government and big business and engendered conflict within the bureaucracy between economic liberals and conservatives. The main big business interest association, the Federation of Korean Industries (FKI), openly criticized the EPB's liberalization programme, whilst after 1985, within government, the EPB encountered growing strategic resistance from the MOF and MCI. These tensions continued into the regimes of Roh Tae Woo (1987–92) and have been further exacerbated during Kim Young Sam's (1992–) presidency. Dramatically illustrating the deteriorating relationship between the corporate sector and the technocratic planners, Hyundai chairman Chung Joo Young defied the National Tax Agency's demand for back taxes, established his own Unification National Party and challenged Kim Young Sam for the presidency in 1992.

Meanwhile, the Kim government's decision to speed liberalization and business deconcentration in the seventh Five-Year Plan (1992–7), maintaining that *chaebol*-centred economic growth had reached the point of diminishing returns, has had the unintended consequence of exposing the network of graft and corruption that permeated government, bureaucracy and *chaebol* relations throughout the 1980s. In particular Kim's decision in 1993 to introduce a 'real name' financial transaction system, to eliminate the dual structure (formal and informal) of financial institutions and improve tax revenue particularly from business conglomerates, exposed the dark side of Korea's corporate growth. The indictment for treason of former Presidents Chun and Roh further revealed the extent to which the more compliant *chaebol* went to promote 'the government–business nexus' that produced 'one of the world's fastest growing economies' (*Far Eastern Economic Review*, 30 November 1995: 6). In December 1995, as a direct consequence of Kim's decision to promote fiscal probity, thirty-six of Korea's leading businessmen, including heads of *chaebol* like Daewoo's Kim Woo Chong, admitted donating contributions to former President Roh's billion-dollar political slush fund, evidently in return for political favours (*International Herald Tribune*, 28 December 1995). The subsequent 'trial of the century' resulted in the chairmen of both Daewoo and Samsung receiving prison sentences for corruption (*The Australian*, 27 August 1996).

Moreover, despite the government's attempt to promote financial transparency, it has failed to reduce monopolistic or oligopolistic economic concentration. Paradoxically, financial deregulation begun by President Chun to reduce the power of the *chaebol* has endowed the conglomerates with greater financial autonomy through access to private borrowing. Indeed evolving *chaebol* resistance to government intervention suggests a limit to the government's capacity to govern the market reflected in the increasing friction between the economic ministries and the EPB, leading ultimately to the abolition of the latter in 1994, and indicating the weakening developmental capacity of the state.

Nevertheless, it would be an exaggeration to maintain, as Chung-in Moon does, that 'the much vaunted developmental state was a transitional configuration which contained its own limits and contradictions. Conditions such as economic backwardness, authoritarian politics and the corporatist culture which underpinned it have now passed' (Moon 1994: 161). Certainly the relationship between the economic ministries and the business conglomerates altered from that of patron–client to one of greater equality, but this by no means implies that government now assumes a neutral role. Although official rhetoric currently adopts a neoliberal tone, government continues to offer 'big leadership' in key sectors. Government incentives promote the fledgeling aerospace industry, whilst, in March 1995, the MCI 'put together a consortium of South Korea's car makers [to] . . . pool resources to make parts' (*The Economist*, 3 June 1995: 17). An analogous interventionism characterizes the inchoate mobile phone industry. Furthermore, the differential access to the Ministries of Finance and Commerce and Industry accorded to conglomerates like Daewoo in the course of the 1980s and Samsung more recently (Rhee 1994: ch. 8; *The Economist*, 3 June 1995: 17) suggests that the corrupt relationship between *chaebol* and government continues to distort the market.

Korean industrial policy has, in fact, evolved towards an increasingly inclusionary corporatist network of consultative mechanisms, and the state technocracy has been central to this evolution. As the World Bank (1993b) observes, much of Korea's economic success in the 1970s, and again in the late 1980s, was a consequence of 'Korea's bureaucracy and planning apparatus, the unique relationship between business and government [and] . . . the pragmatism . . . of policy formulation and implementation' (p. 28). Indeed the bureaucrats responsible for designing industrial policy, unlike the *chaebol*, enjoy high public regard, reflecting a Confucian tradition of 'honoring scholar-bureaucrats' (World Bank 1993b: 30, also see chapter 1). After it was restructured in 1963, the civil service developed into a professional and meritocratic institution. Open competitive examination determines selection to the various grades and candidates are selected from the country's leading universities. The bureaucrats of the EPB, MOF and MCI have successfully planned, implemented, monitored and, where necessary, modified some highly complicated interventionist policies (Leudde-Neurath 1988: 101). Given their high status and responsibility for managing development, 'Korean bureaucrats

... also consider it their national duty to stall foreign interests' (p. 100). In this they reflect a classical Korean xenophobia, for, 'in the minds of many Koreans, foreigners come to Korea essentially to take something away, and bureaucrats see it as their duty to guard against this' (p. 100).

Despite its evident efficiency in promoting the national interest, however, this technocratic *dirigisme* has not been an unmitigated success. Without clear policy direction in 1979–80, the bureaucratic adjustment of the excesses of HCI caused overcapacity, inflation and external debt. In the course of the 1980s, the MOF and MCI increasingly resisted what they considered the doctrinaire, deregulatory policy promulgated by the key planning agency, the EPB. The abolition of the EPB in 1994, in other words, by no means indicates an end to state planning. Instead it offers new opportunities for the more interventionary MOF and MCI.

Continuing state intervention in the finance sector and the consequent weakness of the stock market, as well as the record external debt of $70 billion announced in 1995 (*Far Eastern Economic Review*, 14 September 1995: 83), further demonstrate the endemic conflict between *chaebol* expansion and bureaucratically determined financial policy. Korean banks, despite deregulation, continue to operate as 'handmaiden' serving government industrial policy (Patrick and Park 1994: 360). Indeed, the extreme regulation of the past, coupled with the legacy of bad debt contracted by inefficient *chaebol* like Hanbo, which disintegrated spectacularly in 1997, the excesses of the HCIP and non-performing loans in a vastly inflated Korean property market, means that even liberal technocrats are cautious when it comes to dismantling financial controls and allowing direct foreign investment into the country's highly regulated stock market.

Thus, although South Korea is, in the opinion of the World Bank, 'the most successful NIC' (World Bank 1994: 40), its development has not been unblemished. Certainly, its industrial policy has produced world competitive industries, and sustained impressive GDP growth. Yet even here some sceptics maintain that much of the growth achieved since 1973 has been in capital and labour inputs rather than through gains in efficiency (Young 1995: 657ff), a fact seemingly confirmed by Korea's continuing dependence on Japan for high-technology components. Korea, like all the HPAEs, runs a large trade deficit with Japan, amounting to 3.5 per cent of GNP (*Financial Times*, 17 October 1994). MOF management, moreover, lacks transparency, has acquired a burgeoning external debt and faces continuing inflationary pressure (see table 2.4). Meanwhile, MCI protectionism continues, with average tariffs on imported goods at 8 per cent, whilst in key sectors, like agriculture, it remains as high as 30 per cent (World Bank 1994: 36). In the Korean domestic automobile market, for instance, foreign manufacturers sold a mere 4,000 cars in 1994 (*Asian Wall Street Journal*, 21–2

TABLE 2.4 Inflation, 1994–1995

Country	Annual inflation (%)
Hong Kong	8
Singapore	3
Republic of Korea	6
Republic of China	4
Indonesia	8.3
Malaysia	4
Thailand	4.6

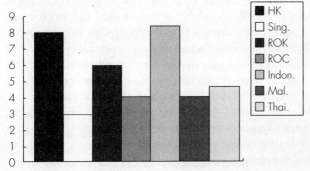

Sources: Fishburn 1994: 94–8; *Far Eastern Economic Review*, 28 December 1996: 124

September 1995). Moreover, as *chaebol* continue to prosper from a mixture of mercantilism and obscure financial practice, the modernized Korean economy suffers from an absence of small and medium-sized industries. Finally, to a very large extent South Korea's development exploited the embedded liberalism of the postwar Bretton Woods global trading system. As Robert Wade contends, South Korea benefited up until 1989 from its location on the fault line of global politics, abutting communist Asia. 'US concern for their economic growth . . . translated into massive aid, good access to the richest market in the world, and US tolerance of their import barriers' (Wade 1992: 312).

In the post-Cold War era, however, the United States has grown less amenable to the trade deficit of between $4 and $9 billion per annum it has contracted with South Korea since the mid-1980s. The increasing readiness of the United States to respond bilaterally to markets closed to American goods further exacerbates the problem of Korea's underdeveloped financial sector and the domestic protection accorded to Korean conglomerates. The state's capacity to deregulate the financial sector and maintain a judicious distance from the claims of the powerful industrial conglomerates without incurring financial embarrassment constitutes the challenge facing Korea's technocracy as the country prepares to enter the ranks of the OECD.

Taiwan Incorporated

The economic development of postwar Taiwan shares some interesting similarities with that of South Korea. After 1950, both HPAEs had few natural resources apart from a plentiful, docile and relatively well-educated labour supply and sustained comparable high economic growth rates. Indeed, Taiwan and Korea 'stand out from virtually all other countries of Eastern Europe and the Third World for having *reduced* the income gap with Northwest European and North American core [economies] between 1980 and 1988' (Wade 1992: 277). Thus Taiwan's gross national product (GNP) grew at an annualized average rate of 8.8 per cent between 1952 and 1992. As a consequence real per capita GNP increased from about $100 in 1952 to $10,000 by 1992 (see table 2.3). The unemployment rate has been below 3 per cent since 1971 (Kuo 1994: 89). In the course of this growth the economy moved from an agricultural to an industrial orientation. The share of agriculture in GDP dropped from 32 per cent in 1952 to 4 per cent in 1992, while the industrial share in GDP rose from 20 per cent to 42 per cent over the same period (pp. 89–90). Significantly, government played an important part in developing manufacturing and promoting export-led growth. In 1992 'The Republic of China [ROC – Taiwan] was the fourteenth largest trading country in the world' (p. 90) with exports of $81.5 billion and imports of $72 billion. The faster growth in exports over imports since 1973 has, moreover, transformed a very weak balance of payments into a very strong one.

Taiwan shared with Korea a Japanese colonial past and the geopolitical benefit of abutting communist Asia, thereby attracting massive American aid after 1950. As in Korea, the Japanese period left an ambivalent legacy of exploitation and development. Japan gained its Taiwanese colony by the Treaty of Shimonoseki in 1895 and the administrative strategy devised by its first Governor, Goto Shimpei, improved infrastructure, public hygiene and education dramatically. The Japanese left 'roads, railroads, port facilities and an electrification system' (Copper 1994: 75) together with rudimentary food processing, textile and fertilizer industries. Manufacturing grew in real terms at 6 per cent per annum between 1912 and 1940 and, even in the colonial period, Taiwan constituted a vital link in a Pacific Asian regional economy 'importing raw materials from Southeast Asia and exporting processed products to Japan' (Wade 1990: 74). By the time Taiwan reverted to Chinese Nationalist rule in 1945, it was the most developed of all the Chinese provinces. When the Nationalist government retreated in disarray to Taiwan in 1949 it determined not to repeat its failure on the mainland and launched sweeping economic reforms. The Leninist structure of the KMT, moreover, together with the absence of links between party mainlanders and the Taiwanese population, facilitated the implementation of radical change. Like Korea, 'Taiwan . . . began its postwar history without an organized political left' and the KMT rapidly established corporate control over labour (Haggard 1990: 80). State autonomy, together with massive US military and economic aid between 1951 and 1965, made possible both agricultural reform and an industrialization programme (Wade 1990: 82–4). Land reform occurred in three phases: a rent reduction programme implemented in 1949; a public land sale policy; followed by the 'land to the tiller' programme, which by 1953 resulted in former tenant farmers owning 71 per cent of public and private land. In 1959, nearly 90 per cent of Taiwan's exports were agricultural (Vogel 1991: 20). Growing efficiency in agricultural production 'prepared the way' for industrialization. The 'combination of a population already well trained under Japanese colonial rule and mainlander technocrats eager to absorb new information', together with US economic aid amounting to 10 per cent of Taiwan's GNP in 1951, 'provided a critical base for industrialization' (pp. 21–2). American aid financed infrastructural development and 'extensive quantitative restrictions and high tariff rates shielded domestic consumer goods from foreign competition' (World Bank 1993a: 131). To absorb abundant labour, the government subsidized some light industries, particularly textiles. Consumer goods industries such as apparel and bicycles developed rapidly. Indeed by the end of the 1950s, industrial production had doubled and the share of consumer goods in total imports had fallen to as low as 7 per cent (Wade 1990: 78).

Nevertheless, many intermediate goods could not be manufactured locally, the demand for foreign imports remained higher than the supply of locally produced exports, and growth in agricultural exports had reached a plateau by 1957. From 1958, the Economic Stabilization Board, established in 1951 under American pressure to centralize government economic planning, supported greater industrial investment and export promotion (Haggard 1990: 86: Vogel 1991: 22). By late 1959 American officials explained to the party elite that they would support export-led industrial growth if 'Taiwan would mobilize all available domestic resources, concentrate on domestic development more than on preparations to retake the mainland and reduce government controls' (Vogel 1991: 23). In 1960, the government introduced a Nineteen-Point Programme for Economic and Financial Reform together with a new four-year plan (1961–4) providing incentives for businesses that produced and marketed for export. In particular the government's third and fourth-four year plans (1961–4; 1965–8) emphasized the development of 'basic heavy industries such as chemical wood pulp, petrochemical intermediates, and large-scale integrated steel production' (Wade 1990: 87). In order to guide development the frequently updated Statute for the Encouragement of Investment (1960) coordinated investment by foreign nationals, overseas Chinese and local investors (Haggard 1990: 96).

As in Korea, then, government initiated the shift to export-led growth, and the super-technocrats of the Economic Stabilization Board played the major role. The combination of US aid up to 1965 and the super-technocrats' direct accountability to Chiang Kai-shek strengthened the autonomy of this super-ministerial unit. From the 1950s until the late 1980s technocrats with scientific backgrounds like K.Y. Yin and K.T. Li 'dominated industrial planning' (Vogel 1991: 25). Not only did they promote pragmatic economic policies, but they went to considerable lengths to recruit and train a cadre of economically literate bureaucrats. Like their South Korean counterparts, they played a role 'much like that of good traditional Confucian advisors' (p. 27). However, their managerial style and the economic content of their policy was scientific, modern and pragmatic. Not only did they manage macroeconomic policy and the exchange rate in a manner that promoted exports, they engineered a mutually supportive combination of state and private enterprise. They arranged the production of basic goods such as cotton, iron, steel and refined petroleum in state firms, and then sold the product cheaply 'to private firms as a way of driving industries such as textiles, machinery, fertilizer, and plastics' (p. 30) that could produce for export. This policy effectively created companies like Formosa Plastic. In 1953, K.Y. Yin considered plastics a suitable target for industrialization and identified Y.C. Wang as an entrepreneur with the vision to undertake the project. Thus 'the first plastics plant for polyvinyl chloride (PVC) was constructed under government supervision and handed to Wang in running order in 1957' (Wade 1990: 80). By the end of the 1960s Formosa Plastics in conjunction with the state-owned Chinese Petroleum Corporation was producing a wide range of petrochemical intermediates sometimes in joint ventures with US firms. In the 1990s Wang's Formosa Plastics Group was the largest and most successful private enterprise in Taiwan.

In the period 1961–72, the Taiwanese government additionally both encouraged private joint ventures in the automobile industry with Toyota and Nissan and promoted Taiwan as a base for relocating the production of sophisticated European electronic and electrical goods to cheaper overseas labour sites. Philips of Holland pioneered the strategy of global manufacturing in Taiwan in 1961 (Wade 1990: 94). In order to attract overseas Chinese capital in producing goods for export, Taiwan opened the world's first export-processing zone in Kaohsiung in 1966; two more followed in the course of the decade.

In addition to coordinating the private sector, the government has also extended the range of state-owned enterprises. In fact, Taiwan has developed one of the largest state-owned sectors in the developing world. State initiatives in the heavier petrochemicals, non-ferrous metals and shipbuilding industries date from the move to export-led growth in the early 1960s. 'The turn to world markets was thus coupled with anticipatory actions aimed at deepening Taiwan's base in intermediate and capital intensive industries' (Haggard 1990: 96). Economic considerations were not the only motivation for creating the large public enterprise sector, which by 1990 included petrol refining, petrochemicals, steel and other basic metals, shipbuilding, nuclear power plants, as well as more conventional utilities. In fact, many of these public enterprises were 'closely linked to the military' and formed 'a vertically integrated, closed production system which is the basis of Taiwan's own defense industry' (Wade 1990: 179).

From a slightly different perspective, the World Bank maintains that whilst the 1960s initiatives had facilitated an inflow of foreign direct investment and joint venture industrialization, the aftermath of the 1973–4 oil crisis witnessed a return to a 'more self reliant development strategy based on industrial consolidation and renewed export growth' (World Bank 1993a: 132). The international derecognition of Taiwan in 1971 followed by the oil-shock of 1973, the slowing of GNP growth to 1.2 per cent and inflation rising to 47 per cent prompted the government forcefully to reassert economic leadership during the 1970s. In order to improve infrastructure, the government launched the Ten Major Development Projects, to modernize highways, railways and ports as well as steel and nuclear power plants (Vogel 1991: 32). Under the management of MIT-trained Chao Yao-tung, Taiwan's China Steel, without natural resources, developed during the 1970s to provide low-cost steel to the expanding machine tool and automobile industries. External events, then, inspired an expansionist technocracy strategy embracing 'non energy intensive, nonpolluting, and technology intensive activities like machine tools, semiconductors, computers, telecommunications, robotics and biotechnology' (Wade 1990: 97–8).

The state bureaucracy also promoted research and development in technology and electronics. The government opened the Hsinchu Science and Industry Park in the late 1970s and in the early 1980s three Silicon Valley Chinese American firms relocated to Hsinchu, with government sponsorship, to promote advanced semiconductor design. In late 1986, the government persuaded Philips to open a joint venture, Taiwan Semiconductor Manufacturing Corporation, with domestic public and private companies to design and produce computer memory chips. In the course of the

1980s, Taiwan developed the biggest pool of chip design talent in Asia outside Japan. Personal computers, peripherals and add-ons, in consequence, came to constitute a major component of Taiwan's exports, rising from zero to 6.9 per cent between 1980 and 1987. By the late 1980s virtually every major electronics multinational had opened a venture in Taiwan and local firms like Acer became global names in the sphere of personal computers (pp. 106–8).

In other areas, state-led development was not so convincing. Technocratic promotion of an indigenous automobile industry has been uncharacteristically incoherent. Given the small domestic market, import-substituting growth in automobiles through a guaranteed domestic market was impractical. Hence the government initially promoted a small-scale parts and components industry. In the course of the 1980s, impressed by the international success of Hyundai, the government planned a large-scale auto plant venture with Toyota. The government 'insisted on an export ratio of 50 per cent and substantial technology transfer' (Wade 1990: 102). Toyota found these conditions increasingly unworkable and in 1984 the joint venture collapsed. Negotiations with British Aerospace in 1991–2 similarly foundered on the rigid insistence on technology transfer and guaranteed export targets. The failure of these projects indicates the weakness of proactive, government-led export promotion.

Nevertheless, despite evident rigidities, the overall ability of the Taiwan bureaucracy to promote export-led growth and proactively manage the shift from labour-intensive industry to high value-added technology has been impressive. A notable feature of Taiwan's technocracy has been its ability both to influence indigenous business through an informal network of connections (*guanxi*) with the ruling KMT and yet remain autonomous from business pressure. Two factors have serendipitously promoted this outcome. Taiwan, partly as a consequence of the small size of the domestic market and partly because of the character of government-promoted joint ventures, never generated the large industrial conglomerates that could seriously jeopardize the management of macroeconomic policy. Moreover, during the first twenty years of development, government officials were mainlanders and local businessmen were indigenous Taiwanese. When they met officially, it was understood that government conveyed directives to business and not vice versa. An attenuated Confucian culture reinforced the expectation that business deferred to the economic bureaucracy. The lack of an organized labour movement and the relatively equitable distribution of the wealth created by growth have additionally facilitated the technocratic capacity to adapt the economy to changing market conditions.

The technocracy, then, has historically promoted export-led growth through an outward-oriented economic policy whilst at the same time maintaining trade barriers in key sectors, a profile that gives Taiwan 'a cascading structure of protection . . . with higher protection on final goods than on raw materials' (Wade 1990: 137). At the same time, 'the banking system, has been publicly owned and tightly controlled' (p. 165). A closely supervised and highly regulated financial sector kept inflation low and the Taiwanese dollar cheap which helped promote export-led growth. By the early 1980s, this policy had achieved 'vast current account surpluses' (Tan 1992: 123). Foreign reserves increased from $9 billion in 1982 to $78 billion by 1987 (p. 124).

However, 'persistent trade surpluses with major trading partners' in Europe and the United States led to increasing demands to restrict Taiwanese access to those markets (World Bank 1993a: 133). In order to mollify American and European critics, Taiwan began in the late 1980s to reduce domestic tariffs on imported final goods. At the same time, the technocracy sought to exploit Taiwan's progress up the technological ladder, allay the rising cost of wages and assuage trading partners by improving the provision of services and reforming the underdeveloped financial sector. In 1987, the government relaxed foreign exchange controls and permitted direct capital movement by the non-bank private sector. Furthermore, the government amended the Banking Law in July 1989, removing controls on both deposit and lending interest rates, allowing fifteen private banks to open and foreign banks to accept savings deposits. Market liberalization, together with low inflation and current account surplus, saw the Taiwanese dollar appreciate against the US dollar after 1985. The rising value of the won further fuelled a bubble in the real estate market and a bull run in equities that saw the Taipei exchange appreciating fifteen times between 1986 and 1990 (Patrick and Park 1994: 342). At the height of the boom 'some 100,000 workers left jobs to speculate on the stock market full time' (Tan 1992: 124). The bubble burst in 1990 and the banking and financial services sector continues to lack maturity. State technocrats, with characterisitic Confucian omniscience, seek to regulate the stock market and direct foreign investment in a manner that is both 'claustrophobic' and counter-productive (*Asian Wall Street Journal*, 15 May 1995).

The liberalization of the banking sector, together with the appreciation of the Taiwanese currency and mounting labour costs, rendered the price of Taiwan's labour-intensive exports increasingly uncompetitive. Characteristically, the technocracy moved proactively to restructure the economy, shifting labour-intensive manufacturing and textile industries offshore. Taiwan's demand for an efficient source of cheap labour fortuitously coincided with the mainland Chinese government's decision to open special economic zones in Guangdong, Fujian, Shandong and Dalian to exploit the foreign investment opportunities and labour-intensive industries made possible by the

rising costs and trade surpluses of the newly developed East Asian economies. By 1989, Taiwan's direct overseas investment had increased to $6.95
billion or 4.6 per cent of GNP and many small businesses relocated labour-
intensive textile and shoe-making operations to Fujian and Guangdong.

However, because of the troubled history of Taiwan's relationship with
the PRC financial and plant investment passes through Hong Kong. Between 1979 and 1992, trade between Hong Kong and Taiwan increased at
an annual rate of 42.4 per cent. Hong Kong, as a result of Taiwanese
investment in the mainland economic zones, is now Taiwan's second biggest trading partner, and in 1991 the balance of trade in favour of Taiwan
amounted to $28.842 billion (Xu 1994: 142). By 1993, PRC customs returns
showed that Taiwan constituted the mainland's fourth largest trading partner (*Straits Times*, 15 October 1993). Characteristically, most Taiwanese
investment in the mainland has been small to medium-sized, with the
amount of money involved usually less than $1 million (Xu 1994: 147). By
the early 1990s 12 per cent of Taiwanese manufacturing jobs and 20,000
small businesses had moved to the mainland. Taiwanese mainland investment takes the form of 'enterprises that import raw materials, process them
using imported machinery, and then export the finished products to overseas markets. Their typical management model is receiving orders in Taiwan, transmitted via Hong Kong, processed in the mainland and then sold
abroad' (p. 148). The evolving economic interdependence between Taiwan,
Hong Kong and the mainland special economic zones enabled the Taiwanese economy to grow at a respectable rate of over 5 per cent per annum
in the early 1990s and mitigated the otherwise potentially economically
harmful effects of the recession that affected Taiwan's key North American
market during the same period.

Meanwhile, on Taiwan itself, government has promoted high value-
added high-technology industries and improved domestic infrastructure.
The government's 1991–6 development plan committed $330 billion to
public sector projects and highlighted the improvement of eight key technologies and ten high-growth industries. In this context, the super technocracy seeks to develop joint ventures that involve significant transfers
of technology to the Taiwanese chemical, computer and biotechnology
industries (Simon 1994: 214–15). To support these efforts, 'the government
has adopted an overall strategy of economic liberalization and internation-
alization including the lifting of foreign exchange controls' (World Bank
1993a: 134).

Yet, although Taiwan by the early 1990s had made progress in reducing
tariffs on non-agricultural products, the average nominal tariff rate still
remained at 9 per cent in 1994. More specifically, tariffs on agricultural
products stood on average at 22 per cent, whilst automobile components

incurred an average duty of 20 per cent and passenger cars and trucks carried effective rates that varied from 60 per cent to 100 per cent (World Bank 1994: 37). Moreover, despite the determined push into high-technology and high value-added sectors in the 1990s, Taiwan's high-tech economy still depends on Japan as 'the source for the equipment and components that are needed to upgrade the technological base of the economy' (Simon 1994: 202). As with Korea, 'Taiwan's exports are mostly built on imports from Japan' (*Business Taiwan*, 19 October 1992). Significantly, in 1993 Taiwan ran a trade deficit with Japan amounting to 6.5 per cent of the former's GNP (*Straits Times*, 21 October 1994). Having developed by moving up the technology ladder, Taiwan remains, none the less, reliant upon Japanese inputs and remarkably exposed to external shocks, especially in its major markets in the United States and mainland China. North American protectionism and a deteriorating relationship with the mainland constitute major difficulties for the development of both a Chinese and a Pacific trading environment in the late 1990s, upon which the prospects of the Taiwanese economy are entirely dependent.

A tale of two cities: Hong Kong and Singapore

Ostensibly, Singapore and Hong Kong share a number of economic similarities. They are commonly included in lists of newly industrialized countries but they are in fact city states historically founded as entrepôts to serve a British trading empire. Since their nineteenth-century liberal imperial inception to promote the China trade, the doctrine of *laisser-faire* has shaped the evolution of both Singapore and Hong Kong. Both share a British colonial past and a familiarity with western business practice, affording a comparative advantage over other East Asian locations in international commerce. Significantly, in the postwar period both adopted externally oriented industrialization strategies when political circumstances removed rural hinterlands. Moreover, both city states, through a mixture of accident and design, created relatively free labour markets with state-controlled or weak labour organization. The city states also possess administrations that in a number of interesting ways resemble the state technocracies of South Korea and Taiwan, possessing 'strong and independent executives, weak, subordinate legislatures, and economic technocrats' who are relatively autonomous (Haggard 1990: 100).

Despite the shared colonial legacy of transport, finance and information facilities, important differences have, however, characterized the postwar economic development of the city states. In fact, 'the approaches of the two cities to industrialization were in some ways almost polar opposites' (Vogel 1991: 67). Hong Kong's civil service has continued the colonial strategy of an almost completely *laisser-faire* course of economic development, whilst, by contrast, Singapore's industrial policy has, like Taiwan and South Korea's, assumed a highly *dirigiste* character. Let us first examine the character of development in Singapore and Hong Kong before considering the economic implications of their growth strategies.

Hong Kong: the regional exception

After the Qing dynasty ceded Hong Kong island to the British in 1842, its commercial role developed quickly. Merchant houses such as Jardine Matheson and Swire established headquarters in the colony, and provided banking, insurance and accounting services. By 1900, Hong Kong handled 40 per cent of China's export trade and 42 per cent of its imports. The interwar period, by contrast, was one of mercantilist rivalry, depression and concern over Hong Kong's future (Haggard 1990: 116). From the late 1920s internal difficulties in China, together with opposition to the 'unequal treaties' that had gifted Hong Kong and the New Territories to Britain, posed acute political and economic problems. The Japanese occupation of 1942–5, and the postwar defeat of Chiang Kai-shek by the Chinese communists, further undermined the entrepôt trade.

After 1945, 'two external events changed the economic life of the colony. First the Chinese Revolution produced a huge influx of migrants, which changed the nature of the entrepreneurial class and had profound consequences for the labour movement. The second shock was the United Nations embargo on trade with China which provided the stimulus to export oriented manufacturing' (p. 117). The industrialists who fled Shanghai between 1947 and 1951 established in Hong Kong a cotton industry whose finance and skill originated in the mainland. The Korean War and the embargo on trade with China facilitated the nascent textile industry's rapid expansion into the American market. 'An economy once geared almost solely to trade now found it both necessary and possible to expand its industry as well' (Youngston 1982: 4). Textile and clothing in the early 1950s constituted the foundation of Hong Kong's postwar recovery, 'hastily expanded in dingy rooms in back streets . . . the clothing industry, more than any other, filled the gap created by the collapse of trade with China' (p. 4). Despite fierce international competition, the clothing trade continues to be a mainstay of Hong Kong's exports.

By the end of the 1950s Hong Kong had established itself as a regional manufacturing centre. Plastics, notably plastic toys and flowers, had been added to clothing and textiles as major external revenue earners. Already in 1962, *The Economist* could describe Hong Kong as 'a show window for capitalism in the East' (p. 7). Practically all manufactured exports during the period 1950–70 were labour-intensive consumer products. Hong Kong found its 'comparative advantage in exporting labour-intensive manufactured goods' and became the first regional economy to promote export-oriented growth. Indeed, some 75 per cent of its manufactured products are sold abroad, and in the 1960s and 1970s commodity trade constituted 'about 150 per cent of GDP' (World Bank 1993c: 6). By the 1990s the ratio had risen above 230 per cent.

Moreover, it was risk-taking, Chinese merchant entrepreneurs in SMEs that largely accounted for the double-digit growth that Hong Kong achieved between 1960 and 1980 (Youngston 1982: 8). Their skill lay in their awareness of business and import-replacing opportunities (Jacobs 1984: 147). Thus, Y.K. Pao emerged as a shipping magnate by ordering ships from Japanese yards at low cost and taking advantage of the export subsidy of the Japanese government. Subsequently, he leased the ships to Japanese shipping firms on long-term contract. 'With these contracts he obtained bank loans to finance the purchase of those ships. This way he was able to add to his fleet with little of his own money and at low risk' (Youngston 1982: 26). Somewhat differently, Li Ka-shing made his first fortune from plastic toys sold cheaply in North America and the United Kingdom. More recently, Jimmy Lai built his Giordano jeans company on a strategy that combined the tightly controlled menu of McDonald's, Wal Mart frugality and Marks and Spencer's value pricing (*Far Eastern Economic Review*, 2 December 1993: 72). The emergence of a distinctive Hong Kong identity gave rise not only to a tourist industry that caters for six million visitors a year, but also to a highly commodifiable local popular culture that has generated an Asia-wide market for Canto-pop stars like Anita Mui and a film industry that is the third largest in the world.

Even as Hong Kong's industrial structure diversified, its industrial reputation remained closely associated with the flexibility, adaptability and focus on short-term profits of small-scale businesses. In 1988, 87 per cent of firms had fewer than nine employees (*Annual Digest of Statistics*, 1990: 72). The small scale of most business ventures clearly weakened the potential for organized labour. Manual workers are not hired on contract and there is little job security. In an economy geared to export, redundancy constitutes an omnipresent fact of life. On the other hand, workers will not hesitate 'to fire the boss' if a better opportunity comes along. Workers, it would seem, accept that labour, like everything else, is a tradable commodity. In consequence 'relatively unobstructed market mechanisms are at work in determing wages and employment' and excessive unemployment tends to be quickly eliminated (England and Rear 1980: 238).

The only sector that deviates from the general pattern of dynamic, family-based, small-scale, entrepreneurial endeavour is Hong Kong's sophisticated financial sector. This evolved rapidly during the 1970s with the growth of the regional market. To secure macroeconomic stability the Hong Kong dollar was linked to the US dollar in October 1983. As the World Bank explains, 'political stability, no exchange controls, a stable currency fully backed by international reserve assets, a well defined and well administered legal system, non interventionist government with low taxation and a geographic location midway between New York and London' (World Bank 1993c: 6) favoured Hong Kong's emergence as the second largest financial centre in the Asia Pacific region in terms of loan syndication, fund management and stock market capitalization. Between 1977 and 1989 the number of banks established in Hong Kong rose from 74 to 165, 135 of which were foreign banks.

Deng Xiaoping's decision in 1979 to create special mainland economic zones opening China to trade and foreign investement further helped Hong Kong's development as the regional financial hub. The reversal of Maoist policy on the mainland also enabled Hong Kong both to resume its nineteenth-century role as an entrepôt and, like Taiwan, to exploit China's vast reserves of cheap labour. As a result, Hong Kong's economy grew at an annualized 6 per cent in the late 1980s, despite the fact that its major European and North American markets had slipped into recession.

Indeed, to the extent that Guangdong province has become the fifth Asian 'tiger' economy, its spectacular double-digit growth since 1980 is largely a consequence of the injection of enterprise, capital and technical skill from Hong Kong. Hong Kong is China's largest financier and also acts as a middleman for investment from Taiwan and South Korea. In the course of the 1980s Hong Kong's low-skilled and semi-skilled manufacturing activity almost wholly moved to mainland Shenzhen and Zhuhai, where labour costs are five times lower (*The Economist*, 10 August 1993). The World Bank estimated that in 1993 3 million mainland labourers worked directly for Hong Kong entrepreneurs (World Bank 1993c: 21).

The revival of the entrepôt trade also meant that re-exports of raw materials, capital goods and consumer durables from the mainland via Hong Kong expanded at the rate of 20 per cent per annum after 1980. Hong Kong entrepreneurialism has in fact created a southern China growth triangle that embraces Hong Kong, Taiwan and the special economic zones of Fujian and Guangdong (World Bank 1993c: 22). Indeed, the increasing economic integration of Hong Kong with that of adjacent Guangdong means that the economic area effectively functions as Greater Hong Kong (Goodman and Feng 1994: 190). Meanwhile, beyond the region, Hong Kong entrepreneurs like Gordon Wu of Hopewell and shipping magnate Tung Chee-hwa have developed Hong Kong's comprador role as an intermediary in developing trade for all of mainland China (p. 190).

The success of Hong Kong and the revival of the entrepôt trade owe a considerable debt to the far-sighted, non-interventionist policies pursued by successive Financial Secretaries of the colonial government. Phillip Haddon-Cave, who succeeded Sir John Cowperthwaite as Financial Secretary in 1971, termed the government's policy 'positive non-interventionism' (Youngston 1982: 9). Hong Kong, unlike the other HPAEs, has not trained a team of super-technocrats to chart successive stages of growth. Indeed, it was only after considerable lobbying that the government offered entrepreneurs the services of a Trade Development Council.

It was, then, the invisible hand of the market, facilitated by a non-interventionary and uncorrupt civil service and the entrepreurial skill of the city's merchant traders, that accounted for Hong Kong's impressive post-war growth. Private enterprise runs the world's second largest container port, and provides public transport, gas, electricity and telecommunications. The government intervenes only in infrastructure, investing directly in roads, railways, subways, water supply and more recently in a new airport. Additionally government provides education, health and public housing. In 1978, the government introduced compulsory education between the ages of five and fourteen and also provided minimal health care chiefly for the benefit of lower income groups (Youngston 1982: 126). More controversially, in view of its ostensible commitment to classical economic principles, the government has become the largest landlord in the colony (p. 128). In 1961, confronted with the problem of squatting and 'insanitary congested tenements' where upward of 600,000 people dwelt, the government embarked upon a programme of public housing (p. 42). By 1990, two-fifths of the population lived in government-subsidized housing. After 1978, the government also began to provide land on special terms to high-technology firms that could not afford rising land prices.

This apart, however, government policy has been non-interventionist with a pro-growth bias. To facilitate grass-roots capitalism, the government respects property rights and the rule of law, keeps taxes low and regularly runs a budgetary surplus. 'Quite unlike other countries, government departments have tended to over-estimate their expenditures and underestimate their revenues. . . . In recent times the accumulated surplus has amounted to about 80 per cent of annual expenditure' (World Bank 1993c: 11). In June 1995, the Hong Kong Monetary Authority's Exchange Fund held $58 billion. As the World Bank concludes, 'the policy mix of a small but effective government, a well administered legal system, free enterprise, and open economy has been unusually effective in promoting growth' (World Bank 1993c: 30). In 1995, the Heritage Foundation considered Hong Kong the world's freest economy (*Asian Wall Street Journal*, 28 November 1995). Between 1953 and 1991, GDP grew at over 8 per cent per annum and by 1995 amounted to $21,987 in per capita terms significantly ahead of its colonial master.

Hong Kong's development after 1997 obviously depends on the continuation of the pro-market strategy that created its dynamic entrepreneurial culture. However, it is clear that a number of the city state's leading entrepreneurs consider this unlikely. Significantly those *hong* businesses that have in the past had difficulty in dealing with Beijing, like Jardine Matheson and the Hong Kong Shanghai Bank, have relocated their central offices regionally. Somewhat differently the Shanghai-born entrepreneur and Hayek enthusiast, Jimmy Lai, who upsets Beijing's gerontocrats with his lack of deference, intends to emigrate to decadent New York when the PRC assumes responsibility for the Hong Kong Special Administrative Region in July 1997. Yet other Hong Kong business enterprises, like Swire Pacific and Hopewell, are more bullish about the prospects for Hong Kong after 1997. They see obvious advantages accruing from the further integration of Hong Kong into the South China economic region. Evidently, after 1997, the rule of law will be less and *guanxi* more important for continued business success. With this in mind, prominent local tycoons, like Tung Chee-hwa, Gordon Wu and Li Ka-shing, have been assiduously cultivating their connections with the higher echelons of the People's Liberation Army (PLA) and the politburo in Beijing.

Singapore Incorporated

In the World Bank's assessment, post-colonial Singapore 'has transformed itself from a resource poor maritime center into a dynamic, industrialized economy. Real GDP growth averaged 8.2 per cent from 1960–1990' (World Bank 1993d: xi). Moreover, since 1990 growth has continued to average over 8 per cent per annum (Abeysinghe et al. 1994: 11). Lacking resources, Singapore developed as a re-export economy. As the world's most efficient container port and with unrivalled air transport facilities, it functions as the hub of a dynamic Southeast Asian economy, whose 'imported inputs are used in the production of some or all export production activities' (Lloyd and Sandilands 1988: 5). Between 1960 and 1990 per capita GDP increased from $3455 to $13,150 (US). By 1995, per capita GDP at $21,493 had overtaken that of the United Kingdom (*Asiaweek*, 11 August 1995: 56; see also table 2.3).

Accounting for this sustained growth, political economists generally concur that, 'Singapore's development relied on a combination of external free trade and strong internal economic control' (Huff 1994: 301). This policy dates effectively from 1961 and the formulation by the United Nations-sponsored Winsemius mission of Singapore's First Development Plan. On the basis of this, the government established the Economic Development Board (EDB) to promote investment and manufacturing, notably in shipbuilding and repair, metal engineering, and chemical and electrical equipment. The EDBs industrial facilities division built large industrial estates, stimulated favourable investment opportunities, through the Economic Expansion Incentives Act (1967), and facilitated good regional communications in order to attract multinational enterprises (MNEs). Internal economic control further required a tight macroeconomic policy, the emasculation of the labour movement and the suppression of communism and communist front activities. The creation of the PAP-managed National Trade Union Congress (NTUC) in 1961, followed by the elimination of alternative labour organizations through the Employment Act (1967) and the Amendment of Industrial Relations Act (1968), together with the creation of the National Wages Council (NWC) in 1971, created 'harmonious industrial labor relations' (World Bank 1993d: 34). As Stephen Haggard more judiciously observes, Singapore presents, 'the clearest case of a link between export-led growth and labor control' (Haggard 1990: 112). After 1965, Singapore's ejection from the Malaysian Federation, the concomitant necessity to foster export-oriented growth, together with the expanded governmental capacity to manage a relatively small city state on corporatist lines (Brown 1994: 82–3), further facilitated state economic management. Successful export-led growth after 1965 was thus 'preceded by institutional reforms that concentrated economic decision making and expanded the economic instruments in the hands of the government' (Haggard 1990: 113). In the view of former Deputy Prime Minister Goh Keng Swee, rapid manufacturing development could be explained by the fact that Singapore 'imported entrepreneurs in the form of multinational corporations and the government itself became an entrepreneur in a big way' (Huff 1994: 330). An unforeseen consequence of this policy has restricted the opportunity for a 'strong local capitalist class' (Tremewan 1994: 34–5), merchant entrepreneurs or indigenous, state-linked *chaebol* to develop in Singapore. This contrasts strikingly both with comparable export-oriented Northeast Asian economies and with Hong Kong.

Instead, the government has participated in business activity through a variety of statutory boards and a large number of state-owned enterprises

(SOEs). These initially took the form of a colonial inheritance which gave the new state a significant stake in the shipbuilding and repair industry. The cumulative effect of government involvement in SOEs created enterprises of two types: first-tier companies, subsidiaries of one of three government holding companies, namely, Temasek Holdings, Singapore Technology Holdings and Health Corporation Holdings; and second- and lower-tier subsidiaries of the first-tier companies. Government holding companies support government-linked corporations (GLCs) like the Neptune and Orient Line shipping fleet, Singapore Airlines and Singapore Telecom. After 1983, the PAP privatized a number of these companies 'to enhance the private sector in the country's future growth', whilst at the same time retaining the holding company as the largest shareholder. By 1990, GLCs accounted for 22.9 per cent of the assets of Singapore's 500 largest firms and provided employment for 18 per cent of the population (World Bank 1993d: 22–3).

This government-initiated and multinational-led, export-oriented growth not only achieved spectacular foreign investment by the early 1970s, it also realized the initial government plan of creating full employment. After 1973, the EDB moved its investment promotion efforts away from labour-intensive manufacturing industries and instead sought to upgrade and restructure the economy. As Goh Keng Swee observed in 1990, investment in education and manpower training meant that Singapore's attraction to MNEs henceforth depended upon not cheap labour, but 'a supply of efficient engineers and technicians' (*Sunday Times* (Singapore), 21 April 1991). Upgrading the workforce and promoting investment in high value-added technology attracted electronics multinationals like Siemens, Sony and Hewlett Packard in the course of the 1970s. These multinationals tended to move to Singapore at earlier stages of product development or for specialized niche work. During the 1980s, semiconductor production declined in relative importance and computer peripherals, especially disk drives and computers, became the more important part of the island's electronics industry (Huff 1994: 330).

This second industrial revolution strategy, however, was not without difficulty. The oil-shock of 1973–4 affected growth rates detrimentally (Quah 1994: 10). From the EDB's omniscient economic management perspective, more perplexing was the unforeseen recession between 1985 and 1987 that precipitated a negative growth rate of –1.3 per cent (Tan 1992: 115). Key sectors of the economy – tourism, shipbuilding and oil refining – simultaneously experienced recession. Significantly, the state technocracy's decision in 1979 to increase wages and pension contributions in order to promote the move to higher technology unwittingly intensified this recession. Between 1979 and 1983 wages rose by 12 per cent whilst productivity rose by a mere 5 per cent per annum (Tan 1992: 120).

The recession necessitated a government-enforced reduction in wages. Nevertheless, the general trend in real wages, particularly as the economy recovered in the late 1980s, was upward. Higher skill and higher rates of foreign direct investment, particularly from Japan, contributed to raising value-added per manufacturing worker. Hourly wage rates rose in US dollar terms from $1.49 in 1980 to $3.78 in 1990 (Huff 1994: 342) and $6.29 by 1995 (*Straits Times Weekly*, 19 August 1995).

A frequently overlooked feature of the government's contribution to growth, particularly in financial and business services, was the provision of public goods like 'the maintenance of honest markets, an environment conducive to easy operation and the stability of the Singapore dollar' (Huff 1994: 342). On the basis of this, in the 1980s, Singapore developed its comparative advantage as a provider of financial, business, retailing and tourist services. The government used both the Development Bank of Singapore (DBS) and the Monetary Authority of Singapore (MAS), established in 1971 and substantially reformed in 1981 as a quasi-central bank, to promote Singapore as the 'Zurich of the East' (Huff 1994: 342). By the end of the 1980s Singapore was the fourth largest foreign exchange market in the world and its development as a financial supermarket created opportunities for financial specialization and fund management. MAS' financial innovation facilitated the Singapore International Monetary Exchange's (SIMEX) becoming globally significant in the derivatives market, as Barings Bank discovered to its cost in January 1995. The provision of these 'brain services' particularly facilitated a shift from dependence upon cheap labour to higher value-added, human capital-intensive jobs.

Singapore's success in upgrading its service sector in the late 1980s, together with its increasingly tight labour market and emerging role as a global city dependent on an open trading environment, constituted the background to the most recent Strategic Economic Plan (SEP, 1991). The plan represents the economic dimension of the 'Next Lap' strategy to build an 'international city of distinction' (Government of Singapore 1991; Low 1993: 169). The SEP encourages private and public sector investment abroad primarily in the Association of South East Asian Nations (ASEAN) region, but also in China and India. In order to minimize entrepreneurial risk, government statutory boards pilot an 'external wing' of investment. The growth triangle initiated in 1989, involving Singaporean synergy with neighbouring suppliers of low-cost labour in relatively under-developed Johor (Malaysia) and Batam (Indonesia), constituted the first manifestation of this strategy. More spectacularly, in 1993, Singapore secured a memorandum of understanding with China's Jiangsu province 'to cooperate in developing an industrial township in Suzhou City' (*Straits Times*, 27 October 1993). The agreement attempted to secure GLC investment in China by 'bud grafting Singapore methods of urban and social organisation onto a Chinese tree' (Lee Kuan Yew, *Straits Times*, 5 December 1993). By 1995, Singapore was the ASEAN region's largest outward investor. Although these investments were concentrated in Malaysia and Indonesia, by early 1995 government-sponsored corporations like Keppel were expanding vigorously into China and Vietnam (Lim 1994: 39).

From a more sceptical perspective, however, the latest economic plan, promoting a state-sponsored investment complemented by the technocratic management of less developed areas of East and Southeast Asia in order to sustain Singapore's growth, might be termed colonialism. To avoid this slur, PAP technocrats contradictorily claim that Singapore is both a fully developed country with a per capita GDP higher than the UK and a fragile Third World country that requires the continuing ministrations of the Party bureaucracy.

Essentially, then, Singaporean economic development after 1959 may be divided into four stages: a period of import substitution from 1959 to 1961; an export-led growth strategy from 1961 to 1973; a second industrial revolution with several hiccups between 1973 and 1989; and the global city with a developing external economy after 1989. Each stage has required government intervention and government direction. Summing up Singapore's industrial policy, the World Bank considered the provision of liberal fiscal incentives together with industrial targeting via investment incentives crucial to subsequent growth (World Bank 1993d: 18). Furthermore, the PAP's proactive choice of industrialization as a developmental strategy; dependence on the private sector, particularly foreign MNEs to establish new enterprises; investment in human capital and infrastructure; management and control of labour; and maintenance of a stable macroeconomic environment through prudent monetary policy provided the necessary environment for this industrial policy to work.

'Good governance' (p. 19), in other words, facilitated successful development. State autonomy combined with an efficient civil service (Quah 1994: 152) and a proliferation of statutory board activity provided the institutional framework for effective and sustained growth. In the course of the 1960s, the PAP leadership forged an alliance with the civil service through 'resocialization and politicization' (Chan 1989: 75). By the early 1970s, the PAP was no longer a party but an administration and the civil service 'became a part of that' (Vasil 1984: 146). Apart from its size and all-pervasiveness, the distinctiveness of the civil service rested in its discipline, efficiency and relative lack of corruption (Quah 1994: 153). Equally significant for Singapore-style development was the role of statutory boards. The early success of the EDB in attracting investment to the city state facilitated the spread of this polyvalent regulatory mechanism to a wide range of social and economic activities, including tourism, trade, infrastructure, family planning, education, transport and productivity. According to one measure, eighty statutory boards existed in 1990 (Milne and Mauzy 1990: 83) presiding over virtually every aspect of socio-economic life.

In the World Bank's assessment, statutory boards were 'atypically effective' (World Bank 1993d: 20). Apart from the EDB's evident centrality to economic development, the statutory boards that have impinged most directly on Singaporean life are those concerned with public housing (the Housing Development Board, HDB) and compulsory saving (the Central Provident Fund, CPF). The CPF scheme, introduced, as in Hong Kong and Malaysia, by the British colonial administration in 1955, represented a compulsory state-run domestic savings scheme. In 1990 the CPF system accounted for 30.1 per cent of gross national savings, an arrangement that facilitated the accumulation of extensive foreign reserves (Huff 1994: 347). The relatively high level of CPF contributions, moreover, constitutes an important part of Singapore's macroeconomic policy to control inflation and maintain exchange rate stability. As the World Bank observes, 'CPF funds have . . . provided much of the government's capital for development' (World Bank 1993d: 36). They further facilitated the government's ability to 'influence the avenues of consumption and savings as well as to exert enormous social, political and economic control' (Asher 1993: 158).

One avenue the forced savings scheme opened was home ownership through the Approved Housing Scheme (AHS), established in 1968. This permitted members to use CPF savings to buy apartments built by another statutory board, the HDB. One of the 'outstanding features of Singapore's economic and social development has been the role of subsidized public housing' (Rodan 1992: 372). Housing and education, in fact, constituted the major props of the first development plan, 'the first by providing low cost accommodation for the work-force and the second by providing it with the requisite technical skills' (Hill and Lian 1995: 118). The compulsory acquisition of land 'at reasonable, non-inflated prices under the Land Acquisition Act' (1966) (pp. 119–20) assisted the process. By 1990, 90.2 per cent of the population owned their own homes and 85 per cent of them lived in public housing (Lim 1989: 183; World Bank 1993d: 20).

By 1995, Singapore had the highest rate of home ownership (91 per cent) in the OECD. None the less ownership of a HDB apartment hardly establishes the independence of the householder. Instead, it has significantly increased 'the PAP-state's social control' (Tremewan 1994: 57). HDB owners are routinely subject to a range of restrictions and regulations that vary from the petty to the punitive. The curiously conditional nature of HDB ownership, together with its link to the CPF system, effectively ties Singaporeans into the PAP's administrative state.

In this context of permanent administration, the PAP consistently presents political decisions as managerial ones and the city state as a rationally managed corporation. The Party's technocratic elite, trained in western graduate schools, form the board of directors and it is their ability to choose the correct pragmatic and proactive economic policies that has maintained economic growth. So effectively has the PAP promoted itself as an 'administrative state' (Chan 1989: 78–82) masterminding development that the World Bank considered the government 'integral to Singapore's rapid industrialization' (World Bank 1993d: 40). The open trading environment and MNE-sponsored industrialization apparently would not have occurred without the 'social and political stability' secured by the Party and its visionary leadership. Even American political economists, seduced by the prospect of bringing the state back in to the study of development, contend that 'single party rule was justified by economic objectives and performances' (Haggard 1990: 260), a finding that supports the view of Singaporean political scientists that the 'absence of parliamentary opposition in Singapore from 1966–1973 enabled the PAP government to switch from its earlier policy of import substitution to that of export substitution in 1967 without any difficulty' (Quah 1994: 10).

Yet this otherwise persuasive account of state-managed, market-oriented growth conspicuously ignores a number of important features of Singapore's recent economic history. To begin with, it was precisely because, like similarly minded nationalist parties in the recently decolonized Third World, the PAP embarked upon a policy of import substitution in the late 1950s that the Winsemius mission found the city state's economy suffering from low growth and underemployment in 1961. Certainly, the effective abolition of political opposition eased the switch to export-oriented growth after 1965, but the fact that the policy change required such drastic measures was largely a testament to the PAP's initial economic incompetence.

Moreover, the successful shift to export-oriented growth after 1965 was rendered relatively painless by the administrative and physical infrastructure developed in the colonial era. Indeed, PAP- and World Bank-sponsored accounts of Singapore's economic success studiously omit the period prior to decolonization. For somewhat problematically for the model of party-led growth, the staple port of Singapore had already grown spectacularly prior to 1939. Although the aftermath of 1945 witnessed regional instability, Singapore possessed both the natural resource of geography and the colonial legacy of an efficient bureaucracy to benefit from an increasingly open Pacific market maintained by a benign *Pax Americana*. As W.G. Huff observes, the PAP 'inherited a successful economy and . . . a stable and efficiently functioning administration' (Huff 1994: 357–8). Singapore, in fact, began from a 'very high base' and significantly capitalized on the embedded liberalism of 'favourable international economic forces' (p. 31).

The city states compared

Despite a shared heritage, a shared commitment to export-oriented growth, and a shared success that has witnessed both countries achieving per capita GDP over $22,000 (see table 2.3), the strategies pursued by the two city states and the political and economic outcomes they have generated offer some intriguing contrasts. From a neoclassical economic perspective, Hong Kong evidently offers the paradigmatic contemporary example of a state blessed with economically rational subjects and minimal, albeit colonial, state administration. Singapore, by contrast, has followed a highly interventionist route to development. This interventionist character has led some neoliberal economists to doubt the sustainability of Singapore's success. In this view, the high rates of growth achieved after 1965 by Singapore, and other 'tiger' economies like South Korea and Taiwan, notably in manufacturing, may not be quite as impressive as the World Bank maintains.

Alwyn Young, in an interesting comparison between *laisser-faire*, but colonial Hong Kong, and state managed, but self-determining Singapore, discovers that both capital and (human capital adjusted) labour inputs have grown considerably faster in Singapore than in Hong Kong. Whilst 'total factor productivity (tfp) growth has contributed substantially to economic growth in Hong Kong, its contribution to growth in Singapore is next to nil' (Young 1992: 16; 1995: 657–9). An 'astonishing mobilization of resources', Paul Krugman avers, accounts almost entirely for Singapore's growth. Interestingly, 'all of Singapore's growth can be explained by increases in measured inputs' of capital, machinery and labour, and 'there is no sign at all of increased efficiency' (Krugman 1994: 70–1). The fact that Singapore's before-subsidy rate of return on capital is currently one of the lowest in the world gives further credence to the neoliberal criticism of such Soviet-style, state-led development. This, together with an overvalued Singapore dollar and a notably inflated domestic housing sector (Cheong 1994: 74–5), suggests not only that the Singapore economy is over-managed, but also that future economic growth relies upon the success of the current strategy to establish Singapore as a 'global city with total business capabilities' (Cheah 1993: 109).

Nevertheless, in promoting this 'external wing' strategy the PAP is significantly helped by the efficiency it has generated in administration, infrastructure and financial services. Total factor productivity in services clearly has improved, yet Krugman and Young significantly fail to measure efficiency in this key sector. Moreover, Hong Kong's development along an unforced learning curve to higher value-added technology is not as unproblematic as proponents of the unfettered free trade model often maintain. Significantly, in *laisser-faire* Hong Kong manufacturing has not advanced into higher technology and 'industrial composition has remained stuck in light industries' (Wade 1993: 155). Indeed, Hong Kong's relatively poor industrial performance in the 1980s and its inability to innovate higher technology products 'may have been partly caused by the absence of industrial policy' (p. 155).

In addition, although it is evident that Hong Kong's flexible merchant traders have shown themselves remarkably adept at adjusting to changing external circumstances in order to sustain growth, the prospects for maintaining this remarkable development after 1997 seem worryingly dependent on the arbitrary whims of Beijing's gerontocracy. Somewhat differently, whilst Singapore successfully engineered corporate growth in the 1980s through exploiting its services and geographical position, the ability to project this model beyond Singapore in order to sustain growth in the late 1990s seems fraught with difficulty. The administrative state, however, cannot entertain any doubt about the efficacy of state-managed growth. Promoting the Singapore model, the EDB concentrates solely on the recent growth of Singapore and neglects both the economic achievement of the colonial past and the worrying shortcomings of an economic policy driven almost exclusively by growth in capital and labour inputs.

Thailand, Malaysia and Indonesia: ersatz capitalism in Southeast Asia

In Northeast Asia state bureaucrats self-consciously applied a Japanese model to the postwar development of their fragile economies. In South Korea's version of this strategy, the technocracy directed and encouraged the formation of large conglomerates. In Taiwan, by contrast, super-bureaucrats facilitated joint ventures and small to medium-sized enterprises. Both states continue to favour successive five-year plans and technocratic intervention to 'pick the winners' to secure future GDP growth. In order to promote domestic industries and develop indigenous technology, both states have at times protected key manufacturing sectors and set limits to foreign direct investment.

Manufacturing in Northeast Asia, nevertheless, depends upon Japan for sophisticated, high-technological inputs, and both South Korea and Taiwan consequently run trade deficits with Japan whilst accumulating trade surpluses with their primary markets in North America and Europe. Indeed, the trade structure of the Asian NIEs, South Korea, Taiwan, Hong Kong and Singapore, 'has been to process capital and intermediate goods imported from Japan and export them not to Japan, but to the United States' (Watanabe 1992: 155). The share of total exports from Japan to the United States increased from 25 per cent in 1980 to 37 per cent in 1987. Similarly the share of total exports from the Asian NIEs destined for the US market increased from 23 per cent to 32 per cent over the same period (p. 157).

The burgeoning trade surpluses that Japan and the NIEs established after 1975 particularly alarmed US manufacturers and prompted US government and European Union pressure both for liberalization of tariff and non-tariff impediments to Pacific Asian markets and the revaluation of undervalued Asian currencies. The subsequent negotiation of the 1985 Plaza Agreement and the 1987 Louvre Accord enabled the industrialized nations to establish concerted foreign exchange intervention and target bands for exchange rates between the leading currencies. The aftermath of the Plaza Agreement witnessed the globalization of financial markets and the rapid appreciation of the Taiwanese dollar, the Korean won and particularly the Japanese yen against the US dollar (Helleiner 1994: 173). This appreciation not only fuelled a liquidity bubble and a property and stock market boom in Tokyo, Seoul, Hong Kong, Singapore and Taipei, it also increased the cost of domestic manufacturing. Consequently, in order to reduce labour costs, Hong Kong and Taiwanese businessmen, Singaporean statutory boards, Korean *chaebol* and Japanese *sogoshosha* sought to relocate lower value-added manufacturing offshore.

Southeast Asia in particular became the major beneficiary of Northeast Asian foreign direct investment in the period after 1985. Investment by Taiwan and South Korea in the 'less developed Western Pacific countries' expanded dramatically (Watanabe 1992: 167). During the period 1986–92, 50 per cent of FDI in Southeast Asia came from the NIEs (World Bank 1994: 43). By contrast, the share of European and US FDI combined was less than that of Hong Kong alone (p. 43). Meanwhile, Japanese investment, both in the Asian NIEs of South Korea, Taiwan, Hong Kong and Singapore, and in the less developed ASEAN economies of Thailand, Malaysia, Indonesia and the Philippines, grew equally impressively. Japanese FDI surged from around $270 million per annum in the early 1980s to nearly $1.5 billion per annum between 1987 and 1991 (p. 47). Japanese FDI in the NIEs increased at over 100 per cent per annum between 1986 and 1988, whilst in the ASEAN economies it grew by 87 per cent in 1987 alone (p. 164). After the Japanese economy entered recession in 1990, the share of Japanese investment in Pacific Asia, notably in China and Southeast Asia, continued to grow steadily by 12.4 per cent in 1990 and 18.8 per cent in

1992 (Park 1994: 9) and averaged approximately $4 billion per annum between 1989 and 1993 (Lim 1994: 37). Moreover, the growing interest expressed by ASEAN in promoting regional trade, particularly after 1993, further facilitated foreign investment. Thus foreign-domiciled company investment constitutes the characteristic mode of development in Southeast Asia (Yoshihara 1988: 5). In 1994, the Pacific Economic Cooperation Council (PECC) found that the 'list of regional multinational groups developing borderless manufacturing structures to serve the fast-growing consumer markets of the Asia–Pacific region, is growing with dizzying speed' (PECC 1994a: 113). The 'massive offshore move' by Japanese industry in response to the persistently high yen, together 'with continued offshore industrial location from the Asian NIEs, induced by shifting comparative advantage', will add to the inflow of investment in the ASEAN countries into the late 1990s (Lim 1994: 38).

For a number of commentators (Watanabe 1992; Lim 1994; Park 1994; World Bank 1994) the evolving pattern of manufacturing, technology and investment between Japan, the NIEs and the ASEAN economies is creating 'a strong complementary relationship' where 'the division of labour among the countries in the region has a diversified and multilayered structure' (Watanabe 1992: 166). Regional institutional arrangements to create an ASEAN Free Trade Area (AFTA) will further accelerate ASEAN's economic integration with Japan (Lim 1994: 37). Indeed, Japanese economists maintain that the Pacific Asian littoral has developed in a harmonious flying geese formation (Akamatsu 1962; 1965; Okita 1989: 47–8), with, of course, Japan 'in the lead position, followed by the so-called four tigers of Asia, the countries of Southeast Asia and finally by China and other low income countries of the region' (Park 1994: 3). The successive 'geese' gain from the experience of the leader, close the technological gap and eventually harmoniously integrate. These developments, the World Bank avers, 'reflect economic adaptations to changing factor endowments, and countries are helped by following . . . the successful policies and technologies of neighbouring countries' (World Bank 1994: 28). Moreover, 'close ties through trade, culture, and history have helped East Asian countries take advantage of each other's experience in production, marketing, management, and policymaking' (p. 28).

By contrast, neoliberal economists discover in Southeast Asia a distinctive pattern of development that contrasts radically with the Northeast Asian version of the Japanese model. ASEAN economies, notably the more successful ones of Malaysia, Singapore, Thailand and Indonesia, are, in the view of *The Economist*, 'much more open to foreign direct investment. . . much less prone to try to second-guess the market through a government directed industrial policy. And . . . much quicker to allow financial markets to develop' (*The Economist*, 24 June 1995: 13). Analogously, in one of the few recent attempts to compare economic development in industrializing Pacific Asia, Andrew Macintyre observes that the patterns of 'state involvement in the economy in the industrialising Southeast Asian countries have generally been quite different from those of the Northeast Asian NICs' (Macintyre 1994: 12). Let us, then, examine the course of economic development in the more successful Southeast Asian economies of Thailand, Malaysia and Indonesia, before reaching some provisional conclusions about the nature of the Pacific Asian economy and its prospects in what a number of its more enthusiastic admirers claim will be the forthcoming Pacific Century.

Thailand

Thailand's economy has grown steadily throughout the postwar period. Initially growth was less than spectacular. Real per capita GDP actually declined between 1950 and 1955, and during the period 1955–88 the economy grew consistently but at a moderate pace of 3.9 per cent per annum (World Bank 1993e: 2). In the late 1980s, however, the economy took off, expanding at an annual rate of 9 per cent between 1985 and 1995. Indeed, in the decade 1985–95, it was the world's fastest growing economy (see table 2.2; World Bank 1993a: 139; PECC 1994b: 52; *Far Eastern Economic Review*, 17 August 1995: 44). Growth has significantly eroded absolute poverty levels. By 1995 per capita GDP had risen to $2600 (see table 2.3), significantly less, however, than that achieved by South Korea, whose growth started from a lower base in the 1950s. Moreover, unlike the Northeast Asian NIEs and Singapore, the profits of growth have been unequally distributed between rural and urban workers. Development has 'been concentrated sectorally (in industry rather than in agriculture) and geographically (in Bangkok and its environs)' (World Bank 1993e: 2; *Far Eastern Economic Review*, 5 August 1993: 46; 14 June1994: 22; Pasuk and Baker 1995: 199–206).

Thailand, like Japan, but unlike the other economies considered here, was never colonized. Thailand's escape from colonial development owes much to the modernizing vision of King Chulalongkorn (1868–1910), who, with the assistance of British advisers, reformed the nation's finances, rationalized administration and developed agriculture, railways and popular education (Wyatt 1984: 272). Like the Meiji reformers in Japan, the Thai monarchy and subsequent military and constitutional leaders attempted to syncretize European economic, scientific and administrative practice with traditional Thai understandings. As Chulalongkorn maintained in 1897, 'there exists no incompatibility between such acquisition [of modern science] and the maintenance of our individuality as an independent Asiatic nation' (Wyatt 1984: 211).

In the immediate postwar context, Thailand benefited from its close relationship with the United States and the consistent anti-communist stance of postwar military leaders like Sarit Thanarat (1957–62) and Prem Tinsulanonda (1980–8). Between 1951 and 1957, Thailand received $149 million in economic and $222 million in military aid. Economic aid paid for the expansion of the port of Bangkok and the improvement of highway and railway communication. It also facilitated a period of economic nationalism and import substitution. Thailand historically exported primary and agricultural products, including precious gems, oil and rice. Government policies emphasized taxation of the resource-based rent associated with the production of these exportable commodities and severely regulated trade (Jitsuchon 1991). In particular the rice premium (1952–70) represented a punitive tax burden on poor tenant farmers (Girling 1981: 63).

American advice prompted a shift towards a more liberal and outward-oriented trade regime from the mid-1950s. In 1955, the government unified the exchange rate and abolished the state-owned rice company (World Bank 1993e: 8). Despite these reforms, Thailand retained substantial import protection for certain industries. During the mid-1960s the government imposed comparatively moderate levels of protection on finished consumer goods and on imported machinery and materials, but after 1971 it resorted to import substitution, most notably for finished consumer goods. The main protected industries were textiles, automobiles and pharmaceuticals. During the 1970s, vehicle imports were banned for a time, creating limitless protection for domestic joint ventures with Nissan, Toyota and Mitsubishi. The government established domestic content requirements to promote upstream suppliers of components and parts, thus raising production costs. Thus, consumers 'were taxed to promote an intermediate goods sector' (World Bank 1993e: 140). Even in the late 1980s, the effective protection rate for motor vehicles remained around 70 per cent. Generally, the most heavily protected industries were capital-intensive manufactures, a policy that discriminated against both labour-intensive agriculture and labour-intensive manufactures. The strong import-substituting strategy had a marked effect on the profile of the Thai economy, with protected heavy industry contributing 42.6 per cent of value added to the GDP by 1979.

Worryingly, however, this industrial policy absorbed a comparatively small proportion of the labour force. Whilst import-substituting and export-promoting heavy industry in South Korea and Japan was highly labour-intensive, this was not the case in Thailand. Thus while industry's share of GDP increased steadily from about one quarter in 1970 to one third by 1988, this industrial transformation has not been accompanied by a comparable shift in employment. Indeed, by 1988, 'nearly 70 per cent of the labour force was still in agriculture, producing 17 per cent of GDP' (World Bank 1993e: 6).

The import substitution policy, exacerbated by the impact of the second oil-shock after 1979, distorted Thailand's pattern of industrialization and culminated in a slump in growth and a ballooning current account deficit in the early 1980s. In 1984, the Bank of Thailand, in order to stimulate export-oriented growth, delinked the Thai baht from the US dollar and allowed it to float against a basket of currencies. In consequence, 'the real effective exchange rate depreciated by nearly 30 per cent between 1983 and 1991' (World Bank 1993e: 11). The government also began removing tariffs protecting local industry.

The government Board of Investment (BOI), established in 1960 to promote import substitution, played an important role in the early stages of the post-1981 export promotion drive. The BOI, advised by the World Bank, established new Criteria in Approving Export Promotion (World Bank 1993e: 11), shifting incentives to labour-intensive, export-oriented, geographically dispersed activities. In an attempt to promote growth beyond Bangkok (which currently accounts for 15 per cent of the population and two-thirds of industrial production), the BOI established the Eastern Seaboard Programme to exploit the natural gas discovered in the Gulf of Thailand and develop a regionally based import-substituting petrochemical industry and export-oriented light industry (World Bank 1993e: 13; *Far Eastern Economic Review*, 14 April 1994: 23). The government also established export processing zones, streamlined customs procedures, abolished unnecessary regulations to expedite export shipments (World Bank 1993a: 141) and substantially reduced tariffs on capital goods, automobile imports and computers. These policy changes dramatically affected growth. By 1986 light manufactures represented 30.6 per cent of a growing volume of Thai exports. Leading sectors included clothing, footwear, artificial flowers, jewellery and integrated circuits.

Direct foreign investment played a major role in the export boom as firms from the Northeast Asian HPAEs moved labour-intensive manufacturing to the Bangkok region. Between 1980 and 1988, direct foreign investment more than tripled. By 1993, more than half of Thailand's total exports were manufactures, mostly etablished directly by foreign investors or in the form of joint ventures. In the textile industry local firms transformed themselves into exporters by building on the business contacts and technology learned from Japanese firms like the Toyo Rayon Company. In the automobile industry Japanese car-making joint ventures now use Thailand as a base for integrating automobile production throughout Asia. With the rise in value of the yen, making domestic car production uncompetitive, Mitsubishi, Nissan and Toyota increasingly used Thai plants as a base both for assembly and for export after 1985. Analogously, Japanese electrical and electronic manufacturers selected Thailand as a key offshore production base in their global network of export-oriented manufacturing. By 1991, electronics and electrical industries were Thailand's leading growth sector, with exports of $4.6 billion (World Bank 1994: 48).

By the early 1980s, moreover, a number of the larger Thai firms, supported by the leading commercial banks, had developed into large, vertically integrated business conglomerates like Saha Union, Shinawatra, Dusit Thani and Charon Phokphand. In the course of the 1980s and early 1990s, these conglomerates were expanding operations into Indochina and Southern China and even venturing overseas, with the Dusit Thani hotel group entering the United States and European leisure markets. These ventures have close links with both government and commercial banks. Thus the computer, telecommunications and broadcasting conglomerate Shinawatra began initially as Chiang Mai silk merchants in Northern Thailand. By the early 1980s Thaksin Shinawatra, building upon family business and government links, began selling IBM hardware to the public sector. In 1993, the conglomerate launched a telecommunications satellite and planned to expand its telecommunications 'footprint' across Pacific Asia (*The Economist*, 20 November 1993; Pasuk and Baker 1995: 165). Meanwhile, Thailand's largest agribusiness conglomerate, Charon Phokphand, spent over $2 billion expanding operations into Southern China in 1995 (*Asian Wall Street Journal*, 21–22 July 1995).

A noteworthy feature of Thailand's development across the period 1955–95 has been its macroeconomic stability. Sound money has played a crucial role in maintaining the preconditions for growth. After the coup that established General Sarit's supremacy in 1958, the government, in consultation with the World Bank, established a National Economic and Social Development Board (NESDB) and the Bureau of the Budget (BOB). These agencies were directly responsible to the Prime Minister and together with the Ministry of Finance and the Bank of Thailand formed the core macroeconomic agencies. Sarit's reforms empowered the budget bureau to scrutinize public spending by line ministries and reduce subsidies to state enterprises. These reforms cut losses, stabilized fiscal management and ensured the effective monitoring of public investments.

The success of these reforms stemmed from a number of factors: the autonomy of the budgetary agencies that implemented them; a shared *esprit de corps* inspired by a long tradition of fiscal conservatism inherited from British advisers; and the monarchy's fear that debt would lead to the erosion of sovereignty. Transmitted primarily through the Ministry of Finance and the Bank of Thailand, this 'Gladstonian orthodoxy' favoured a liberal exchange and trade regime (World Bank 1993e: 22–3). Each fiscal year the fiscal agencies cooperate in planning government spending. The budget bureau dominates the implementation of the fiscal decisions in the manner of a 'Victorian housekeeper' (p. 26). The 1959 and 1974 budgetary laws reinforced the deflationary bias of the technocrats by limiting government deficits to no more than 20 per cent of government expenditure. Conservatism and a degree of autonomy enabled the fiscal agencies to limit foreign borrowing in the 1970s, against military pressure to the contrary, and to devalue the baht by 15 per cent in 1984. Fiscal conservatism has also meant that, although Thailand has borrowed externally to finance development projects and defence spending, strictly enforced NESDB guidelines kept foreign debt in check (Rao et al. 1994: 51). In consequence the Thai rate of inflation 'has been one of the lowest in the developing world; government, trade and current account deficits have all been managed well above Third World standards; and the foreign exchange regime has been mainly liberal and market conforming' (Laothamatas 1994: 210).

The strength of Thai macroeconomic policy and the relative openness of the economy in the 1980s facilitated Bangkok's development as a regional financial and related services centre. Financial services are considerably more evolved than in Northeast Asia. To comply with the Uruguay round of GATT, the government deregulated the banking sector in the course of the 1990s. Offshore banking has enabled foreign banks to open for 'limited business' (*Far Eastern Economic Review*, 17 August 1995: 48). A bond market and a thriving mutual fund industry have emerged and the government plans to open further the financial services market to foreign firms. Increasing competition, moreover, has prompted domestic commercial banks to compete internationally. By 1995, Thai banks like Thai Farmers Bank had opened offices in Indochina and China to explore these emerging markets (*Far Eastern Economic Review*, 17 August 1995: 49).

Sound macroeconomic management in the 1980s was central to economic growth (World Bank 1993e: 30). In the course of the 1990s however, fiscal policy, loosened and exposed the NESDB and the Bank of Thailand to political manipulation and speculative pressure. In particular the Bank's decision to bail out stock market speculators in November 1995 contradicted its traditional conservatism. At the same time, indifference to a consumption and credit boom has allowed inflation to rise above 5 per cent and the current account deficit to exceed 8 per cent of GDP in 1995. In the same year external debt rose by 33 per cent (*The Australian*, 20 March 1996; World Bank 1996).

Whilst competence has, on balance, characterized Thai fiscal policy, technocratic initiatives undertaken by the BOI and various line ministries to promote industry have been less impressive. Since the 1950s, the government has vigorously promoted particular industries and favoured specific conglomerates. Prior to 1980, the trade regime and the BOI consistently favoured large and heavy industry. Yet such interventions 'have not been important in explaining Thailand's economic success' (World Bank 1993e: 7). Thai industrial policy significantly deviated from the Northeast Asian norm. Technocrats were not guided by a strategy of picking winners and instead succumbed to patronage and rent seeking (Laothamatas 1992: ch. 1). This was certainly the case in the 1950s era of the bureaucratic polity when the private sector functioned largely as 'the creature of leading politico-bureaucrats' (Laothamatas 1994: 197). The economic nationalism that characterized the 1950s further promoted often corrupt clientilistic arrangements between the evolving bureaucratic polity and ethnically Chinese private sector entrepreneurs in Bangkok. By the late 1950s, ethnic Chinese, who constituted less than 10 per cent of the population, accounted for 70 per cent of 'large and smaller business owners or managers in Bangkok' (Laothamatas 1994: 197). The Chinese in particular dominated the commercial banking sector, controlling four of the five major commercial banks (Hewison 1985; Redding 1993: 32). In this period, the private sector effectively functioned as 'pariah entrepreneurs' (Riggs 1966).

However, from the 1960s, notably during the Sarit regime (1958–63), and reinforced during the Prem regime (1981–8), the bureaucratic polity abandoned the patrimonialism of the mid-1950s and began instead to develop the private sector rather than rent seek from it. The shrewd management of fiscal policy, especially after 1981 (Laothamatas 1994: 199–201), demonstrated growing technocratic competence. At the same time, the assimilation of ethnic Chinese business families into the modernized Thai state further helped business interests. By 1973, 63 per cent of Chinese-dominated trade association members and 87 per cent of their presidents held Thai citizenship (p. 202). A process of miscegenation additionally facilitated assimilation, as family members of the indigenous bureaucratic elite entered the ranks of the Chinese-dominated business elite in significant numbers. By the late 1970s one fifth of business leaders were children of government officials (p. 202). This developmental process, together with the emergence from the late 1970s of a range of Thai business associations, has both promoted closer government business relations and enabled the business sector to initiate, deflect and even block government policy. Government–business cooperation reached its apogee with the formation of the Joint Public–Private Consultative Committee (JPCC) in 1980, to help business associations communicate with leading technocrats and economic ministers. These inclusionary arrangements enabled business associations to influence financial and industrial policy in the course of the 1980s, particularly the crucial decision to rationalize the financial sector and devalue the baht in 1984 (p. 210).

This evolving partnership between big business and government, moreover, has led to the growing involvement of powerful business figures in politics. After Thailand's most recent coup (1991), the military elite briefly appointed Saha Union chairman Anand Panyarachun Prime Minister. He again held office briefly in 1993. After elections in 1995, Thaksin Shinawatra briefly became Deputy Prime Minister. Both businessmen demonstrated an ability to work in conjunction with the financial technocracy. Technocratic rule, consequently, appears to offer the best hope for Thailand's economic, if not its political, development.

By contrast, Thailand's bouts of quasi-democracy have been most commonly associated with corruption, dubious financial deals and land scandals. Certainly, this was the case with the government of Chatichai Choonhavan between 1988 and 1991 and repeated by the Chart Thai-led coalition of Prime Minister Banharn between 1995 and 1996. Yet because of the fluid nature of Thai politics, corruption has not been quite the drag on economic development that it is elsewhere in Indochina. Nevertheless its often deleterious effect upon business–government relations constitutes a significant difference between the Thai developmental experience and that of Hong Kong, Taiwan and Singapore.

In 1994, the World Bank reported that although Thailand had performed remarkably well since 1981, it still required 'a more transparent and coherent trade regime . . . to improve efficiency . . . sustain growth and preempt unilateral and bilateral pressures from the country's major trading partners' (World Bank 1994: 37). Thailand's postwar development story has on balance, then, been uneven. Certainly, the fiscal orthodoxy and the deregulated financial environment created after 1981 made possible an economic boom between 1985 and 1995. Meanwhile, Thailand's flexible conglomerates are well placed to exploit business opportunities in Indochina and Southern China. Yet, despite growth of 8.6 per cent in 1995 and a 23 per cent growth in exports, both industry and wealth remain worryingly concentrated in Bangkok and its environs. The failure to develop effective regional light industry, especially in the poor Northeast, and the urban nightmare that constitutes commuter travel in Bangkok are enduring testaments to the failure of Thai planning. Industrialization, moreover, has failed to absorb the pool of underemployed urban and rural labour. Although labour remains cheap, docile and mobile, it has come under pressure from even lower cost neighbouring countries like Vietnam and Southern China.

TABLE 2.5 Trade deficits on current account 1995 (per cent)

Country	%
Republic of Korea	-2
Indonesia	-2.2
Malaysia	-7.4
Thailand	-6.3

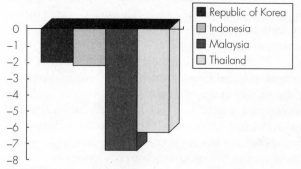

Sources: *Asian Wall Street Journal*, 16 January 1996; *Business Times*, 10 March 1996; *Far Eastern Economic Review*, 17 August 1996; 21 March 1996

Thailand's economy is moving from a position of dependency on cheap labour to dependence on capital goods and more advanced technology. Layoffs in the textile industry have prompted the formation of increasingly aggressive labour unions. Here again government planning has been ineffective. The state provides only six years of compulsory education, so that Thailand encounters difficulty promoting workers into higher value-added technologies. This limits Thai industrial exports to 'processed primary products, garments, textiles and other labour intensive products' (Yoshihara 1988: 117). Thailand, consequently, remains economically dependent on foreign companies. Consequently, when Thai wages increase, 'Thailand cannot develop new industrial exports and thus upgrade the composition of its industrial products' (p. 117). Clearly, the Thai attempt to plan development has not been as successful as its Northeast Asian counterparts. During the corrupt administration of Banharn, moreover, even the previously sound technocratic management of the Bank of Thailand was subject to damaging political manipulation. As the 1985–95 boom ended, the Thai economy had developed a worrying combination of a trade deficit amounting to 8 per cent of GDP (*Far Eastern Economic Review*, 15 August 1996: 40; see table 2.5) and foreign debt corresponding to 46 per cent of GDP (*The Economist*, 24 August 1996: 58).

Malaysia

Since independence in 1957, the Malaysian government has sustained economic growth, promoted structural transformation and attempted to distribute wealth equitably in an ethnically diverse society. Except for a severe recession between 1984 and 1986, Malaysia has experienced relatively uninterrupted growth since 1957. Between 1960 and 1990, real GDP increased sevenfold at an annual rate of 6.8 per cent. Indeed between 1988 and 1995 the growth rate accelerated to over 8 per cent per annum (*Straits Times*, 29 August 1994; *Far Eastern Economic Review*, 28 September 1995). Per capita real GDP multiplied sixfold, rising from US$534 in 1980 to US$3,500 by 1995 (see table 2.3; World Bank 1993f; *Straits Times*, 29 August 1994; *Asiaweek*, 21 July 1995). Significantly, inequality in income distribution has been reduced, particularly between ethnic groups. With a population of only 17.8 million, Malaysia, unlike the rest of Southeast Asia, is relatively under-populated. This has enabled the government to eradicate poverty and change the pattern of wealth distribution. Thus whereas in 1970, the indigenous Malay *bumiputeras* owned an estimated 2.4 per cent of corporate equity, by 1990 their share had increased to 20.4 per cent (Jesudason 1990: 108; World Bank 1993f: 1).

Like Singapore, which briefly formed a part of the federation between 1963 and 1965, Malaysia developed under British colonial rule before 1957. By 1957 Malaysia had achieved a relatively high standard of living compared with neighbouring countries, effective communications and a growing economy dependent on commodities like tea, coffee, tin and rubber. In 1960, agriculture employed 60 per cent of the workforce and was dualistic in character, consisting of large, mainly British-owned plantations, on the one hand, and Malay rubber and rice farming smallholders, on the other. The colonial legacy also included sizeable ethnic Chinese and Indian communities attracted initially by the prospect of work in the plantation and mining industries. By the early 1960s the Chinese community not only constituted 37 per cent of the population, they had also established a formidable presence in tin mining, banking and trade. In 1963 the departing British added the timber- and oil-rich Bornean states of Sabah and Sarawak to the infant federation, further exacerbating the problem of ethnic identity.

The UMNO-led *Barisan Nasional* coalition of ethnically based parties that has governed Malaysia since independence initially continued the colonial free trade regime. The two major export commodities, tin and rubber, commanded particularly high export shares during the 1960s (Watanabe 1992: 67). The government, however, did intervene extensively to promote rural development and develop infrastructure. Subsequently, limited import-substituting policies, introduced in the late 1960s, attempted to reduce imports of consumer goods and develop domestic processing of natural resources to create industrial employment (World Bank 1993a: 134; 1993f: 4). Although economic growth averaged 6 per cent per annum throughout the 1960s, there was little reduction in the level of absolute poverty, coupled with relatively high unemployment amongst the *bumiputeras*. This, together with a growing concentration of private enterprise in the hands of the Chinese community, contributed to discontent resulting in ethnic riots in 1969.

Communal violence contributed to a major socio-economic rethink and a New Economic Policy (NEP) introduced in 1971. The NEP aimed to achieve growth with equity, eradicating poverty and redressing the economic imbalance between the predominantly urban Chinese and the Malay rural poor. The policy began an era of state activism in resource allocation, production and trade primarily through public enterprise trusts like *Perbadanan Nasional Bhd* (*Pernas*) and *Permodalan Nasional Bhd* (PNB) in order to promote a *bumiputera* interest in commerce and industry (Gomez 1994: 3). The NEP established affirmative action employment quotas to reflect the ethnic composition of the population and sought to achieve a 30 per cent *bumiputera* stake in Malaysian industry by 1991. In 1975, the government introduced the Investment Coordination Act (ICA) in an attempt to manage industrialization and reinforce the NEPs equity objectives by requiring manufacturers to acquire licences. The granting of a licence was conditional upon compliance with NEP guidelines. To achieve the ownership target, PNB and *Pernas* began a programme of nationalization by buying out and restructuring the equity of foreign-held resource-based companies like Guthrie and Sime Darby.

The new strategy also sought to promote export-oriented growth through export incentives, tax breaks and indirect subsidies to pioneer industries in Export Processing Zones (EPZs). These incentives, combined with the availability of low-cost, semi-skilled female workers, attracted the first wave of Japanese, South Korean and Taiwanese foreign investment. By 1980, 70 per cent of Malaysia's manufactured exports originated from foreign-owned firms located in the new EPZs. Foreign investment in labour-absorptive semi- and low-skilled light industrial production resulted in Malaysia becoming the world's leading producer of semiconductor devices by 1978 (Jesudason 1990: 174). The discovery of substantial reserves of oil and natural gas offshore from Sabah and Sarawak and in eastern peninsular Malaysia further boosted economic growth. Malaysia became a net oil exporter with a surplus that grew to $3.4 billion by 1980.

Buoyed by these resources and revenue derived from the 1980 oil price rise, Mahathir Mohamad, the new Ultra Malay Prime Minister, inaugurated his rule in 1981 by launching a 'Look East' policy and a state-led

programme of heavy industrialization under the auspices of the Heavy
Industries Corporation of Malaysia (HICOM). The fourth four-year plan
(1981–5) envisaged the creation of a new Malaysia Incorporated. Mahathir
and UMNO technocrats like Daim Zainudin looked somewhat contradictorily towards Japan and to a lesser extent South Korea both as a model of
the state-led industrialization and as a source of FDI. Economic imitation
extended even to creating Malaysian-style *sogoshoshas* in a self-conscious and
largely unsuccessful attempt to project Malaysian enterprise abroad (Lim
and Gomez 1994: 232ff). In the period up to 1985, state-run enterprises
constituted the vanguard of state-led industrialization policy. The corporate incursions of UMNO's investment arm, Fleet Holdings, subsequently
the Renong Group, exemplified Mahathir's vision of 'how *bumiputeras*
could actively participate in business' (Gomez 1994: 8). The rapid conglom-
eratization of the Renong Group, with its various media, property, industrial, stock exchange and tourist interests (p. 131), further demonstrated
the extensive patronage, in the form of soft loans from government banks,
that characterized the evolving relationship between the UMNO elite and
bumiputera business interests.

The Malaysia Incorporated strategy thus sought to achieve Mahathir's
twin nationalist policy objectives: economic restructuring and accelerating
industrialization, combined with the social and political goal 'of redistribut-
ing national income to help the Malays, who were the group least active in
the industrial sector' (Bowie 1994: 177). The HICOM-sponsored national
car, the Proton Saga, symbolized this policy. By the 1990s the national car
had captured 70 per cent of the Malaysian market and achieved success
overseas in the United Kingdom and Australia (Jomo 1994b: 263).

State intervention, however, had its drawbacks. Chinese business groups
in particular maintained the ICA constituted 'a sword hanging over the
private sector' (World Bank 1993f: 10). Private, especially Chinese, domestic
investment fell away sharply after 1975, and this had a negative effect on the
level of foreign direct investment. Moreover the government-funded heavy
industrialization strategy caused a worrying escalation in the level of foreign
debt. By 1987, 'public enterprises accounted for more than one-third of the
public sector's outstanding debt, and for more than 30 per cent of total debt
servicing' (Gomez 1994: 12). In 1983, the government used two-thirds of its
total expenditure to finance twenty-seven of the country's larger public
enterprises. At the same time, the collapse in world commodity prices after
1984, especially for oil, tin and rubber, plunged the Malaysian economy
into recession. In 1985 real GDP fell by 1 per cent. By 1988 the total public
sector debt had risen to a worrying $16.7 billion. 'Money politics', the
involvement of ministers and politicians from the ruling coalition in the
misappropriation and diversion of funds, further exacerbated the financial

drain. The Carrian affair involving a Hong Kong-based affiliate of Bank Bumiputra Malaysia cost the UMNO-supported bank $1 billion when the Hong Kong property market crashed in 1984 (Clad 1991: 52). Equally suspect was the government decision in 1987 to grant the contract for its largest infrastructural development project, the North South Highway from Johor to the Thai border, to an UMNO front company, United Engineers Malaysia, that had no previous experience in highway construction (Bowie 1994: 182). Moreover, as most UMNO-related companies developed through active stock market intervention and had grown on the property and development boom of the early 1980s, they suffered heavy losses when the country slid into recession. A notable feature of speculation on the Kuala Lumpur exchange involves insider knowledge of what are or are about to become UMNO shares. Money politics, dubious share dealings and stock swaps cement the patrimonial ties between government and business that have evolved since 1981. The blurring of government and party and the overlap between state and market have distorted economic development in Malaysia (Bowie 1994: 183). At the same time, the NEP has failed to create a *bumiputera* entrepreneurial class 'that can venture out without political crutches' (World Bank 1993f: 26).

In order to remedy the detrimental effects of industrial restructuring and the inefficiency of public enterprises, Mahathir and his key economic adviser, Finance Minister Daim Zainuddin, embarked on a programme of privatization and a relaxation of the *bumiputera* affirmative action provisions. In particular the Promotions of Investment Act (PIA, 1986) offered a wide range of incentives for investment in manufacturing, agriculture and tourism. In 1990, Mahathir announced a new National Development Policy (NDP) to replace the NEP. The new policy remained committed to achieving a 30 per cent *bumiputera* share of the economy, but overall growth would henceforth take precedence (*Straits Times*, 17 August 1992). The NDP set an annual growth rate of 7 per cent to achieve a fully developed Malaysia by 2020.

To secure growth targets the government, therefore, relaxed the rules governing foreign investment. Liberalization and the search for FDI fortuitously coincided with *endaka*, the strengthening yen, and encouraged a wave of Japanese and Taiwanese investment together with Japanese overseas development aid (ODA). By 1990 Taiwanese investment in small semi-skilled manufacturing components ventures amounted to $2.3 billion, and George Wang, Taipei's Economic and Cultural Centre Director, considered Malaysia the base for subsequent Taiwanese ventures into Southeast Asia (*Straits Times*, 10 August 1994). This notwithstanding, Japanese FDI has since 1985 had the greatest impact on Malaysian industrialization (Ali 1994: 105). Between 1986 and 1991 alone Japanese investment exceeded

$2 billion. About 50 per cent of this was invested in the electrical and electronic industry, primarily located in Special Economic Zones (SEZs) in the Klang Valley, Selangor and on the East Malaysian island of Penang (Anazawa 1994: 82). Japanese SMEs and multinationals have participated both in import-substituting heavy industry joint ventures and more recently in export-oriented electronics and textile manufacturing. Almost all Japanese import-substituting companies in Malaysia, like the initial collaboration between HICOM and Mitsubishi to produce the Proton Saga, are joint ventures. By contrast, export-oriented companies are almost wholly owned Japanese subsidiaries managed without domestic interference (p. 83), an arrangement made possible by the liberal terms of the PIA and the sixth Malaysia Plan (1990–5), which sought to attract $12 billion of FDI in Malaysian manufacturing. Significantly, 82 per cent of foreign projects export more than 50 per cent and 75 per cent export more than 80 per cent of their output. In 1990, manufacturing accounted for 27 per cent of GDP, compared with agriculture's 19 per cent, and 60 per cent of total exports. Structural transformation has in fact increased the economy's dependence on trade. Exports increased from 56 per cent of GDP in 1960 to 65 per cent by 1990 (World Bank 1993f: 2). By 1995, unemployment had disappeared and UMNO had relatively equitably distributed the wealth created by development.

The creation, moreover, of an investment-friendly climate and the evolution of a relatively sophisticated banking sector has seen Kuala Lumpur emerge as a potential competitor to Singapore in the financial services sector. By 1995, the Kuala Lumpur Stock Exchange (KLSE) ranked as the largest bourse in Southeast Asia and the eleventh largest in the world. In July 1995, Deputy Prime Minister and Minister of Finance Anwar Ibrahim outlined a liberalization package designed to take trade in Malaysian shares away from the Singapore exchange and attract foreign fund managers to the KLSE (*Far Eastern Economic Review*, 31 August 1995: 56–60). Meanwhile, the government has inaugurated a 'raft of colossal infrastructure projects . . . [that] include the world's tallest office towers, Southeast Asia's largest hydroelectric dam and one of the region's most modern airports' (*Far Eastern Economic Review*, 28 September 1995: 84). Eclipsing all this is the proposed new administrative city, Putrajaya, at a projected cost of $8.1 billion. The UMNO Economic Planning Unit promotes this proactive urban development to avoid the inefficient gridlock that blights the growth prospects of contemporary Bangkok.

UMNO has, on balance, then, managed development competently since 1957. Indeed, the evolving capacity of UMNO technocrats to both sustain growth and infrastructural development and guarantee political stability has attracted foreign investment to Malaysia. This, combined with legal restrictions on trade union activity, a docile and compliant labour force, low inflation and competitive wages, 'rated highly in the decision of Japanese companies to locate in the country' after 1985 (Denker 1994: 54). Moreover, the maintenance and extension of the Employers' Provident Fund (EPF), introduced, like the Singaporean CPF, by the colonial authority in 1951 as a form of forced saving, has proved both an effective source for government domestic investment and an important limitation on domestic consumption. By 1990, contributions to EPF accounted for 20 per cent of net wages (Asher 1993: 13) and 40 per cent of GDP in 1991 (p. 17).

Yet, although technocratic management, economic liberalization and FDI engendered a spectacular acceleration of growth after 1985, a number of unresolved problems threaten future development. Japanese, Hong Kong and Taiwanese investment has certainly transformed Malaysia into a centre for low-cost, low-technology electronic manufacturing, and in the process 'counteracted the weakness of national actors in providing employment' (Jesudason 1990: 196). However, although FDI provided employment, it has not developed links with domestic manufacturers. Export-oriented Japanese manufacturers maintain regional intercompany networks as part of a global strategy. Consequently, Japanese multinationals have not transferred any technology. Even in joint ventures like the Proton Saga, Mitsubishi ships ready-assembled engines from Japan (Jomo 1994b: 280). The practice of transfer pricing, moreover, enables Japanese parent companies to repatriate profits from Malaysian plants (Anatory and Jomo 1994: 149). Such practices, combined with an acute shortage of skilled manpower, severely constrain Malaysia's capacity to move up the technological ladder to higher value-added technologies (*Far Eastern Economic Review*, 31 August 1995). Meanwhile as wage costs rise and multinationals encounter increasing difficulty in both finding and retaining skilled and semi-skilled workers, Malaysian manufacturing faces growing competition from Vietnam and Southern China as these sources of low-cost production compete for FDI (*The Economist*, 24 June 1995: 27–8).

Ultimately, Malaysia's success in courting Japanese investment could prove self-defeating. Malaysia, like Thailand, South Korea and Taiwan, runs a growing trade deficit with Japan. In 1991 Japan accounted for 15.9 per cent of Malaysia's exports but 26.1 per cent of imports. The terms of trade are unequal both in quantitative and in qualitative terms. Japan's trade with Malaysia accounted for only 2.6 per cent of total trade in 1991. Moreover, whilst Japan exports high value added technology to Malaysia and repatriates the profits of its export-oriented growth to Japanese parent companies, its interest in Malaysian products extends only as far as commodities (Aslam and Piei 1994: 23–32). Tariff and unofficial trade barriers keep Malaysian textile and agricultural exports out of the Japanese market, whilst

Japanese manufacturers are keenly interested in Malaysian raw materials, in particular tropical hardwood. Japan currently imports 64 per cent of its hardwood from Sarawak. As K.S. Jomo observes, Japan plays 'a significant role in Malaysian deforestation' (Jomo 1994a: 182).

The growth through borrowing and foreign investment strategy pursued since 1985 has created a burgeoning savings investment gap increasingly covered by foreign borrowing. Although government reduced the level of foreign debt in the course of the 1980s, it remains over $23 billion. Moreover, as this debt is for the most part denominated in yen, it appreciates when the yen strengthens. The rise in imports to sustain rapid growth has pushed Malaysia's current account into burgeoning deficit. In 1994 the deficit stood at $4 billion, or about 7.7 per cent of GDP, and rose to 8.3 per cent of GDP in 1995 (*Business Times*, 10 March 1995). This, together with external debt amounting to 39 per cent of GDP, contracted to fund pretentious infrastructural schemes like the Petronas towers, renders the Malaysian ringgit highly susceptible to speculative pressure. Moreover, the Malaysian Central Bank's practice of speculating with the national assets in the international money markets and incurring losses estimated at $6 billion between 1992 and 1994 (*International Herald Tribune*, 31 August 1994: viii) hardly engenders confidence in the probity of Malaysia's fiscal management.

These factors, together with growing inflation, high interest rates and the murky relationship between UMNO politicians and indigenous business groups, give some credence to the view that Malaysian-style capitalists are 'paper entrepreneurs' who relentlessly pursue 'opportunities for acquisitions, mergers, restructurings and leveraged buy-outs' (Yoshihara 1988: 4) at the expense of developing indigenous manufacturing and technology. The forty-year development process, moreover, has increasingly marginalized the smaller indigenous Chinese entrepreneurs. Significantly, the big Malaysian Chinese trading conglomerates, like Quek Leng Chan's Hong Leong Group, the Robert Kuok Group and Vincent Tan's Inter Pacific Group, specialize in hotel chains, media enterprises and transport, industries diversified across Pacific Asia. Moreover, Quek, Kuok and Tan cultivate close links with key figures in the UMNO elite and function as their 'business proxies' (Gomez 1994: 37–9). Such arrangements ensure that the UMNO elite's business activity occurs 'outside the purview of the party' (p. 43). Thus, whilst indigenous Chinese entrepreneurs are either marginalized or co-opted into UMNOs business politics, the majority *bumiputera* community have become worryingly inured to a 'subsidy mentality' (p. 55).

Control and accountability constitute crucial issues, therefore, for the continued management of Malaysia Incorporated. Speculation and peculation have marked Malaysia's post-1985 corporate development and the government bureaucracy has developed an 'institutional interest in preserving corporate freedom from public scrutiny' (Ling 1993: 125). Thus, although the UMNO party state has astutely manipulated domestic and foreign investment since 1985, the shadier aspects of this strategy have generated a disturbing air of insubstantiality indicated by the growth of imports, mounting foreign debt and rising inflation (see tables 2.4 and 2.5).

Indonesia

Indonesia is by far the largest HPAE in terms of both size and population. Archipelagic Indonesia consists of 13,000 islands, 300 ethnic and linguistic groups, and has a total population in excess of 184 million, larger than all the other HPAEs combined. Five large islands (Java, Sumatra, Sulawesi, Kalimantan and Irian Jaya) account for 92 per cent of the area and 94 per cent of the population. Two-thirds of the population live on Java. Ninety-five per cent of the population are ethnically Malay, and as elsewhere in Southeast Asia there is a small (2.5 per cent), commercially active, urbanized, ethnically Chinese minority (World Bank 1993g: 1). Unlike the Northeast and Southeast Asian HPAEs, which have achieved either developed or middle-income status, the World Bank places Indonesia in the low-income category. Average GDP per capita is substantially lower than both Northeast and Southeast Asian HPAEs, although it has risen from the extremely low base of $50 in 1965 to $940 in 1995 (p. 2; see also table 2.3). Indonesia also possesses a much richer resource base, including oil, gas and precious metals, than other East Asian economies and has until recently generally pursued a resource-intensive rather than a labour-intensive, export-oriented growth strategy. Nevertheless, over the past thirty years per capita income has risen at an average rate of 4.5 per cent and since 1986 at an impressive 7 per cent per annum (p. 3; *Far Eastern Economic Review*, 18 May 1995: 56).

Like Malaysia, Singapore, South Korea and Taiwan, Indonesia experienced a protracted period of colonization, and owes its basic territorial configuration to its former colonial power, the Netherlands. The Republic of Indonesia was 'born with a classic colonial economy based on plantation estates producing for export' (Macintyre 1994: 246). To the extent that there was a local business class at all at the time of decolonization in 1949 it consisted of small, predominantly Chinese, merchants and regional traders. A military-bureaucratic elite, which established a ruling estate 'free of control by parties or other nonbureaucratic forces' (Robison, 1993: 68), occupied the socio-economic vacuum left by the departing Dutch. After a brief and confused period of multiparty democracy, this estate evolved into Sukarno's guided democracy (1957–65). Informed by a heady mixture of charisma, socialism and economic nationalism, the government after 1958 embarked upon an orgy of nationalization and import-substituting industrialization. Under the rubric, 'Guided Economy', the government established a regime of import monopolies, confiscated foreign assets, and ran them as state-owned enterprises. Military adventures, including the confrontation (*konfrontasi*) with Malaysia (1963–6), together with the construction of grandiose national monuments, led to increased external borrowing. The result was economic and political chaos. Inflation accelerated to 1000 per cent by 1965 and debt service fees exceeded foreign exchange earning. Per capita income actually fell by 15 per cent between 1958–1965. By the mid-1960s most observers despaired of Indonesia's economic prospects. In 1966, Gunnar Myrdal maintained there was 'little prospect of rapid economic growth in Indonesia' (Myrdal 1968: 489).

An attempted coup followed by a military-inspired purge of communists between 1965 and 1966 constituted the Old Order's denouement and dramatically altered Indonesia's developmental path. Banning the *Partai Kommunis Indonesia* (PKI) in March 1966 committed General, subsequently President, Suharto's New Order to the western industrial democracies (Bresnan 1993: 68). Despite its fragility, the New Order government moved quickly to restore macroeconomic stability and introduce market-minded reforms. It had to. In the course of the 1960s, foreign borrowing had risen to $2 billion and interest repayments on debt exceeded export earnings (Schwarz 1994: 52; Nitisastro 1994: 18). In an attempt to resolve the economic crisis and impress both the IMF and the Paris Club of developed economies with Indonesia's rediscovered fiscal probity, Suharto installed a 'Berkeley Mafia' of western-trained economists based at the University of Indonesia in key economic ministries. The rescheduling of the debt enabled the Indonesian government to access financial resources after 1970 and 'move forward to a process of sustained growth' (Nitisastro 1994: 19). In return as Widjojo Nitisastro, the guru of the new economic technocrats, points out, the Indonesian government undertook to 'put its own house in order by carrying out effectively a comprehensive program of economic stabilization' (p. 19). Under technocratic guidance the New Order cut spending on SOEs, loosened trade barriers and overhauled investment laws. The technocrats removed most domestic price controls and returned some nationalized enterprises to private ownership. The government passed a 'balanced budget' law in 1967 prohibiting budget financing through foreign borrowing or money creation. By 1969, this fiscal policy reduced inflation to a manageable 20 per cent per annum and the external accounts were brought into balance. Following the devaluation of the currency and unification of the exchange rate in 1971, the capital account was fully liberalized (World Bank 1993g: 6).

The economy recovered surprisingly quickly from the Old Order's economic utopianism, recording double-digit growth for the first time in 1968

(Hill 1994: 61). With the economy stabilized, the government focus shifted to long-term development. The first five-year plan, *REPELITA 1* (1969–74), emphasized agriculture, particularly rice farming, and infrastructure. In fact, despite its evident utility in 1966, the New Order's embrace of economic liberalism was always less than passionate. The official *pancasila* ideology and the constitution of 1945 favoured *gotong royong* or cooperative capitalism rather than the individualist 'free fight' variety (Hill 1994: 66; Taubert 1991: 132). Consequently, Indonesian industrial and economic policy during the New Order is an unresolved debate over more or less government intervention. Even economic technocrats like Widjojo, who remained a key policy adviser throughout the New Order, were sympathetic to economic nationalist ideas and never committed themselves completely to economic liberalism (Hill 1994: 66; Bresnan 1993: 82–3).

The windfall tax revenues afforded by the OPEC-inspired oil price rises of 1973 and 1979 offered a new opportunity for state *dirigisme*, social distribution and *gotong royong*. Net oil and gas earnings rose from $0.6 billion in 1973 to a peak of $10.6 billion in 1981. By that time oil and gas accounted for 75 per cent of export earning and 70 per cent of budget revenues (World Bank 1993g: 7). The massive increase in terms of trade between 1973 and 1985 (Hill 1994: 56) made a renewed economic nationalism feasible. 'Huge sums were pumped into SOEs in such industries as steel, fertilisers, aluminium, oil, paper, petrochemical refining, and cement' (Macintyre 1994: 250). Early beneficiaries were 'big ticket industrial projects like the Krakatau Steel plant' (Schwarz 1994: 55).

The banking and financial sector suffered a similar interventionary fate. Dominated by the five state banks and the long-term development bank Bappindo, the government intervened to determine the pattern of bank lending. State and private bank lending expanded from 86 per cent to 92 per cent of total loans. Domestic gains came at the expense of foreign banks. Joint ventures and foreign investment inexorably declined. Indeed, after the 1974 student-inspired Malari riots against corruption, capitalism and the visit of Japanese Prime Minister Tanaka, the government positively discouraged foreign investment (Bresnan 1993: ch. 6). For 'most of the oil boom decade, entry procedures for foreign firms remained opaque, complex, time consuming and costly' (Hill 1994: 68).

Nationalist economic thinking had further implications for trade policy. Import restrictions increased and the New Order returned to an ISI policy. 'The proliferation of tariff and, especially, non-tariff barriers intensified in the wake of the second oil boom' (Macintyre 1994: 251). The government extended coverage to an ever-expanding list of manufacturing and raw material processing industries. The wealth attracted by increased oil revenues also made possible a characteristic New Order corporatist style of management that permeated both economy and society. As the power of the state expanded, moreover, 'the well being of the people improved so that those living in intolerably poor conditions declined from well over half the population to around 20 per cent by the end of the 1980s' (Vatikiotis 1993: 109).

The state became the great provider. Corporate control extended to labour and business. After the demise of the PKI in 1965, the New Order organized labour through an officially sponsored All-Indonesia Workers, Union (*Serikat Perburuhan Seluruh Indonesia* – SPSI) introduced in 1973. The evolution of a system of corporate controls and the military–bureaucratic management of functional groups rendered labour both pliable and subject to military control and interference (Bresnan 1993: 98, Human Rights Watch 1994: 43). Business representative bodies like the National Chamber of Commerce and Industry (*Kamar Dagang Dan Industri* – KADIN), although not as tightly controlled as the SPSI, similarly function as instruments of the state.

The evolving corporatism of the New Order necessarily entailed the extension of traditional patrimonialism to the domestic economy. In particular, domestic corporate conglomerates, closely connected to 'the centres of military bureaucratic power' (Robison 1990: 104), proliferated. Despite official commitment to indigenous *pribumi* entrepreneurs, the corporate giants that emerged after 1975 were Chinese Indonesian with close ties to President Suharto. State-allocated monopolies constituted the source of this new wealth. Thus Liem Sioe Liong's Salim Group, with interests in 'everything from cement to noodles' (*Forbes*, 13 February 1995), dates from Liem's relationship with Suharto in 1950s Semarang. Significantly, many of Salim's ventures involve at least one of Suharto's children and the group has become deeply embedded in Suharto's 'patrimonial network' (Schwarz 1994: 113). By 1990, the group's revenues amounted to $9 billion with about 60 per cent coming from its Indonesian operations. A similar *cukong* relationship exists between the second largest conglomerate, the Bob Hassan Group, and Suharto. Indonesia's 'plywood king' also began his entrepreneurial career by supplying goods to Suharto's Diponegoro Division in 1957. By 1995, as chairman of Apkindo, the Indonesian plywood association, Hassan had a 'hammerlock' on Indonesia's plywood trade (*Asian Wall Street Journal*, 20–21 January 1995). Hasan's group also includes two banks, substantial manufacturing interests, an airline and a shipping line. The group's timber and airline interests are also linked to conglomerates owned by Suharto's second son, Bambang, and youngest son, Hutomo.

Indeed, apart from the *pribumi* Bakrie Group, Suharto's children own the only indigenous conglomerates of substance. In fact, second son Bambang's Bimantara Group and eldest daughter Tutut's Citra Lamtoro Gung Group are on a par with the Chinese conglomerates in terms of size and capitalization. As Andrew Macintyre observes, 'the business careers of Suharto's children highlight the fundamental importance of clientilistic connections as the key to gaining access to state generated rent taking opportunities and thence to commercial success' (Macintyre 1994: 254). Tommy Suharto's experience in the Indonesian cigarette market illustrates this. In 1990, a Tommy Suharto company, BPCC, tried to establish a monopoly on cloves, the main ingredient in *kretek* cigarettes. The endeavour spectacularly failed when cigarette firms refused to accept the monopoly price, and in 1991 BPCC needed a $325 million government loan to avoid bankruptcy (*Asian Wall Street Journal*, 26 March 1992; *Far Eastern Economic Review*, 30 April 1992: 58).

The system of licensing and monopolies that evolved in the course of the 1970s made possible corruption, rent seeking and graft on an unprecedented scale. It also made possible some spectacular financial collapses, most notably that of the state oil monopoly, Pertamina. In 1973, Ibnu Sutowo, the Director of Pertamina, the 'strategic cornerstone of the Indonesian economy' (Robison 1990: 104), sought to deepen import substitution and create a business empire by extending Pertamina interests into shipping, steel and construction. In the process the Director abandoned internal auditing procedures. In 1976, he departed from the scene, 'after it was revealed that Pertamina had run up debts of $10.5 billion – approximately 30 per cent of Indonesia's gross domestic product at the time' (Schwarz 1994: 55). Pertamina's overdraft required further recourse to foreign borrowing, in the process doubling Indonesia's foreign debt (p. 55).

Nevertheless, despite its potential for both patrimonialism and corruption, the oil boom also made possible the alleviation of poverty and the achievement of self-sufficiency in rice production. Based on a strategy of massive investment in agricultural infrastructure and services, a favourable incentive regime and strong central direction by the National Logistics Agency, Bulog, rice output grew by 4 per cent per annum between 1965 and 1990 and increased from 12 million to 22 million tons per annum between 1970 and 1980 (Bresnan 1993: 124).

The oil boom decade also supported the development of Indonesian manufacturing industries. Manufacturing employment grew at an annual rate of about 5.6 per cent for the whole sector from 1975 to 1986 (Hill 1994: 82) and labour productivity rose sharply over the period, 'among large and medium firms it grew at about 9 per cent' (p. 81). The Ministry of Industry played an interventionary role in promoting heavy, capital-intensive projects like steel-making and oil-refining. In the course of the late 1970s, the Ministry attempted to 'deepen' the industrial structure and impose local content quotas (World Bank 1993g: 39). At the same time, the Ministry of Research and Technology, dominated by the German-trained aeronautical engineer B.J. Habibie, enthusiastically promoted the development of indigenous technology and telecommunications, transportation, energy, agriculture and defence as the 'natural vehicles of Indonesia's transformation' (Bresnan 1993: 214; Schwarz 1994: 90–7). In 1989, Suharto expanded the Ministry's mandate and placed ten state-owned enterprises under Habibie's direct management (World Bank 1993g: 39).

The decline in oil prices after 1981, however, once more necessitated a modification of state-led industrialization and an industrial policy that had largely failed to pick winners. Initially, reappraisal took the form of more prudent macroeconomic management and a large currency devaluation in 1983. However, in 1986, Indonesia suffered a severe economic slowdown and confronted, once again, an alarming balance of payments problem rescued only by recourse to foreign borrowing. 'Put simply, economic necessity demanded a change of policy' (Macintyre 1994: 255). After 1986, again in consultation with the World Bank, the government adopted 'bold deregulation packages, a larger role for the private sector, and an emphasis on exports' (Hill 1994: 80). Intent on diversification away from dependence on the oil sector, the economic technocrats, who reasserted an uneasy economic ascendancy, sought to create a more attractive investment climate. The National Planning Agency, *Bappenas*, introduced an export incentive package in May 1986 followed by a large devaluation of the rupiah in September and a series of trade reforms in October 1986. A further dismantling of quantitative restrictions and trade-promoting measures were introduced between January 1987 and June 1991 (World Bank 1993g: 31; Hill 1994: 70). Almost immediately, the stabilization and adjustment programme boosted manufacturing output, exports and investment. The removal of 'the stifling bureaucratic and regulatory regime' and the subsequent surge in exports seemingly vindicated the neoliberal strategy (Hill 1994: 82).

After 1986, Indonesian dependence on oil and gas revenues declined. Oil exports fell from a high of 81.9 per cent of total merchandise exports in 1981–2 to an estimated 44.9 per cent in 1990–1. Meanwhile government revenues from oil and gas fell from 70.6 per cent of total revenues in 1981–2 to 44.2 per cent in 1990–1 (p. 82). During the same period non-oil manufacturing grew at an annual average rate of 12.2 per cent and banking and finance grew at an annual average rate of 10.7 per cent. By 1990, Indonesia's GDP 'was by far the largest in the region at $107.2 billion' (p. 284).

The decline in oil revenue and the opening of Indonesia to FDI, as in Malaysia and Thailand, coincided with the appreciation of the Northeast Asian currencies and facilitated an influx of foreign investment capital. Japan, in particular, had, since the birth of the New Order, taken a keen interest in Indonesian primary resources. Indeed, the Japanese government 'gave more economic aid to Indonesia than to any other country in the world between 1967 and 1990' (Bresnan 1993: 282). Unsurprisingly, as elsewhere in Southeast Asia, the 'principal sources of foreign private investment in manufacturing in Indonesia after 1985 were Japan, Hong Kong, South Korea and Taiwan' (p. 265).

Much of the manufacturing growth was in plywood, but by the late 1980s 'the base had broadened considerably to include garments, textiles, footwear, furniture, fertiliser, paper and many other products' (Hill 1994: 83). The rapid growth in manufacturing, moreover, has structurally changed the economy, but in a significantly different way from the other HPAEs. Unlike those economies, natural resource-based products still formed over 30 per cent of Indonesia's manufactured exports in 1991 (World Bank 1993g: 31; Hill 1994: 83).

By contrast, imports are relatively skill- and technology-intensive, reflecting Indonesia's increasingly liberal policy on technology imports and foreign investment. Indonesia, thus, moved to labour-intensive export-led growth at a much later stage than other East Asian countries. The devaluation of the rupiah by 65 per cent against the yen in September 1986 boosted Indonesia's comparative advantage in labour-intensive production, making it, China apart, the cheapest source of unskilled labour in the region (World Bank 1993g: 31).

Deregulation had its most dramatic impact, however, upon the banking and financial services sector (Bresnan 1993: 265). The banking system's assets grew at a rate of 26 per cent per annum between 1988 and 1990. Forty new domestic banks opened in the same period, together with fifteen new joint venture banks. In 1991, the World Bank judged deregulation to have given Indonesia 'one of the most dynamic and least distorted financial sectors in the developing world' (World Bank 1993g: 6–8; *Jakarta Post*, 29 December 1993).

Trade and domestic liberalization continued between 1991 and 1995 both to comply with the completion of the Uruguay round of GATT and to 'strengthen export and overall economic performance' (World Bank 1994: 35). Between June and October 1993, the cabinet's economic team introduced measures reducing tariffs on the import of 'upstream industrial products', opening business sectors previously closed to foreign investment and permitting 100 per cent foreign ownership of manufacturing ventures. In May 1995, the government again reduced tariffs and surcharges on a range of imports to facilitate Indonesia's incorporation into AFTA by 2003.

Trade liberalization packages continued to generate impressive GDP growth, which averaged over 7 per cent per annum between 1992 and 1995. In 1994 alone, Indonesia attracted $23.7 billion in foreign investment. Exports increased from $33.9 billion in 1993 to $40.5 billion by 1994.

Meanwhile, oil and gas as a percentage of export earnings continued to decline, accounting for $9.69 billion in 1994 down from $10.67 billion in 1993. Labour-intensive textile and garment manufactures ($5 billion), plywood ($4.07 billion) and wood products ($5 billion) contributed the bulk of export earning, whilst electronic and electrical exports rose dramatically from $870 billion in 1993 to $1.3 billion in 1994 (*Far Eastern Economic Review*, 18 May 1995: 58). Between 1992 and 1994, Indonesia maintained a healthy trade surplus of over $8 billion. Since 1995, however, the current account has sunk into deficit (*Jakarta Post*, 29 December 1993; *Far Eastern Economic Review*, 18 May 1995: 56; 16 May 1996: 40).

Indonesian economic development has oscillated between periods of high state intervention and periods of reluctant deregulation. Even after deregulation, important areas of the economy remain on 'the negative list – closed to foreign investment' (*Straits Times*, 24 May 1995). The results of New Order development have, therefore, been mixed. Development since 1966 has reduced the level of poverty, improved health and cut the birth rate by half. The government has also established a system of almost universal primary education and between 1965 and 1990 achieved high growth rates in both agricultural and manufacturing production by regional and global standards.

Yet despite, or perhaps because of, its vast and often untapped, or poorly utilized, resources, Indonesia remains the poorest of the HPAEs. The growth achieved, moreover, has been inequitably distributed both amongst the population as a whole and between the capital, Jakarta, and the provinces. Whilst the GDP per capita of Jakarta had grown to $1,145 by 1995, that of peripiheral, but oil-rich, Aceh was less than $500 per capita (*The Australian*, 17 August 1995). The growing perception of a widening income gap between rich and poor and the absence of an efficient legal framework to deal with labour and property disputes has prompted an intermittent recourse to urban and rural *jacquerie*. Only military intervention suppressed labour riots and wildcat strikes at Tanjung Priok (Jakarta) in 1984 and more recently in Medan, Sumatra, in April 1994.

Exasperation with Chinese business ownership and the corrupt 'state officials who work with the Chinese colonizers and surrender Indonesia into Chinese hands', as one labour activist maintained (Human Rights Watch 1994: 66–7), is the main source of labour discontent. It reflects a wider resentment of the close *cukong* ties between Chinese conglomerates, like the Salim Group, and the Suharto regime. Deregulation of the economy, moreover, has only served the interests of the Chinese conglomerates and increased their popular opprobrium. As Christianto Wibisono observes, 'the constellation of Indonesia conglomerates involves a complex mixture of interrelationships between state owned firms and crony capitalist and bureaucratic capitalist, as well as the genuine private sector business conglomerates' (Wibisono 1995: 97–8; *Straits Times*, 26 January 1994). Of the 300 largest Indonesian enterprises, 65.7 per cent are Chinese and they account for 77 per cent of total sales (Witsibono 1995: 97).

The perception of Chinese business dominance allied to a burgeoning income gap has prompted contradictory demands both for greater economic liberalization and for greater government intervention. Those associated with the interventionist Minister of Research and Technology, B.J. Habibie, and his Indonesian Muslim Intellectuals Association (*Ikatan Cendekiawan Muslim Indonesia* – ICMI) look favourably to the distributive success of Malaysia's NEP. Fiscal and industrial policy in the 1990s has degenerated into an increasingly acrimonious debate between deregulating technocrats like Saleh Afiff and Mar'ie Muhammed, respectively Coordinating Minister for the Economy and Finance Minister, and interventionists like Habibie and Ginanjar, the current head of the National Planning Board, who favour a strategy of government intervention, both to inspire a 'national awakening to a higher technology', symbolically realized in the flight of the N250 commercial aircraft developed by Habibie's Agency for Strategic Industries, and to promote *pribumi* businesses.

Yet any attempt to introduce an Indonesian version of an NEP is additionally complicated by the role played by Suharto's children in indigenous conglomerates linked to Chinese conglomerates. Their interlocking business relations make it extremely difficult to distinguish between private enterprise, state enterprise and crony capitalism as well as between Chinese and *pribumi* conglomerates. Such complex ties obscure the distinction between government and business. They also render the best intentions of technocratic deregulators hostage to crony capitalism and military-bureaucratic pressure. Illustrative of the increasingly dynastic character of crony capitalism is the recent deal between Tommy Suharto's Humpuss Group and the South Korean conglomerate Kia to manufacture a national car – the Timor – with 60 per cent Indonesian content by 1999. The government's preferential classification of the national car project permits the Kia venture to undercut joint venture competitors by between 30 and 50 per cent (*Far Eastern Economic Review*, 14 March 1996: 50) and occasioned speculation that Suharto and his family are shifting government policy from an export orientation to import substitution (*Far Eastern Economic Review*, 16 May 1996: 42).

At the same time, the much vaunted liberalization of financial services has not proved an unmixed blessing for the Indonesian economy. The rapid reform of the financial sector constituted a case of 'too much too fast' (Schwarz 1994: 74). The rapid flow of money into the Indonesian banking system after 1989 led to a rise in lending, especially by state banks, and a growth in money supply. It also led to inflation (see table 2.4). Property speculation and an overheating economy required the Ministry of Finance to raise interest rates to 30 per cent in 1991. Although subsequently reduced, interest rates remain high at 13.3 per cent and loan to deposit rates reached a disturbing 82 per cent by December 1994. The state banks are adrift on a pool of bad debt, estimated at $85.88 billion in 1995 (*Far Eastern Economic Review*, 18 May 1995).

Financial scandal has further eroded faith in the banking sector. In 1990 Bank Duta, a bank with links to Hasan and several Suharto-supported charitable foundations, lost $419 million in foreign exchange trading, but hid the figure in its financial statements (World Bank 1993g: 28; *Asian Wall Street Journal*, 20–21 January 1995). In 1993 the State Development Bank, Bappindo, was at the centre of a $620 million loan scandal involving Chinese businessman Eddy Tansil's Golden Key Group. The loan swindle, which occurred between 1989 and 1993, cast doubt upon the activities of former Finance Minister J.B. Sumarlin (*Jakarta Post*, 6 September 1994) and 'strengthened the public's belief in conspiracies between the government and big entrepreneurs' (*Indonesia Business Weekly*, 6 January 1995). In 1994 another loan scandal rocked the Kanindo textile group run by former luxury car thief Robby Tjahjadi. In order to service the high interest on bank loans, indebted businessmen like Tjahjadi resort to '*ekspor fictif*', falsifying their export claims, in order to avail themselves of cheap credit (*Kompas*, 5 September 1994; *Jakarta Post*, 3 September 1994).

The recent government practice of running budget deficits has further eroded confidence in an already unstable financial sector. Budget deficits rose from $2.3 billion in 1993–4 to over $3 billion in 1994–5 and have occurred notwithstanding the 1967 law requiring a balanced budget. More disturbing still is the level of foreign debt sustained by the expanding Indonesian economy. By 1995 foreign debt had risen to $100 billion, 40 per cent of which is denominated in yen. Worryingly, for each '1% rise in the yen compared with the U.S. dollar, Indonesia's total foreign debt increases an estimated $350 million' (*Asian Wall Street Journal*, 12 May 1995), making the Indonesian rupiah an ideal target for international currency speculation.

Thus, although the Indonesian government has attempted to manage development through import substitution followed by export-led growth and bureaucratic planning, the strategy has been less effective than elsewhere in Southeast Asia. The World Bank observed in 1992 that 'selective interventions on Korean lines could not work in countries like Indonesia because of weaker administrative and institutional structures, less clear economic objectives and skill limitations' (Macintyre 1994: 262). A recent survey of the evolving Indonesian pattern of business government relations concludes that, 'with limited state capacities and widespread rent seeking activity . . . there is a significant threat to continued high economic growth' (Macintyre 1994: 262).

The overseas Chinese and ersatz capitalism in Southeast Asia

Any survey of the political economy of Southeast Asia necessarily requires an assessment of the role played by overseas Chinese capital in the economic development of the region and, more recently, of South China. A pattern of trade between Southern China and the *nanyang*, or what came to be known as Southeast Asia, established itself from the earliest times. During the colonial period, for political and economic reasons, migration and settlement became pronounced. In the boom years of the 1920s over a million Chinese emigrated yearly from the Southern Chinese ports of Hong Kong, Amoy and Swatow (Fukuda 1995: 34). In Malaysia the Chinese sojourners (*huaqiao*) established an all-pervasive economic presence in the nascent tin mining and rubber plantation industries. In Thailand they dominated the rice and timber trade and established commercial and banking networks, whilst in Indonesia they played the role of comprador capitalists and petty traders (ch. 5).

The character of British and Dutch colonial rule, which maintained the customary laws and preserved traditional hierarchies, lent itself to Chinese commercial enterprise. As Ruth McVey explains, 'in much of Southeast Asia a three tiered system developed in which the upper level of business was dominated by Europeans and the middle by Chinese, while the indigenous population was restricted to the margins of petty trade. The natives were peasants or (if of gentle birth) officials, and any taste they developed for entrepreneurial advancement was firmly discouraged' (McVey 1993: 19). Moreover, as they adapted to this colonial environment, the Chinese immigrants 'acculturated to the style of the ruling groups', which in the case of Malaysia and Indonesia were western, 'and this resulted in further estrangement between them and the indigenous elites' (p. 19).

The post-colonial era offered both opportunity and threat in equal proportion for this urban Chinese business class. Nationalism of the Phibun variety in 1930s Thailand and in the early days of the bureaucratic polity could lead to the attempted economic ostracism of the 'Jews of the East' (Terwiel 1991: ch. 5). Nevertheless as the Dutch, French and British commercial presence faded under the onslaught of economic nationalism in the 1950s and 1960s, a distinctive pattern of ethnic Chinese domination of indigenous Southeast Asian business came to replace it. Indeed, the scale of Chinese economic success presents a serious political problem for the new Southeast Asian ruling elites engaged in the seemingly endless task of 'nation building.'

Given the insecurity of the infant Malaysian, Indonesian and Thai states in the postwar era, a number of possibilities opened both for the evolving Chinese business conglomerates and for the indigenous bureaucracies. One effective strategy involved abandoning Chinese ethnicity and assimilating to local cultural practice. This was the approach adopted by the Chinese business community in Thailand in the course of the 1950s. Thus *Teochiu* merchants like Tan Piak Chin formed powerful conglomerates like Asian Trust and the Bangkok Bank Group during the 1950s. Pragmatically adopting Thai nationality and acquiring a Thai name (Tan became Chin Sophonphanich), he subsequently invited members of the Thai military-bureaucratic elite to serve on the board of his companies. Finally, intermarriage between the Chinese family and the Thai bureaucracy secured the future of the newly indigenized conglomerate (Suehiro 1992: 44ff).

In Malaysia, the ramifications of the NEP required the most successful Chinese conglomerates to adopt a different strategy. Here, Chinese tycoons formed alliances with prominent Malay political patrons (Heng 1993: 132). The Kuok Group, 'the most successful Chinese conglomerate in the country', exemplifies the practice. From sugar trading, the Kuok Group diversified into shipbuilding, flour, property, the Shangri-la Hotel chain and newspapers. To preserve a business empire that extends from Hong Kong to Australia, the Kuok Group has developed extremely close ties with 'the highest circles of UMNO', whilst members of the Malay aristocracy sit on the board. Indeed, the 'Malay directors represented on the group's publicly listed companies reflect a judicious mix of individuals from different power centres within the Malay establishment' (p. 133).

Differently again, in Indonesia, the success of New Order Chinese conglomerates depends on the *cukong* relationship established either with the military bureaucracy or more directly and importantly with the Suharto family. Thus Liem Sioe Liong's Salim Group involves more than 300 companies and covers 'a strikingly diverse array of interests' (Mackie 1995: 53; Schwarz 1994: 110). In 1990, Salim's domestic sales alone constituted about 5 per cent of Indonesia's GDP. Liem built his empire 'with a true entrepreneur's eye for business opportunities and a talent for attracting first rate partners' (Schwarz 1994: 110). The ability to exercise this talent, however, depended on Liem's greatest asset, 'his relationship with Suharto' (p. 110). Liem's access to Suharto has enabled the Liem Group to exercise domestic monopolies on a range of commodities. In return, he looks after Suharto's financial interests. Thus when Bank Duta lost $420 million in 1990, Liem made good half the bank's losses (p. 112).

Evidently, the economic success of the approximately 20 million overseas Chinese and the increasingly visible Chinese conglomerates 'is out of proportion to their numbers in the ASEAN countries' (Redding 1993: 57). This social fact has prompted speculation about the cultural basis of such entrepreneurial flair, its peculiar character and the extent to which it constitutes the basis of an interdependent regional economic system (McVey 1993; Redding 1993; Mackie 1995; Yoshihara 1988, 1995). A number of commentators emphasize the role that cultural values, notably the Confucian ethic of relationship, and the Chinese cultural practices of *guanxi, xinyong* (mutual trust) and filial piety have played in facilitating the emergence of Chinese regional commercial dominance (Yoshihara 1988; Redding 1993). This Confucian ethic is sometimes compared disadvantageously with the 'weak' work ethic of the Southeast Asian indigenes (Yoshihara 1995: 77). Given the prevalence of eugenic discourse in contemporary Southeast Asia, such views find overt and covert support among a variety of Southeast Asian, primarily Singaporean, Chinese politicians and academics (*Straits Times*, 23 November 1993, 19 May 1995; Wong 1994: 40).

The 'hard' Confucian culture of the overseas Chinese and their minority status lend credence to the further claim that their conglomerates constitute an emerging 'supra-national' regional network 'stitched together by capital flows, joint ventures, marriage, political expediency, and a common culture and business ethic' (Sender in Mackie 1995: 36). Indeed, there is some evidence of interconglomerate activity. Robert Kuok's Malaysian conglomerate runs the Salim Group's flour mills and both Kuok and Liem sit on the board of the International Association of Fuzhous. Together with fellow board member, Malaysian timber *taipan* Tiong Hiew King and the Hong Leong Group, they collectively run a number of regional and Hong Kong-based newspaper and communication ventures and actively promote investment in their 'home' province of Fujian, South China.

However, although these and other ventures certainly evoke fear of an international Chinese conspiracy amongst some of the region's Islamic activists of a fundamentalist hue, in fact, interconglomerate ties are loose and personalistic. Although Chinese conglomerates constitute an important element in the political economy of Southeast Asia, they do not represent 'a controlling one' (Mackie 1995: 36). Moreover, although high Confucian values, modified for contemporary mass consumption, certainly inform the technocratic process of East Asian modernization, the historic particularity of conglomerate evolution in Southeast Asia cannot be ignored. The contingencies that shaped conglomerate development explain the central features of Chinese entrepreneurial practice. Indigenous suspicion of Chinese capitalism and its 'pariah' status, which continues to inflect attitudes to Chinese enterprise in contemporary Malaysia and Indonesia, necessitated a recourse to networks of affiliation based on family, clan and language group as the basis of *xinyong* (trust). Dependent upon elite patrons, Chinese entrepreneurs could not, however, rely on state protection. Political isolation forged a Chinese economic network and fostered a common cosmopolitan outlook. Moreover, in the absence of well-developed capital markets, they allocate capital among diversified activities and often link primary inputs and intermediate goods within their firms (Doner 1991: 833). As groups, they perform many of the special functions required for entrepreneurship in developing countries (Mackie 1995: 56–8), spreading entrepreneurial risk and, in uncertain times, distributing their multifarious interests across the region. Ultimately, it was these 'circumstances rather than a special entrepreneurial genius [that] determined the Southeast Asian Chinese centrality to contemporary Southeast Asian development' (McVey 1993: 21).

The peculiar socio-economic conditions that shaped the diversified Chinese conglomerate structure, together with the poor quality of Southeast Asian government intervention, further determined, Yoshihara maintains, the peculiarly ersatz character of Southeast Asian capitalism. Insecure Chinese entrepreneurs concentrate either on financial and banking services or on property, tourism, communications and distribution, enterprises that are regional, potentially global and increasingly independent of their domestic base. Moreover, when the conglomerate ventures into manufacturing, whether of electronics, cement, noodles or cars, it is merely as a comprador, regional conduit for foreign, usually Japanese, technology. Southeast Asian industrialization is in consequence 'technologyless' and lacks the 'scientists, engineers, and skilled workers' necessary to overcome 'the export barriers an economy faces as its income rises' (Yoshihara 1988: 111; 1995: 77). This, as James Mackie argues, seems an unduly harsh assessment of the foreign investment-driven and export-led manufacturing growth in Southeast Asia and the role of Chinese entrepreneurs and bankers in facilitating it (Mackie 1995: 58). It does, however, return us to our initial concern with the role of the Japanese model in Pacific Asian development and the emergence of distinctively different Northeast and Southeast Asian approaches to economic growth.

The difficulty of Asia Pacific economic cooperation in the new world trading order

Directly or indirectly, the Japanese model of state-directed, export-led growth has profoundly affected the political economy of Pacific Asia. The attempt to follow, like flying geese, the Japanese example has given these late developing economies certain commonalities. All the HPAEs have established state technocracies with varying degrees of autonomy from domestic and external pressure. With the exception of Hong Kong, these bureaucracies devise developmental targets and outline successive four- or five-year plans in which to achieve them. Such plans have often involved strategically calculated shifts from import-substituting industrialization to export-led growth. State technocracies, with varying degrees of success, select and develop manufacturing 'winners'. An important precondition for subsequent growth has in all cases been a docile and compliant labour force and restrained domestic consumption. Further, all the HPAEs have fostered, directly or indirectly, high rates of saving to facilitate domestic investment and share a penchant for universal education at least to secondary school level. With the exception of the city states of Hong Kong and Singapore, the HPAEs maintain considerable levels of tariff and non-tariff protection in both agriculture and key areas of manufacturing. With the exception of Malaysia, all the HPAEs have facilitated directly or indirectly programmes to reduce population growth and have effectively curtailed the number of young people entering the workforce. All the HPAEs have pursued export-led growth in order to sustain consistent economic expansion over a long period. Again, with the exception of anomalous Hong Kong, all the HPAEs have increasingly favoured corporatist mechanisms that draw business associations into technocratic planning in order to sustain future growth as the economy matures (Campos 1993: 21–3). Consequently, government encourages domestic consumers, small businessmen, state technocrats and conglomerates to consider themselves members of a team running, as Singapore's Prime Minister explains, 'the next lap of development together' (Government of Singapore 1991: 13). In fact, the realization of an organically interdependent body politic is potentially more total in the HPAEs (Hong Kong apart until 1997) than it has been in the Japanese case.

Nevertheless, there are a number of substantial differences within the individual economies surveyed, and between the broadly different regional patterns of development, both in Northeast and Southeast Asia and between the city states, that render the notion of a monolothic developmental model and the flying geese analogy unsustainable. Broadly, whilst Northeast Asia has followed a strategy of bureaucratically planned growth through the development of domestic manufacturing or joint ventures and succeeded in generating internationally competitive industries, Southeast Asian development relies much more on foreign direct investment and technologyless growth. Conversely, Southeast Asian macroeconomic planning, as a consequence of its higher degree of financial deregulation, has generated a more open investment climate and a more mature financial and banking service sector than Northeast Asia, where banks and even stock exchanges are treated as 'handmaidens' or 'bureaucratic stewards' of government policy

(Patrick and Park 1994: 364). Indeed, the opacity and immaturity of financial and banking services in Northeast Asia has facilitated a worrying escalation of non-performing bank loans on real estate in Taipei, Seoul and Tokyo. In Taiwan this has left the property sector highly 'distorted' (*Far Eastern Economic Review*, 8 June 1995) and the Japanese banking sector cruelly exposed to asset deflation, insolvent *jusen* and up to $170 billion bad debt.

However, it would be inaccurate to assume that the relatively deregulated financial markets of Southeast Asia constitute an alternative or more efficient Asian capitalism, as some neoclassical commentators maintain. Southeast Asian deregulation and the foreign investment it made possible actually opened these later developing HPAEs to Japanese and NIE investment on an unprecedented scale. Northeast Asian conglomerates and SMEs came, particularly after 1985, to use Malaysia, Thailand and Indonesia as low-cost manufacturing bases for low-level technology, assembly and subsequent export in a relationship of evolving dependency. Moreover, the more attractive investment climate in Southeast Asia has by no means expunged the fiscal predation facilitated by government–business collusion in maintaining opaque property and financial practices. Indeed the early 1990s have witnessed a 'massive overbuilding' of real estate and office space across developing urban Pacific Asia from Jakarta to Shanghai and Seoul. Low planning standards and equity funding not subject to accountable financial institutions have created the prospect of a 'colossal crunch' in Pacific Asian real estate values (*Asian Wall Street Journal*, 24–25 November 1995). The pursuit of FDI and foreign loans, coupled with mounting current account deficits, moreover, renders Thailand, Indonesia and Malaysia potentially susceptible to the kind of 'meltdown' that devastated the Mexican economy in 1994 (*The Economist*, 24 August 1996: 13).

A more enduring problem for future Pacific Asian development resides in the distinctive triangular pattern of trade between Japan, the NIEs of South Korea, Taiwan, Singapore and Hong Kong, the ASEAN economies of Thailand, Malaysia and Indonesia, and the large and relatively open US market, which both accounts for the impressive export-induced growth of Pacific Asia and which is unlikely to be sustained into the next century. The large-scale relocation of labour-intensive export-oriented manufacturing to low-cost, FDI-seeking countries in Southeast Asia enabled Japan and the NIEs to divert, via these third countries, their burgeoning trade surpluses with the United States. At the same time, Japanese *keiretsu* were notably reluctant to transfer high value-added technology offshore. Consequently, whilst all the HPAEs run trade surpluses with the United States, they equally maintain trade deficits with Japan, deficits increasingly exacerbated by the rising cost of the yen. The following pattern thus emerges: Japan runs trade surpluses with the United States, the Asian NIEs and ASEAN countries; and the Asian NIEs and ASEAN countries maintain trade surpluses with the United States but deficits with Japan. By 1995, the trade flows between Pacific Asia and the United States accounted for 32.5 per cent of total US trade (Rodner 1995: 403). This has prompted demands both from the US Senate and the European Union for reform of the international trade order to address the continuing impermeability of the Japanese market, the tariff and non-tariff mechanisms deployed by the HPAEs and the trade imbalances they continue to generate.

In other words, the external trading environment which facilitated Pacific Asian export-led growth is in the process of change. Moreover, under the provisions of the post-GATT World Trade Organization, the change will demand evidence of market opening. The alternative will be managed or strategic trade grounded on a bilateral *quid pro quo* basis or the emergence of protectionist trading blocs. In this context, a number of recent innovations in the strategic management of Pacific Asian and intra-Asian trade have profound implications for the future development of Pacific Asia.

Conclusion: cooperation versus protectionism in the Pacific Basin

In order to address the increasingly vexed issue of Asia Pacific trade, the Australian Prime Minister, with the evident support of the MITI (*The Australian*, 4 January 1996), inaugurated a process of Asia Pacific Economic Cooperation (APEC) in Canberra in 1989. This loose grouping of initially fifteen Asia Pacific economies included Australia, New Zealand, the United States, Canada, Hong Kong, Taiwan, South Korea, Japan, China and the ASEAN six. As an intergovernmental forum, APEC evolved from earlier non-governmental arrangements, notably the PECC, which in the course of the 1980s established confidence in broader intergovernmental cooperation. APEC was notable, given the previous history of Asia Pacific economic agreement, for its rapid development into an annual summit of Pacific Asian leaders (Kahler 1994: ch. 2). By the first APEC summit held in Seattle in November 1993 membership had expanded to seventeen countries, including Mexico and Papua New Guinea, and offered the seductive prospect of increasingly free Pacific Asian trade through a somewhat paradoxical process of 'open regionalism'. At the Bogor summit in 1994, the group had expanded to eighteen countries, including Chile, and accepted the report of its Eminent Persons Group proposing a framework for what the American delegation termed 'steadily increasing liberalisation' (*Straits Times*, 1 October 1994). The Bogor Declaration of 15 November 1994 committed APEC members 'to adopt the long term goal of free and open trade and investment in the Asia Pacific'. Industrialized countries were to achieve this goal by 2010 and developing countries by 2020 (Setyawan 1994: 379; *Straits Times*, 17 November 1994). Bogor, it seemed, presaged a new era of Pacific Asian growth and interdependence premised on a regional commitment to the principle of free trade that would both erode trade imbalance and create a broad range of economic and political interdependencies.

However, despite these auspicious beginnings, it soon appeared that APEC members interpreted their commitment to free trade in very different ways. On the one hand, Pacific Asian countries embraced a distinctively Asian understanding of both free trade in particular and trade agreements generally. Expounding this Asian way at Bogor in 1994, President Suharto explained 'consensus must be broad and flexible, decisions should be made collectively and there can be no quick or delayed implementation' (*Straits Times*, 12 November 1994). Such a gradualist and voluntarist approach to free trade contrasted strongly with the growing desire of the various branches of American government and its business lobby for a strict rule-based approach to Pacific Asian trade with sanctions for non-compliance (*Far Eastern Economic Review*, 30 November, 1995: 14).

Whilst the rapid development of APEC intimated to the US diplomatic and 'epistemic' community the prospect of a structured, coherent, multilateral organizational basis for regional economic and political development, in practice this was not to be the case. Already in 1990, President Bush had inaugurated the North American Free Trade Area (NAFTA) as an alternative to Pacific Asian cooperation. NAFTA intimated a potential 'fortress America' antipathetic to Pacific Asian exports (Eden and Molot 1993: 219). Moreover, increasingly abrasive exchanges with China over issues of human rights and trade surpluses and with Japan over its reluctance to open its automobile market indicated growing trade friction rather than cooperation. Reflecting this, the Office of the United States Trade Representative decided in May 1995 to impose 100 per cent duties on thirteen Japanese car models. The subsequent decision not to invoke Section 301 of the US Trade Act (1974) and to refer the matter to the WTO only heightened US Senatorial frustration with market opening in Pacific Asia. This frustration was further exacerbated by South Korea and Japan's attempt in the course of 1995 to 'water down' APEC's commitment to regional free trade by excluding agriculture from the deal (*The Australian*, 1 October 1995; 25 October 1995). Although, at the subsequent Osaka summit in November 1995, APEC announced a timetable for trade liberalization to begin in 1997, its flexibility and absence of penalty for non-compliance leaves APEC with 'an agreement that is not enforceable or even binding' (*Far Eastern Economic Review*, 30 November 1995: 14). Significantly the increasingly protectionist

American Senate called in November 1995 for a 'cooling off' period before entering into further trade agreements with the Pacific Asian states (*The Australian*, 16 November 1995).

Interestingly, mounting US disenchantment with APEC has its Asian corollary in demands for a pan-Asian economic nationalism which eerily mirrors the Greater East Asian Co-prosperity Sphere briefly inaugurated by Japan in 1942. Asian nationalists like Mahathir Mohamad and Shintaro Ishihara have consistently questioned the value of a continued American economic presence in Pacific Asia. In 1990, Mahathir proposed, as an altern- ative to APEC and NAFTA, an East Asian Economic Caucus (EAEC) comprising ASEAN, South Korea, Japan, Taiwan, China and Hong Kong. In 1993, Mahathir declined to attend the APEC summit in Seattle and appended an annex to the Bogor Declaration of 1994 dissenting from its provisions. 'East Asian countries', he maintained, 'should have their own forum' (*Straits Times*, 17 November 1994). Although in 1993, the ASEAN Annual Ministerial Meeting agreed that the EAEC might form a group- ing within APEC (*Straits Times*, 30 August 1993) and represent a building block to a multilateral trading order (*Straits Times*, 25 April 1995), it could only do so realistically, as the Malaysian Minister of Trade, Rafidah Aziz, explained, if APEC was 'under no obligation to achieve free trade' (*The Australian*, 8 November 1995). Whilst a number of ASEAN states, notably Singapore and Indonesia, expressed reservations about the utility of a pan- Asian economic grouping, they, together with the other ASEAN states, have nevertheless agreed to form an ASEAN Free Trade Area (AFTA) committing member states to reduce tariffs on almost all items of intra- ASEAN trade to 5 per cent by 2003 (*The Economist*, 16 December 1995: 69). Such an arrangement constitutes a potential Southeast Asian insurance policy 'should the EC and NAFTA at some future date decide to block ASEAN products' (Emmerson and Simon 1993: 31; Goldsmith 1994: 55– 75). Thus we can identify two clearly contrasting scenarios for the future economic development of Pacific Asia. On the one hand, an increasingly open, integrated, borderless and interdependent multilateral trading envir- onment might emerge under the auspices of a benign APEC leading Pacific Asia into a borderless world. Alternatively, reluctance to conduct trade fairly, let alone freely, could facilitate an emerging Pacific Asian trading bloc inevitably dominated by Japan.

Hence, we can provisionally conclude that Pacific Asian governments have in the period 1950–95 effectively exploited the embedded liberalism of the post-Bretton Woods international trade regime. In so doing the more efficiently organized and coherently planned Northeast Asian economies succeeded both in managing trade and picking industrial winners. Latterly and less coherently, Southeast Asian economies have also sought export-led growth through a haphazard exploitation of natural resources, cheap labour and FDI. This planned growth and bureaucratic mobilization of both capital and labour in a favourable external environment sustained impressive growth over long periods. Yet, as recent, more sceptical studies by Alwyn Young and Paul Krugman have demonstrated (Young 1992, 1995; Krugman 1994), the high growth achieved by the HPAEs can be explained by an effective mobilization of inputs like the rise in participation rates, transfer of labour from agriculture to higher value-added work, investment in machinery and the education of the workforce (Young 1995: 673–5). In other words, the most effective HPAEs have efficiently mobilized resources. They have not, however, achieved a 'miracle' in terms of total factor productivity. Moreover, in the process of mobilizing capital, South Korea, Thailand, Malaysia and particularly Indonesia have accumulated disturbingly high levels of external debt, together with burgeoning current account deficits rendering the latter three currencies highly susceptible to international financial speculation (*Fortune*, 6 March 1995).

Finally, the long-term effects of the growth strategies pursued by the HPAEs have caused the unintended consequence of mounting the Pelion of trade surpluses with the open United States market upon the Ossa of protected domestic markets, destabilizing international currencies in an era of globally traded derivatives, and adding unnecessarily to the debt burden of weaker HPAEs whilst simultaneously threatening deflation in Japan. Meanwhile, the attempt to manage trade has engendered countervailing American and European responses that make the emerging multilateral framework of Asia Pacific Economic Cooperation less conducive to management and more fractious than during the era of benign American hegemony. The international ramifications of this emerging pattern we shall subsequently consider in our discussion of the structure, or lack of it, in Pacific Asian international relations in the emerging New World Disorder, the subject of chapter 4.

3
Democratization, Civil Society and the Pacific Asian Nouveaux Riches

A prevailing understanding in the study of political and economic development holds that economic modernization creates an irresistible pressure for liberal democratic political change. Authoritarian rule may offer the initial stability necessary for economic growth, but as fully developed modernity approaches it becomes increasingly redundant and reluctantly withers away. Depending on one's theoretical preference, the overt or covert hand promoting this change is an articulate, urban, and self-confident middle class (see Lipset 1963; O'Donnell et al. 1986; Przeworski 1992; McVey 1994). In the technical argot of development studies, the presence of this new socioeconomic phenomenon intimates both liberalization and democratization.

Accordingly, after thirty years of sustained economic growth, we would expect to find the HPAEs of South Korea, Singapore, Malaysia, Indonesia, Thailand and Taiwan metamorphosing into polyarchic democracies with Asian characteristics. Indeed, a growing literature traces the inexorable rise of bourgeois democracy and civil society in Pacific Asia. Thus, after 1987, South Korea, we are told, spawned an increasingly self-confident middle class that terminated an 'authoritarian cycle' of rule (Han 1989: 292). In Taiwan, the middle class has become so 'politicized and powerful' (Robinson 1991: 2) it has forged the 'first Chinese democracy' (Chao and Myers 1994: 213). Meanwhile in Southeast Asia, the Thai middle class is developing a 'separate identity based on liberal democratic values' (Samudavanija 1991: 76) and growing democratic 'revolt' in Malaysia stems from 'a type of middle class politics' (Saravanamuttu 1992: 50). In Singapore, the burgeoning confidence of an educated middle class constitutes an 'extremely important precondition for political liberalization' (Rodan 1993a: 104), whilst in Indonesia a 'middle class has grown larger and is demanding more public information' (Chalmers 1991: 21).

Thus, from this perspective, 'the middle class transforms society. Some elements of that class . . . start to demand those effete and non-material things which are associated . . . with western lifestyles and philosophies. The items include political participation, multi-party politics, an end to corruption, a freer press, environmental clean up. Already these things and others can be seen emerging on the East Asian scene' (Jones 1994: 27). This understanding of economic growth and democratic political development finds regular confirmation in the influential columns of journals like *The Economist*, the *Far Eastern Economic Review* and the *Asian Wall Street Journal*.

Equipped with some version of this model, its proponents nevertheless concede that the role played by the new middle class in Pacific Asia is a curious one. In South Korea the new middle class is highly sensitive 'to a stable social order' (Dong 1993: 89). In Taiwan, the middle class between 1960 and 1990 was either 'intolerant' or largely 'apolitical' (Lu 1991: 36). Meanwhile in less developed and therefore more authoritarian Southeast Asia, the middle class has 'ambiguous political consequences', operating in Malaysia, for instance, both as democratizing agents and as supporters of continuing authoritarian rule (Crouch 1993: 40). In Indonesia, the emerging middle class contradictorily both threatens 'the pact of domination' that maintained the Suharto regime (Robison 1989: 52) and supports the Indonesian equivalent of a 'Bonapartist state' (Robison 1993: 104). In Thailand Anek Laothamatas detects a similar ambivalence, where the middle class 'did not appear to believe that democracy could take care of its own faults and flaws' (in Hewison 1996: 151). Even more curious, and generally unremarked, is the fact that the only political entity to generate the type of autonomous civic activity consistent with the middle-class model is Hong Kong, a notably dynamic economy that flourished under a liberal but problematically colonial dispensation until 1997 (Lo 1996: 174–9). Worryingly, then, not only is the political conduct of the emerging middle-class ambivalent, but the explanatory utility of the term becomes increasingly redundant.

The apparent inconsistency in both the behaviour of the class and the application of the term evidently stems from the prevailing understanding of the relationship between political and economic development. Broadly, we can identify two not necessarily incompatible schools of thought: the first presents the emergence of an increasingly educated, wealthy and self-assured middle class as an important precondition for the transition to democracy; the second, more circumspectly, views the middle class playing an increasingly important reforming role after an authoritarian regime initiates the democratization process. This process assumes that a ruling elite liberalizes in order to decompress social tension and so provides an opening for autonomous organization in civil society. As civil society strengthens, moreover, the associative life of the middle class increasingly facilitates the transition to full democracy (Przeworski 1992: ch. 2). Yet neither the precondition or process model, or some synthesis of the two, adequately accounts for the seemingly incoherent behaviour of the new middle class in Pacific Asia. For a discipline that infers causal connections between otherwise discrete social, economic and political phenomena in contingently situated units of rule, to consider such regionally incoherent behaviour 'aberrant' (Emmerson 1995: 223) or explain it away by some neo-Marxist sophistry concerning the structure of class coalitions (Hewison et al. 1993: ch. 1) is clearly inadequate. What, we might then ask, is the actual character of this new middle class and how does this affect its political role? Secondly, how do the incumbent ruling arrangements in newly industrialized Pacific Asia respond to or manage this emerging social phenomenon? Finally, what light does the emerging pattern of political change in Pacific Asia shed upon the phenomenon of Pacific Asian democracy?

The middle-class culture of dependency in contemporary Pacific Asia

Reporting the East Asian Miracle, the World Bank found that the 'HPAEs are unique in that they combine rapid, sustained growth with highly equal income distributions (World Bank 1993a: 8). The most significant social phenomenon produced by this sustained economic growth is a materialistic, upwardly mobile and highly urbanized middle class. Whilst economic growth classically entails increasing income disparities between rich and poor, and town and country, a distinctive feature of the economies of Pacific Asia has been their ability both to distribute increasing wealth relatively equitably and telescope the historical time taken to modernize. The Gini coefficient produced by the World Bank to cover the period 1965–90 indicates that 'rapid growth and declining inequality have been shared virtues' among the HPAEs (World Bank 1993a: 30–1). As a consequence of this 'miracle' (p. 8) the Pacific Asian states of South Korea, Taiwan, Singapore and Malaysia and to a lesser extent Thailand and Indonesia have become increasingly middle-class polities.

As we have shown in the first two chapters, this economic transformation owes nothing to constitutional democracy and little to neoclassical economic policy. In fact, it was government-planned, export-led growth, coupled with the wealth it generated, that ultimately legitimated the rule of the autocratic generals or 'quasi-Leninist' political parties that governed post-colonial Korea, Taiwan, Singapore, Indonesia and Malaysia (World Bank 1993a: 157). The vision is one of planned development, what Singapore's

Lee Kuan Yew refers to as 'one step at a time', where no aspect of social, economic or political life is left to chance (*Straits Times*, 15 February 1992). Between 1960 and 1995 these emerging economies both achieved, and continue to generate, growth rates in excess of 7 per cent per annum. In order to secure the political stability considered vital to sustain growth, the technocratic elite increasingly entrusted with development policy in the HPAEs exploited and sometimes selectively reinvented Asian traditions of deference, bureaucracy and consensus. In fact, a growing band of comment-ators now assert that Asian values of legalistic bureaucracy and Confucian deference in emerging South Korea, Taiwan and Singapore and traditional practices of merit and status in Thailand and cooperation and consensus building in Indonesia and Malaysia explain Pacific Asian economic dynam-ism, social order and the capacity to industrialize without incurring undue social dislocation.

It is important to realize, however, that the customary values that Asian scholar-bureaucrats now contend shaped the developmental process in Paci-fic Asia have, as we have indicated in chapter 1, been largely reinvented for the ideological purpose of channelling popular energy to collectively achiev-able developmental targets. Significantly, the first-generation leaders who assumed power in the unstable world of post-colonial Pacific Asia viewed the recovery of lost tradition with considerable scepticism. Ideologically committed to building progressive nations, they thought traditional hier-archical practice had failed either to prevent the indignity of colonization or promote the capacity to modernize.

It was, in fact, only during the period of sustained economic growth after 1960, and the rapid urbanization that accompanied it, that traditional understandings came to play an increasingly important integrative role in the nation building process. As a number of anthropologists and political scientists noticed at the time, the rapidity of modernization in these late developing economies generated identity confusion at both a personal and a national level (Henderson 1968: 282–3; Geertz 1993: ch. 9; Gold 1993: 170–1). Whatever else it might be, the modernizing East Asian identity was an anxious one. Thus, in 1965, we find Indonesian scholar Soedjatmoko wondering whether the 'dynamics of the operation of developmental values only come to life in a wider structure of meaning', and worrying that 'the progressive breakdown of traditional social structures with their established customs and the difficulty of relating to emerging new ones' created growing 'uncertainty and anxiety leading in some case to a genuine crisis of identity'. Indeed, such a 'brooding preoccupation with the national self' was widely considered an 'unavoidable phase in a nation's adjustment' (Soedjatmoko 1965: 3–4). In order to resolve the seemingly unpatterned desperation gen-erated by the shock of the new and the deracinating transition from agrarian to urban, governments turned increasingly to traditional understandings of relationship and order, now centrally disseminated through the powerful modern media of television, school and press, to reconstitute in the burgeoning modern Asian city the values fast disappearing from the rural hinterland.

Consequently, it is after 1965 and the bloody instauration of Suharto's New Order that Indonesian commentators observe a renewed emphasis upon paternalistic guidance, or *bapakism*. In Singapore programmes to inculcate shared Asian values become matters of educational and political urgency only in the 1980s (Quah 1990: ch. 1) whilst in the same decade UMNO in Malaysia sought to revitalize and purify traditions drawn from the golden era of the Malacca sultanate, but amended to support an 'untraditionalistic leader' devoted to building 'Malaysia Incorporated' (Kessler 1993: 133–54). Thailand, somewhat differently, enjoyed an unbroken tradition of Buddhism, monarchy and independence. Nevertheless, it is only during the autocratic regime of Marshal Sarit (1958–63) that the monarchy, nation and religion are symbolically constituted as the focus of national loyalty (Wyatt 1984: 277ff; Jackson 1991: ch. 7) In South Korea, similarly, the claim to have inherited a Confucian legacy dating from the end of the Yi dynasty substantiated the Republic of Korea's claim to be the legitimate vehicle of the Korean nation. Yet it was only during General Park Chung Hee's autocratic but effective programme of state-managed industrialization (1961–79) that official ideology came to emphasize a new nation ruled not by laws but by superior men. In Taiwan, more problematically, scientific Confucian education after 1988 had to pay increasing attention to indigenous cultural practice. Nevertheless, although education policy still remains officially committed to mandarinization, the KMT has been peculiarly successful, 'through its exclusive control over the socialization agents, the schools, and mass media', in constructing an 'ideologically underestimated popular coalition where all members of society believe the KMT embodies the interest of all classes' (Chu 1992: 17; see also Hsiao 1992: 65).

Significantly, the World Bank maintains that the efficient provision of primary and secondary education was a crucial factor in both creating a disciplined workforce and sustaining economic growth in the HPAEs. The World Bank in particular, and political economists generally, refers only tangentially to the values actually inculcated in state-administered schools. This notwithstanding, the educational bureaucracies of the HPAEs from the 1970s onward devoted increasing attention to the role of public schooling in creating loyal and efficient citizens. The more Confucianized polities of Singapore, Taiwan and South Korea required state schools to inculcate nation building values like filial piety and Confucian conformity. In Indonesia an awareness of *pancasila* ideology and in Malaysia of *rukun negara* (national values) became significant features of the school curriculum, whilst in Thailand schooling inculcates 'correct' behaviour, a Buddhist awareness of karmic determinism and an acute awareness of social status (see Ho 1989: 686; Hsiao 1992: 65; Tien 1993: 103–5; R.L. Cheng 1994: 386–91). Such schooling, moreover, occurs in an educational context of intensely competitive public examination, rote learning and machinic obedience. Officially controlled or state-licensed newspapers and television, often contractually obligated to promote national development, further reinforce the socialization message received in school (Quah 1990: ch. 4; *Far Eastern Economic Review*, 9 December 1993; Khoo 1993: 44–77; *The Economist*, 3 June 1995).

Consequently, it was as these Pacific Asian states educated and trained their populations that culture, which 'once resembled the air men breathed and of which they were seldom properly aware' (Gellner 1987: 16), became visible. The literate, mobile, urban and formally equal lifestyle of the East Asian miracle contrasts radically with the stable, immobile and discontinuous cultural practices of the relatively recent past. Yet, it was in the process of this transformation that a national culture, officially promulgated through centrally supervised, specialized educational agencies, came to constitute the admission card to employability and citizenship. 'The Age of Nationalism [thus] arrives' (Gellner 1988: 206).

It is not without political significance, then, that the middle classes of the East Asian Miracle constitute both the material beneficiaries and the class most exposed to national values. Moreover, the reinvented values absorbed in state education programmes and mass media campaigns emphasize community rather than autonomy, status rather than equality and moral certainty rather than tolerance. It is the middle-class products of the state educational system, many of whom subsequently enjoy state employment and patronage, who are expected to respond positively to official demands for greater unity.

In Singapore, Taiwan and South Korea, the middle class consists mainly of professionals, civil servants or businessmen with bureaucratic connections. In Singapore, Rodan argues, the 'workforce accounted for by administrators . . . managers, professionals and technicians' rose from 7 per cent in 1956 to 13.6 per cent in 1980 (Rodan 1996a: 30; 1996b: 50). It has grown consistently since then with an expanding bureaucracy offering an important source of employment for recent graduates. In Taiwan, the middle class form 'one third of the total adult population', they include 'owners of small and medium sized enterprises, managers in public and private banks and corporations, KMT and government bureaucrats, elected representatives, teachers and professionals' (Tien 1992: 36; see also Chu 1996: 216). In South Korea, scholars generally distinguish between a 'new' middle class of white-collar workers in both private and public institutions, and an 'old' middle class of small owner-managers. The new middle class comprised about 17.7 per cent of a class that altogether constituted a third of the population. A further distinction exists between a 'mainstream middle class', with an economic interest in a stable capitalist order, and a peripheral middle class, consisting mainly of 'highly politicized' university lecturers (Koo 1991: 486–94; see also Cotton and Kim 1992: 362).

The graduates produced in growing numbers by the tertiary education sector in Taiwan, South Korea and Singapore increasingly seek employment in the expanding public or semi-public sectors. State education followed by bureaucratic training inculcates a respect for expert knowledge, and a lack of interest in wider political issues. Specialization, deference and a professional code of status group conformity facilitate social practices that have significantly illiberal political implications. In Singapore, these factors, exacerbated by the claustrophobic nature of Singaporean life, favour a middle-class identity founded on political indifference mixed with high anxiety. Its most significant manifestation is the local cultural practice of kiasuism. *Kiasu*, from the Hokkien 'scared to lose', is one of the few identifiably indigenous words to find its way into the forthcoming edition of the *Macquarie Dictionary*. *Kiasu* behaviour is premised on the belief that if 'you are not one up you are one down' and condones otherwise anti-social activity provided the progenitor succeeds in achieving collectively desired but scarce social goods whilst maintaining conformist anonymity. The selfishness central to *kiasu* behaviour stems not from self-confidence, but from its absence, which makes fear of failure the dominant concern in a competitive and highly regulated society.

The government-controlled media are notably ambivalent in their response to displays of Singaporean kiasuism. Significantly, the *Straits Times* considers it 'synonymous with Singapore's famous competitiveness', whilst the newspaper's editor interprets it as 'a duty to care' (*Straits Times*, 19 August 1992). In fact, the middle-class anxiety that kiasuism reflects, combined with a migrant heritage and its attendant deracination, responds positively to the ruling PAP's claim to technical, rational and managerial guidance. Incontrovertible rationalistic certainty provided by state experts consoles the neurotic parvenu who recoils at the prospect of a free choice. This lack of confidence, therefore, welcomes the activist and interventionist PAP style of rule.

Meanwhile in Taiwan, the ruling KMT, in its various guises – as government employer, political machine and entrepreneur – remains the major source of middle-class employment (Baum 1994: 62–6). Prior to 1986 its stable, tutelary rule encouraged the *guanxi* (connections) through which the middle classes could attain the socio-economic security which their exposure to a Confucian education in moral certitude required. Significantly, like their Singaporean counterparts, *arriviste* Taiwanese are 'not always able to express themselves adequately'. Inadequacy allied with deference found assurance in a political 'culture of intolerance' (Kuo and Myers 1988: 189). Thus, 'whatever its size, the middle class has yet to find a political voice. It does, however, have certain traits in common with middle classes in other [Asian] countries; it is politically pragmatic with an overriding interest in preserving the status quo' (Metraux 1990: 58).

Consequently, the continuing erosion of the KMT's capacity to wield paternalistic authority after 1987 has important ramifications for middle-class political behaviour. Growing political uncertainty has in fact amplified middle-class political and social insecurity. In this context, the rise of autonomous social movements, the growth of the opposition Democratic Progressive Party (DPP) and the articulation of dissent within the KMT constitute a growing source of anxiety for a middle class still largely dis-interested in the polymorphous joys of pluralism. Although some com-mentators argue that political liberalization has fostered the emergence of a more tolerant, open, yet still Confucian civic culture, others note a growing dependence upon factional connections in both local and national politics (Bosco 1994a, 1994b; Chao and Myers 1994). Attachment to a faction, moreover, offers a means of avoiding the unwanted consequences of polit-ical liberalization. Consequently, a middle class worried by the uncertainty of democratic change continues to seek reassurance in the technocratic guidance of the KMT, even if this now requires democratic endorsement.

Like its counterpart in Singapore and Taiwan, the South Korean middle class also finds solace in an intolerant social conformity. The military-backed authoritarian regimes of Generals Park, Chun and Roh actively promoted the virtue of conformity. This collective pursuit, combined with a Confucian regard for absolute loyalty to moral rule, has engendered in the Korean middle class a respect for *ch'ijo*, or an inflexible stand on matters of principle (Kim 1990: 50). The practice of clientilism further intensified respect for intolerant commitment. In particular, President Park's regime strategically cultivated regional bonds of kinship, training or personal con-tact (*inmaek*) in order to maintain political dominance (Back 1992: 238–41). Since 1987, regional factions have formed the basis for those political parties that are constitutionally tolerated. Consequently, 'political parties especially are notable for their factional strife, for parties in truth are collectivities of individuals who have banded together to enable a leader to attain and maintain power' (Jacobs 1985: 26). In a society that exhibits such a high regard for group loyalty premised upon intolerant commitment, the open-handed discussion of different interests and the possibility of political compromise offers little persuasive appeal.

If the attractions of a civil society that promotes the articulation of differ-ence seems ill-suited to the insecure, inarticulate *arriviste* of Seoul, Taipei or Singapore, what of their equivalent in the reinvented Buddhist monarchy of Thailand and the moderately Islamized realms of Indonesia and Malaysia? Once again a familiar pattern of middle-class dependence and clientilism asserts itself. In Thailand the period since 1961 has seen a notable rise in those engaged in middle-class occupations. Employment in professional, technical, administrative, executive, managerial, clerical and service-related occupations grew from about 10 per cent of the economically active population to 26 per cent by 1986 and in numerical terms from 1 million to 5 million. Equally significantly, the new middle class is concentrated in metropolitan Bangkok, where 54 per cent of the population enjoyed middle or higher incomes by the mid-1990s (Hewison 1996: 145–55). The expansion of the tertiary education sector from 360,000 students in 1970 to 1.8 million in 1991 reflects the growth of this literate, urban and upwardly mobile new class (p. 145). Clearly the emergence of this group, together with its concentration in the politically dominant capital, has significant but highly unpredictable political implications.

This unpredictability may be explained by the uncertain response of the middle class both to its recently discovered economic power and to the continuing influence of traditional expectations. Up until the 1980s the bureaucracy constitued the main source of middle-class employment. Reinvented traditional values informed both the bureaucratic polity and state education. Thus, a university education at Chulalongkorn University, the key civil service training college, inculcates in the aspirant government employee respect for seniority, order, tradition, unity and spirit (Girling 1981: 148). The urban middle class in both the public and the private sphere continues to enjoy relationships of hierarchy, dependency and an acute awareness of bureaucratic rank, the contemporary equivalent of the Ayudhyan *sakdi na* system. In Lucien Pye's view, 'Thais rejoice in the fact that relations are hierarchical and conducted in terms of superior and inferior' (Pye 1985: 108). Moreover, the Thai disposition to *mai pen rai* (never mind) in order to accommodate oneself to the broader demands of society further reinforces the joy of dependence. When middle-class professionals consult their astrologers, their preoccupation is not with self-realization and autonomy but with success in adapting to the social environment already determined by the cosmological one. Indeed, to achieve in Thai society 'does not depend so much on one's competence as one's ability to perceive and choose the right means and opportunity that leads to success in society' (Cook 1990: 238).

Up until the 1970s, dependency took the form of patron–client relationships within the military and civilian bureaucracy. Even though economic growth eroded attachment to the bureaucratic polity and facilitated a number of constitutional experiments after 1973, it by no means entailed the transformation of Thailand into a pluralistic society of interest-articulating, self-confident individuals. Whilst middle-class employment in the private sector has rapidly expanded as the economy boomed after 1985, the only additional value this seems to have inculcated is a taste for consumerism. Characteristically, this consumerist style blends a penchant for mobile phones and designer labels with a postmodernized Buddhist understanding of merit and nostalgia for the gentle paternalism that facilitated material improvement.

Moreover, excluded by the evolution of the private sector from the dependency relationships it craves, the new middle class has become both highly critical of the military-bureaucratic elite and disillusioned with the factionalism and corruption that characterize Thailand's periodic bouts of electoral politics. Indeed, the middle class broadly supports traditional Thai institutions provided they accommodate the joys of consumerism. As Anek Laothamatas observes, 'they rejected authoritarianism only in principle whilst in practice holding that there could be good authoritarian rule' (in Hewison 1996: 155). Consequently, this new and increasingly powerful extra-bureaucratic force, whilst perhaps more tolerant and less anxiety-ridden than its Taiwanese and Singaporean equivalent, remains both fragmented as a group and unsure of its political role.

The ties of dependence are even more prominent in multi-ethnic Malaysia. Here the *bumiputera* or indigenous Malay middle class is the direct creation of post-1971 government intervention in the economy. In the aftermath of ethnic riots in 1969, the UMNO-dominated BN coalition government introduced a New Economic Policy designed to promote the indigenous Malay interest. In the course of Dr Mahathir Mohamad's premiership (1981–), UMNO has attempted both to manage communal differences and forge a new Malay national consciousness through an assertively *bumiputera* affirmative action policy. UMNO policy successfully expanded not only the size of the middle class, but also the *bumiputera* element within it. The Malay middle class, as former UMNO representative Tawfik Tun Ismail explains, is largely 'a creation of the government' (*Far Eastern Economic Review*, 2 July 1995). By 1988, the middle class comprised 36 per cent of the total population, whilst *bumiputera* ownership of corporate equity rose from 2.3 per cent in 1970 to 20.3 per cent in 1990 (Saravanamuttu 1992: 48–50). Whilst Chinese middle-class entrepreneurs have been politically neutralized, the *bumiputera* middle class has either actively supported Mahathir Mohamad's attempts to create a centralized and interventionist one-party state or remained politically apathetic. This is hardly surprising as the state bureaucracy or businesses with UMNO links constitute the main source of Malay middle-class employment. UMNO, in other words, provides a political and economic 'crutch' for the 'unimaginative' *bumiputera* entrepreneurial class (World Bank 1993g: 26; see also Gomez 1994: ch. 2; Jesudason 1990: ch. 4; 1995: 347).

As Professor M.K. Mahadzir observes, the Malaysian 'nouveau riche do not have the same reasons for contributing to politics or speaking out because they would rather not change the system so long as they are the beneficiaries'. It is, Mahadzir maintains, 'snob appeal that motivates the middle class', a motive that reinforces a traditional Malaysian pattern of deference, hierarchy and consensus. Whilst traditionally these bonds obtained with feudal rulers, now the ties that bind are those with the party and its new men of prowess. State largesse facilitates UMNO's patrimonial rule where patron–client relations within both UMNO and the wider business community negate the possibility of open disagreement or a public debate. UMNO's press control, patronage, judicious manipulation of the constitution and 'money politics' has consequently augmented the state management of politics, business and a fortiori the middle class (Straits Times, 13 July 1994).

In Indonesia, a more troubled evolution witnessed the middle class growing together with the state bureaucracy after the traumatic transition to President Suharto's New Order in 1965. By the 1980s, 'everything from patronage to rice emanated from the state' (Bresnan 1993: 280). It is the middle class that most obviously benefits from the bureaucratic 'management of the nation's affairs. It has a stake in the economic and social progress that has been achieved, it has a stake in the status quo, in continuity' (p. 279). Significantly, the New Order has vastly increased the size of the civil service, which after 1967 grew faster than the rise in population (Vatkikiotis 1993: 109). Together with a regular salary, the bureaucracy provides its 4 million middle-class employees 'with rice, housing, transport to and from work, and comprehensive medical care' (p. 109). In return, the government expects loyal conformity.

Such an arrangement, moreover, fortuitously corresponds to traditional Javanese understandings of self-control and lack of initiative seeking. Indeed, the corporate management of New Order Society sedulously cultivates dependency ties through reinvented tradition. A syncretic blending of technocratic development with traditional deference has made New Order rule increasingly exclusionary rather than participatory. Such a development appears nevertheless well-suited to a docile, pessimistic and dependent middle class. Indeed, a survey for the banned Editor magazine found in 1990 that the 'better off the middle class were, the more reluctant they were to go onto the political stage' (Straits Times, 13 July 1994), a conclusion that confirms the view expressed by a number of local commentators that the new class is politically 'barren' (Soetrisno 1984: 27).

From this survey of the character of the new Asian middle class certain salient features emerge. As the major economic and social beneficiary of thirty years of economic growth, the new middle class is highly dependent upon state patronage. Its defining characteristic is the deracinated anxiety of the parvenu and the consequent search for political and social ties that guarantee stability and certainty. In return for this reassurance, the dominant single party or paternalist leaders expect their dependent middle classes to demonstrate actively their collective commitment towards the latest government-sponsored nation building initiative. Mere acquiescence is insufficient. Traditional high culture, whether of an Islamic, Javanese, Buddhist or Confucian provenance, centrally promulgated for mass consumption reinforces the view that the only alternative to a bureaucratically determined consensus is unwanted conflict between right and wrong. From this perspective, political pluralism, and the open communication of an autonomous civil society, appears disturbingly anarchic.

The managerial techniques of contemporary corporate capitalism further reinforce this illiberal political culture. Pacific Asian technocracy postulates an economic rationalism in which management, entrepreneurialism and administration develop the population as a resource. Instead of an urban bourgeoisie forging a polymorphous civil society out of an otiose authoritarianism, in Pacific Asia the middle class produced by the developmental state is effectively in its thrall. What we might next consider are the political ramifications of this relationship between these developmental technocracies and their dependent middle classes.

Maintaining the balance: state strategy towards the illiberal middle class in Pacific Asia

Having established the apolitical, state-dependent and ambivalent character of the emerging Asian middle class, how then do we account for political change in contemporary Pacific Asia? Clearly, there is not the conflict between the ruling elite and the middle class in the HPAEs that liberal democratic universalism demands. Instead of tension, we discover a ruling elite often ideologically, economically and sometimes ethnically homogeneous with the middle class. Consequently, constitutional change to the extent that it does occur represents a technocratic strategy to manage proactively either the anticipated aspirations of the middle class or the anticipated problem of political succession.

This is most evidently the case in Malaysia and Indonesia. Here the middle class is noticeably state-dependent and quiescent. Political debate, to the extent that it is officially tolerated, reflects elite concern with pursuing the most effective strategy to maintain the stability that attracts economic investment and avoids the errors perpetrated in the West by what Mahathir Mohamad terms 'fanatical' liberal democrats (*Straits Times*, 7 October 1993).

This proactive management of the future, nevertheless, can generate factional and generational tension. Factionalism within UMNO is the usual harbinger of political change. Divisions have become increasingly marked during Mahathir Mohamad's abrasive prime ministership. A ripening conflict between the dynamic, technocratic, Deputy Premier, Anwar Ibrahim, and the aging and increasingly irascible Mahathir may potentially undermine the possibility of non-contentious consensus building. In part this tension illustrates the problem of managing leadership transition in a Southeast Asia that continues to value the 'man of prowess' (Wolters 1982: 102–3), but it also reflects disagreement within UMNO over Mahathir's *Vision 2020* for a fully developed Malaysia and the role of the new Malaysian middle class in this plan.

Mahathir, paradoxically, has become the victim of his own success in destroying feudal attachments and forging both an increasingly centralized Malaysian state and an anxious new Malay identity. The very effectiveness of his modernization strategy has created choices that provide grounds for elite dissensus. As Professor A.B. Shamsul observes, there exists tension within UMNO between the pro-business team led by Anwar and the UMNO traditionalists whose support is 'rooted in the Malay villages' (*Straits Times*, 3 November 1993). Moreover, although modernizers like Anwar and Mahathir both agree that 'the Asian traditions themselves need to be revitalized and purified . . . from the excesses of an oppressive, autocratic and feudalistic past' (Anwar Ibrahim in *Far Eastern Economic Review*, 2 June 1994), the Malay middle class does not necessarily share their reforming zeal. Neither does it seek greater autonomy. Worryingly, deracinated urban Malays, favoured by UMNO-style affirmative action, increasingly seek consolation either in the myth of an idealized *kampong* lifestyle or alternatively in the chiliastic certainties of a purified and fundamentalist Islam (*Far Eastern Economic Review*, 26 May 1994; Kahn 1994: 37). The fact that young, urban Malays found solace in the messianic Islamic faith promoted by Al Arqam prompted the government to invoke the draconic provisions of the Internal Security Act (ISA) to suppress this Sufi sect and intern its leaders in July 1995. Ironically, the young, privileged Malays attracted to Al Arqam frequently discovered their Islamic faith during their state-sponsored studies at British and North American universities. Whilst UMNO leaders officially worried at the exposure of Malay youth to decadent western liberalism, those educated in the West discovered there an Islamic authenticity that denies the market-friendly version of Islam carefully nurtured by UMNO since 1971. In Malaysia, therefore, political change reflects both intergenerational tension and a conflict over identity created by rapid modernization. The vast majority of the middle class, whether Chinese, Indian or Malay, have become either politically apathetic or actively support UMNO's growing control of social and economic life. Elections held in April 1995 saw political opposition reduced to insignificance as the UMNO-led BN coalition won an impressive 64 per cent of the popular vote. As one government critic observed, the Malay middle class 'doesn't care' about political liberalization 'as long as they live comfortably, people are satisfied' (*Far Eastern Economic Review*, 2 July 1995). Moreover, that small minority of middle-class Malays who oppose UMNO manifest their dissent by embracing an intolerant fundamentalism ideologically opposed to the diversification of interests and ideas promised by a liberalized civil society.

A related but more uncertain pattern of development is at work in contemporary Indonesia. President Suharto's New Order has extended state power to all corners of society. Yet the success of state-managed, cooperative *gotong royong* capitalism and public welfare since 1965 increasingly poses new difficulties. The evolution of the New Order had, by the late 1980s, increased the number, variety and complexity of private groups. The problem of managing succession to Suharto further exacerbates the difficulty of managing this evolving complexity. These unwanted dilemmas and the absence of constitutional mechanisms to contain them have created increasing political unease. Burgeoning uncertainty in turn casts doubt both on the continuing legitimacy of the armed forces' dual function (*dwifungsi*) as guardian of the revolution and of the republic, and on the New Order's technocratic capacity to absorb growing labour unrest and widespread financial irregularities in the recently deregulated banking sector.

This uncertainty briefly made possible between 1992 and 1994 a new 'openness' in Indonesian politics. For proponents of the liberalizing middle-class thesis, this obviously constituted an overdue response to middle-class aspirations. However, what appears progressive from a liberal democratic perspective looked very different to a New Order elite accustomed to harmony and corporately managed consensus. Openness, in fact, signified an ill-defined arena where previously depoliticized voices were hesitantly invited to articulate their views in order, somewhat optimistically, to refresh the national consensus. In this context, the technocracy with its economically rationalist programme, Minister for Research and Technology B.J. Habibie's Association of Indonesian Muslim Intellectuals, ABRIs continuing concern with national unity and the previously depoliticized, mass-based Islamic organization *Nahdatul Ulama*, associated with Abdurrahman Wahid's democratically pluralist aproach to Islamic development, promote worryingly different approaches to future development (Ramage 1996: ch. 1). In Indonesian terms, such difference represents a loss of direction, not the reluctant embrace of a newly discovered pluralism. Imprisonment of journalists and MPs critical of late Suhartoism and increasingly militant student demonstrations against the *haram* national lottery in December 1993 illustrate the growing sense of a loss of direction. Moreover, when radical students claim that 'we have been cool for fifteen to twenty years but now we're thinking of democracy' (*Far Eastern Economic Review*, 9 December 1993), they evince no necessary commitment to pluralism and the rule of law, but rather a renewed interest in a purified Islamic *umma* (Budiman 1994: 227–9).

Increasingly, it appears that the apolitical middle class in general and the armed forces (ABRI) in particular consider 'openness' a threat, rather than the 'refreshing' reinvigoration of 'national stability' that Suharto sought when he launched the new policy in 1992. There is no Indonesian tradition of public debate or loyal opposition. Accustomed to the deference carefully cultivated by the New Order, Indonesian officials find both public criticism and the potential consequences of a free vote rebarbative. As Amir Santoso explains, 'victory and defeat are more transparent in the voting process (*mufakat lonjong*, or elongated agreement) while our culture considers it demeaning to the highest degree for a person to be made to lose face in public' (*Jakarta Post*, 10 November 1993; Santoso 1992: 84ff). The inability to tolerate the free speech that openness initially permitted ineluctably fuelled demand for a reimposition of censorship. The subsequent closure of critical political journals like *Detik*, *Editor* and *Tempo* in 1994, the removal of Megawati Sukarnoputri from the leadership of the PDI in June 1996 and the ruthless suppression of dissent in the aftermath of riots in support of Megawati in Jakarta in July 1996 illustrate the continuing importance of the armed forces to the maintenance of public order and to the political succession. However, the growing politicization of Islam and emerging student radicalism suggest that the succession to Suharto lacks institutional safeguards and the prospect of liberalization remains uncertain.

Thus, to the extent that the middle class is active at all in Malaysia and Indonesia it seeks a resolution of its continuing search for security in a non-liberal, non-indigenous, purified Islam; an Islamic solution, moreover, that might very well be democratic, but certainly will not be liberal or market-friendly.

By contrast with these Southeast Asian states, however, some change of a constitutional democratic character has occurred both in Buddhist Thailand and in the more Confucian and economically developed states that we have discussed. Both Thailand since 1973 and South Korea since 1987 appear to offer examples of middle-class pressure promoting constitutional democracy. Thus we find in Thailand, in the 1970s, that it is the extrabureaucratic capitalist and middle-class groups together with militant students that put pressure on the military-bureaucratic elite to 'decompress' and open government to political participation and constitutional rule. Thus, in 1973, middle-class, particularly student, pressure terminated military rule and the bureaucratic polity. Yet this 'premature' constitutionalism rapidly gave way to the strong man rule of General Prem and subsequently to a military-backed civilian Prime Minister, General Chatichai Choonhavan, in 1988, without any evident middle-class expression of dissent. This curious behaviour notwithstanding, the events of 1991–2 that saw Chatichai removed in a coup, the introduction of a military-inspired National Peace Keeping Council (NPKC), and the decision of the coup leader General Suchinda to declare himself unelected Prime Minister after elections in March 1992 ultimately prompted the Bangkok middle class onto the streets to demand a return to constitutional rule. Elections in 1993 returned an 'angelic' coalition of urban-based, middle-class parties like the Democrats and the Palang Dharma Party (PDP) who had most vigorously opposed the actions of the military coup group. The events of the early 1990s at last seemed to confirm the intimation of the 1970s that the growing economic and political impact of the middle class would dissolve patrimonialism and institutionalize constitutional democracy.

Events particularly since 1994 have largely disappointed these political expectations. The new coalition government of Mr Chuan Leekpai, like its less idealistic predecessors, soon encountered difficulty in introducing political reform and fell victim to factional rivalries both between the five parties comprising the coalition and within parties like the PDP. In early 1995, the coalition disintegrated to be replaced after elections by a new coalition dominated by Banharn Silpa-archa's Chart Thai party. Problematically, for those attracted by the prospect of a liberal democratic conclusion to Thai political development, Chart Thai has close associations both with the military and with provincial 'godfathers' (*jao pho*). Rampant vote buying, which earned him the sobriquet 'Mr Mobile ATM', characterized Banharn's campaign. Yet this money politics did not discourage the previously idealistic PDP and the New Aspiration Party of democratic General Chavalit from joining the new Chart Thai coalition. In keeping with the evolving pattern of Thailand's quasi-democracy, however, Banharn's coalition lasted only thirteen months before collapsing in allegations of corruption and bribery. Vote buying and the tendency to use political office to rent seek and reward supporters, together with the coalitional nature of Thai democratic practice and intra-party factionalism, has left Thai government notably weak and corruption-prone.

What these seemingly endless permutations, confusions and revolutions of government indicate is not middle-class pressure for constitutional rule but a mixture of middle-class ambivalence and indifference. Thus, whilst 1973 demonstrated student and middle-class alienation from military rule, the subsequent failure of parliamentary government to provide stability or direction saw the middle class rapidly abandoning its recently discovered constitutionalism. By 1976 the middle class proved a fertile recruiting ground for the nationalist *Nawaphon* (New Force) movement that promoted an unswerving loyalty to 'nation, religion and king' and endorsed the teachings of a revivalist and illiberal Buddhism that held 'killing communists is no demerit' (Girling 1981: 156–7; Wyatt 1984: 301). Similarly, the middle class either actively supported or remained indifferent to the military coup that terminated Chatichai's civilian government in 1991. Moreover, whilst the middle class actively resisted the arbitrary government of Suchinda in 1992, it also remains unconvinced by the constitutional rule that has replaced it and which is so evidently prey to the corruption and 'vote banks' of provincial 'godfathers' and 'dark forces' masquerading as local business interests (*Far Eastern Economic Review*, 1 December 1994: 25; Pasuk and Sungsidh 1994: ch. 3).

The advantage in finding an influential bureaucratic patron, therefore, remains as strong in the 1990s as it did during the Ayudhya dynasty. *Karuna* (the ability to guide subordinates) and *kamlungjie* (the motivation provided by a superior) continue to occupy an important place in Thai political behaviour. Indeed, those involved in corruption consider their actions legitimate under the patronage system, in spite of their technical criminality. 'This conflict . . . has existed for a long time in Thai politics. Thai politicians and Thai elites resolve the conflict by adhering to tradition rather than to modern standards of political practice' (Pasuk and Sungsidh 1994: 5; Pasuk and Baker 1995: 352–4).

Curiously, to the extent that political parties like Chart Thai endure, they have done so by extending traditional patrimonialism into the constitutional order. The National Assembly thus constitutes a conduit for provincial bosses to extract their share of corruption revenue in a way that adapts a democratic form of constitutional rules to traditional patrimonial practice.

In the Thai case, then, the middle class demonstrates no consistent commitment to democratization and harbours a suspicion both of corrupt politicians and of a self-serving military. Instead, as Anek Laothamatas maintains, it increasingly seeks efficient, technocratic rule (see Hewison 1996: 155). Efficient, apolitical administrations, as the caretaker administrations of Anand demonstrated, do not necessarily require elections. Yet such an administrative state has yet to be institutionalized. Consequently, since 1973, Thai government has oscillated between autocratic, military rule and periodic bouts of constitutionalism, notably in 1973–6, 1988–91 and in the period since 1992. These democratic and quasi-democratic experiments have been punctuated by increasingly desperate military coups in 1976, 1981, 1983 and most recently in 1991. The problem for Thai political stability is that neither the military bureaucracy nor civilian government can deliver the techno-paternalistic management that the middle class evidently requires.

South Korea, it is maintained, offers another example of middle-class pressure promoting constitutional democracy. Postwar Korean politics oscillated between developing autocratic centralization punctuated by brief and often violent moments of intransigent resistance and constitutional reform. This pattern, moreover, seemed to resemble Yi dynasty (1392–1910) practice, where government constituted a great vortex, 'summoning men rapidly into it, placing them briefly near the summit of ambition and then sweeping them out, often ruthlessly' (Henderson 1968: 31). Violence marked every leadership transition from Syngman Rhee (1961) to Roh Tae Woo in 1987. In April of that year, incumbent President Chun Doo Hwan reneged upon an earlier promise to grant a new constitution. Instead, he arbitrarily appointed General Roh Tae Woo to succeed him. This act brought the urban middle classes onto the streets. Faced with massive unrest, General Roh acceded to constitutional demands and direct presidential elections took place for the first time in December 1987.

Most commentators maintain that this bourgeois resistance began a new historical cycle of constitutional democracy, a prediction seemingly confirmed by presidential elections in December 1992 which witnessed both an uncharacteristically peaceful leadership transition and the election of the first civilian President of South Korea. The new President, Kim Young Sam, moreover, embarked upon a series of bureaucratic and judicial reforms that promised greater political accountability. 'A new political era has dawned', Daryl Plunk avers, characterized by 'an unprecedented opening up of the government's decision making process' (Plunk 1991: 105).

Yet the view that South Korea now functions as a liberal democracy with a vibrant and autonomous civil society is a highly misleading one. Both freedom of the press and freedom of political organization remain severely curtailed. All periodicals must register with the government and specify their editorial objectives. Moreover, when the press fails to practise self-censorship, the Agency for National Security Planning is on hand to offer Confucian guidance, a practice that, as the Professor of Journalism at Korea University notes, 'is possibly contrary to the idea of a free press' (*The Economist*, 25 September 1993). More worryingly, a national security law introduced in the 1950s continues to impose severe penalties on those who commit an 'ideological crime' like commemorating the death of the Great Leader of North Korea. As a recent study of Korean democratization reluctantly concluded, 'formal and informal restrictions on the basic rights of citizens to a free press and free association' remain in force (Lim and Kim 1992: 225).

The continuing fragility of South Korean politics reflects, in fact, a middle-class disposition whose constituting feature is the search for order, certainty and security, a characteristic that casts doubt upon the view that its resistance to Chun Doo Hwan in 1987 announced the arrival of a self-confident, bourgeois, liberal democracy. In the mid-1980s the middle class was politically timid (Han 1989: 292; Eberstadt 1991: 266; Ahn 1993: 101; Dong 1993: ch. 5). Indeed, prior to 1987, the 'role played by the entrepreneurial-management sector as far as the process of political democratization was concerned [was] . . . passive if not negative' (Dong 1993: 85). Yet in 1987, this conformity-obsessed, timid bourgeoisie suddenly became politically assertive and actively demanded political reform.

However, the constitutional aftermath found this newly articulate bourgeoisie executing a notable *volte-face* and electing their erstwhile oppressor, General Roh Tae Woo, President. A number of Korean writers observed this curious conduct and termed it 'sentimental'. Those who demonstrate violently against their autocratic rulers, whether, Rhee, Park, Chun or Roh, it is maintained, subsequently come to regret their action. Yet, having noticed this practice, little has been made of its implications for Korea's nascent democracy.

It is at least plausible to maintain that such behaviour may be interpreted not as a demand for autonomy but as a plea for reassurance, a possibility seemingly confirmed by the fact that somewhat surreally in the events of June 1987 the Korean middle class took to the streets chanting the decidedly unrevolutionary slogan 'order' (p. 91). As it became increasingly obvious that military autocracy no longer guaranteed political certainty, middle-class demonstrators demanded constitutional democracy to allay continuing uncertainty concerning orderly leadership transition. As Dong Won Mo commented in 1991, the Korean middle class 'appears to be more concerned about issues of . . . constitutional order . . . than with issues of distributive justice' (p. 91). Indeed the shift from political passivity to radical action reflects a Confucian legacy of moral absolutism rather than a new-found interest in civil liberties. From this perspective, arbitrary rule builds up resentment, or *han*, that erupts in moral indignation and is conducted in terms of *ch'ijo* (moral absolutes) and *inmaek* (clientelism). Thus, although constitutional change has taken place in South Korea, as the paradoxical consequence of a middle-class desire for order, the prevalence of intolerant regionalism tied to group conformity hardly conduces to a liberal democratic practice. Instead we have a form of patrimonial democracy where political parties are amalgams of regional groups, disagreement takes the form of confrontation rather than debate, and participation occurs through the manipulation of factions rather than by any self-chosen activity. Local elections held in July 1995 further entrenched an increasingly irreconcilable regionalism oiled by the judicious application of financial inducements (*Business Times*, 29–30 July 1995). Recent revelations of former President Roh Tae Woo's billion dollar slush fund not only illustrate the extent of corrupt links between *chaebol* and politics, but also demonstrate that former opposition faction leaders like Kim Dae Jung and current President Kim Young Sam were on the government payroll in the 1980s. Moreover, Kim's current attempts to render government and business more transparent and prosecute the past corruption of Generals Chun and Roh indicate not so much a new-found penchant for greater openness as a classical attempt to remove all competitors from the vortex of power (*Far Eastern Economic Review*, 30 November 1995: 66–72; *The Australian*, 2–3 December 1995). Significantly, whilst Kim's opponents are subjected to the full rigour of the treason law, the President himself remains above the law and demonstrates an increasing intolerance with any publicly articulated criticism of his presidential style or future successor (*The Australian Financial Review*, 3 April 1996; *Choson Ilbo*, 20 August 1996).

Ironically, whilst the military elite and their technocratic advisers premised constitutional reform upon the assumption of a growing middle-class demand for autonomy, middle-class values remain distinctly conservative and seek new certainty and new civilian patrons through a constitutionally inscribed orthodoxy; a fact seemingly confirmed by a 'univariate analysis' of 'democratic orientations' among the Korean public that found an overwhelming '83.2% of the population' believed democratization 'would enhance the quality of their lives', whilst only 3 per cent of the survey group had actually experienced any benefit from the apparent 'transition from authoritarian rule to democracy' (Chey and Shin 1992: 264–9). Such data not only suggest a triumph of hope over experience but also the extent to which democracy offers the seductive prospect of a new organically binding certainty; a certainty that gives Korea's nascent civic culture a strangely conformist character which, as one of its more excited proponents unwittingly admits, 'gradually filtered from the upper to the lower classes until there are no particular cultural differences among classes, age groups or resident types' (Back 1992: 238). Korean democracy, it would seem, represents the uncertain outcome of the pursuit of moral certainty and as such offers no obvious prospect of an autonomous civil society guaranteeing the rule of law. Indeed, reform may only sustain a new '*dicta blanda* dexterously hiding its authoritarian nature behind the façade of formal electoral competition' (Lim and Kim 1992: 225).

An equally ambivalent search to resolve the question of maintaining stability in the face of an unwanted dilemma also explains political change in Taiwan. The lifting of martial law in 1987 and the subsequent erosion of KMT autocracy clearly facilitated more open political debate, the emergence of a political opposition and the reform both of the national legislature and of local government. Despite abandoning paternalism, however, the KMT remains the dominant party and there is little evidence to suggest that the opposition has either the desire or the capacity to mount a serious political challenge. Moreover, the massive financial resources commanded by the KMT, 'the richest ruling party in the non-communist world' (*Far Eastern Economic Review*, 11 August), together with its continuing penetration of social and economic life, casts doubt on the widely promulgated view that Taiwan now functions as a constitutional democracy. In fact, it is increasingly evident that the KMT elite proactively managed the change from autocracy to accountability after 1987 both to guarantee a smooth transition from Chiang Ching-kuo to the current indigenous Taiwanese President, Lee Teng-hui, and to address the incoherence surrounding Taiwan's political identity.

By the late 1980s external political factors, primarily Taiwan's troubled relationship with the People's Republic of China, rendered the ruling party's legacy of patriarchal tutelage inherited from Sun Yat-sen and Chiang Kai-shek unsustainable. Unfortunately for this otherwise appealingly Confucian doctrine, the KMT could not decide whether they continued to constitute the *de jure* rulers of the Chinese mainland or the *de facto* rulers of an independent island state. Moreover, the loss of United Nations membership in 1979, followed by an increasingly difficult Pacific economic trading environment after 1989, acutely exposed this dilemma. In the course of the presidency of Chiang Ching-kuo (1977–88) and more significantly during the current presidency of Lee Teng-hui (1988–), growing elite uncertainty about Taiwan's identity compelled the KMT leadership to permit open debate and gradual constitutional reform. Under Lee Teng-hui's technocratic guidance, the KMT strategically promoted reform in order to ensure its continuing guidance of Taiwanese affairs.

The inchoate nature of opposition politics and the evident uncertainty of middle-class voters further diminishes the potential for an electoral challenge to KMT dominance. Thus, Yun-han Chu finds that the DPP has no mass basis or extensive organizational links with 'the mobilized sectors of civil society' and observes that 40 per cent of the voters who articulated a preference for the DPP in 1989 actually voted for the KMT (Chu 1992: 65). Moreover, the KMT's developing capacity to mobilize factional machines at the local and national level, its extensive mechanisms of patronage and vote buying, its access to the National Security Bureau and an extensive network of popular surveillance, together with its continuing control of the island's three main TV channels (*The Economist*, 18 September 1993; Bosco 1994: ch. 4), effectively countenance the notion that Taiwan's middle class now function as autonomous agents in an open and what one commentator considers 'demanding' civil society (Hsiao 1992: 57). Moreover, the fact that the mainstream KMT currently supports 'Taiwanization, technocratization or youthification' by no means implies 'that the ruling party is disposed to alienate its control over political outcomes' (Meaney 1992: 103). In this context, Lee Teng-hui's overwhelming victory in presidential elections held in March 1996 against a backdrop of escalating tension with the mainland illustrates not so much the KMT's new-found zeal for democratic values as its success in strategically renegotiating the KMT's tutelary grip on Taiwanese politics. Indeed, after Lee Teng-hui's comprehensive victory in presidential elections in March 1995, the opposition DPP fragmented to such an extent that reformist elements within it sought to drop the party's intransigent commitment to independence and enter a coalition with the mainstream KMT (*The Economist*, 13 April 1996).

The problem for the KMT, then, arises not from any middle-class pressure for autonomy and political pluralism, but from its own uncertainty about how to proceed in the emerging new world disorder, an uncertainty ill-suited to Taiwan's anxious and factionalized middle class (Chu 1996: 216). Indeed, after almost a decade of democratization, the largely apolitical middle class takes an increasingly captious view of new constitutional arrangements, considering 'aggressive queries and the farce in the National Assembly and the legislative yuan, as well as the clashes in the streets and confrontations in the campuses' distastefully un-Confucian. As Lu Ya Li points out, Taiwan has failed to generate a 'healthy civic culture or proper democratic norms' (*Straits Times*, 24 July 1994). Their absence has created a climate of partisan intolerance and factionalism that periodically erupts into violence in the National Assembly. Confrontation, moreover, does not seem to form part of a democratic learning process, but rather represents a loss of face intolerable in an essentially conservative political culture. Continuing disorder worries both businessmen and ordinary citizens and 'the turmoil and confusion are often attributed to the unruly and ungovernable nature of democracy' (Chu 1996: 173). Indeed, alienation from 'proper democratic norms' has led more conservative Taiwanese to compare their experience of liberalization unfavourably with the apolitical, one-party rule of Singapore. As Diane Ying contends, the anxious Taiwanese middle class perhaps does not want 'greater freedom and democracy'. Certainly, it admires Singapore, 'run like a corporation with a common vision, a sense of mission and visible strategies' (*Commonwealth*, June 1994).

Remarkably, it would seem that the continuing ability of the PAP to dominate both Singaporean politics and socio-economic development is peculiarly suited to the anxiously apolitical new middle classes of Pacific Asia. In the course of its thirty-year domination of both government, judiciary, bureaucracy and economy, the PAP has syncretically blended an apparent commitment to a liberal market economic policy with a reinvented concern for Asian values of hierarchy and deference in order to build what the Ministry of Information and the Arts considers a 'Tropical Paradise'.

Singapore's party-led bureaucracy attempts to manage the city state like a multinational corporation. In the political philosophy of the PAP, the ruling party executive forms the board of directors of Singapore plc and citizenship represents a form of share ownership with attached voting rights. As current Prime Minister Goh explained at his National Day rally speech in 1996, 'I regard my cabinet as a Board of Trustees and myself as its elected Chairman. Like a publicly listed company, the account must be presented and approved by you, the shareholders' (*Straits Times*, 18 August 1996). Centrally enforced national savings schemes and government-subsidized housing imbricate the citizen in a network of state tutelage (see Chua 1995: ch. 6). From this perspective regularly held elections test the rationality of the electorate and endorse efficient technocratic rule rather than pass a verdict on the competence of the technocratic elite. The Singapore polity, then, constitutes an enterprise association mobilized towards a collective goal of excellence. Central to this strategy has been the ability to mould a multicultural population into 'one people, one nation, one Singapore' in pursuit of a collectively achievable vision, through a developing control of all aspects of public discourse. Indeed, the party state's relatively uncorrupt, but absolute, power to direct environmental, economic and social policy offers a model and a practice of apolitical development and public administration for developing Asia and Africa.

Political reform or constitutional innovation in contemporary Pacific Asia, then, neither constitutes an inevitable authoritarian response to middle-class pressure nor reflects any wider societal demand for a modular civil society and a communicatory democracy. Instead, the political development that occurs is the sometimes contradictory, but always proactive attempt by a technocratic elite to maintain harmony, order and economic growth in an uncertain world. In this context the selective promotion of specific customary practices disseminated through agencies of central government promotes behaviour appealing to the psychological needs of a rapidly developed middle class and in turn explains its political behaviour. In other words, traditional constructions of power in Asia and their relationship to Asian practices of self-enactment and self-disclosure evidently have crucial implications for the evolution of distinctively Pacific Asian political cultures and shed some illumination on political change in Pacific Asia. Indeed we might have to abandon the somewhat lineal constraints of the developmental model altogether and consider whether the success of the HPAEs might not imply that whereas Protestant individualism and its contingent democratic politics may have initially favoured the modernized industrial order, once that order 'has come into being, and its advantages are clear to all, it can be better run in a Confucian-collectivist spirit' (Gellner 1994: 60).

Conclusion: democratization and its discontents

The literature currently devoted to democracy and globalization character-istically portrays democratization as an evolution from authoritarianism to liberal, bourgeois democracy. The technocratic response to the diverse tastes of an articulate middle class produces political pluralism. Diversity and complexity in turn require tolerance and the consequent 'weakening' of the formerly authoritarian state. Democratization connotes both the state's recognition of the hitherto unacknowledged premonitory snufflings of civil society, 'the devolution of power from a group of people to a set of rules' (Przeworski 1992: 14), and the 'appearance of uncertainty' (p. 50).

However, the evolving political practices of East and Southeast Asia confound this pattern. In Northeast Asia political reform continues to favour single-party rule, whilst in Southeast Asia the prospect of even moder-ate decompression seems improbable. Indeed, the selective cultivation of traditional high cultural values of passivity and group conformity and their subsequent promulgation through universal education programmes militate against individualism, the rule of law and critical public debate. Yet, the dominant paradigm, in both its process and preconditions manifestations, requires evolution in the direction of bourgeois liberalization. The con-sequent lack of fit between political science and political practice in Pacific Asia promotes incoherence. This incoherence springs in part from what Ernest Gellner has shown to be the circularity in the use of the term 'demo-cratization', which combines and confuses a type of rule with an ethical value. Given such 'misleading associations' (Gellner 1994: 185), Gellner prefers the term 'civil society' to describe an arrangement based 'on the sep-aration of the polity from economic and social life' (p. 212), and that holds that economic growth, 'by requiring cognitive growth, makes ideological monopoly impossible' (p. 211). Such an individualistic, modular society seems to have been the particularly successful, but historically contingent, product of Anglo-American political and economic development. As such it may prove ultimately both transitory and unappealing to modernized soci-eties formed by a different history and influenced by a different ethic.

Certainly modular civil society is not emerging in Pacific Asia. Instead political change here reflects a conservative, managerial strategy to amplify political control through forging a new relationship with an *arriviste* middle class. The success of this policy depends upon not the independence or assertiveness of the middle class, but the efficiency of state technocracies in defining acceptable interests and then consulting them through state-regulated feedback mechanisms.

Central to an understanding of the political role of the middle class in Pacific Asia is the fact that not only do the state managers require a leadership principle, but the middle class, too, desires the certainty and established relationship that such techno-paternalism provides. This anxious pursuit of hierarchically coded relationship is daily manifest in the personalized factionalism and 'money politics' of the ostensibly communitarian politics practised in East and Southeast Asia. Hence political participation in the HPAEs actually involves an anxious pursuit by the middle class for clientelist access to those individuals who actually or potentially distribute state largess. Consequently, liberal communicatory democracy exercises little appeal, and when it appears represents a comminatory intrusion upon the conservative pursuit of harmony and consensus.

A reinvented Asian understanding of power as the capacity to harmonize, balance and, particularly in the case of Confucianism, transmit an ethical understanding further facilitates this managerial project. Power is personal and subjects, particularly middle-class ones, actively seek the security that relationships of dependence provide. This means that any alteration in the distribution of power should not automatically be thought of in Pacific Asia as progress from rule by good men to rule by law and the institutionalization of constitutional procedures. Indeed, Asian constitutions, as we saw in chapter 1, are somewhat transient affairs frequently adjusted to the current requirements of an apolitical technocracy and an insecure middle class.

Nevertheless, we may identify the lineaments of an Asian model. Given the understanding of leadership as the power to absorb difference and establish balance and harmony, the 1970s assertion of depoliticized authoritarianism became increasingly cumbersome. It entailed potential or actual confrontation with new urban groups. Such conflict worryingly symbolizes imminent dissolution in East Asian political thought. Consequently, in the course of the 1980s, East and Southeast Asian states devised a number of managerial strategies not only to facilitate the authority of the state, but also to assuage the anxieties of emerging urban middle-class groups and render them both more visible and more manageable in order to re-establish the desired equilibrium.

However, the state managers are not always able to control this process. Thus, democratization in East and Southeast Asia necessarily creates tension between, on the one hand, the incorporative endeavours of the state technocracy and, on the other, the problematic emergence of factions among the state elites and the ensuing difficulty in projecting power. The variation in political practice amongst the East and Southeast Asian states reflects their success in accomplishing this manoeuvre. In other words, rather than the process of democratization, it is political technique reflected through a paradoxically conservative weave of tradition and national development that explains political differences in Pacific Asia.

4

Living in Interesting Times: International Relations in the Asia Pacific

Happy is the country that the rest of the world finds boring. It quietly gets on with its business in life, which mostly is business. Every so often a dazzled economist or a stranded journalist, marvels at its growth rates and its per capita everythings. (*The Economist* [discussing East Asia], 10 May 1986)

The Pacific Century may turn out to be far from peaceful. (*The Economist*, 5 January 1996)

In the 1980s the growing economic interdependence of Pacific Asia and its ramifications for international relations and international political economy constituted largely neglected phenomena. The HPAEs emerged under the cloak of a 'boringness factor' made possible by a felicific mixture of American protection and access to American markets. Cambodia apart, Pacific Asian development occurred in a regional environment largely untroubled by major conflict after 1975. Indeed, *The Economist* observed in 1986 that 'some of the most contentedly placid countries in the world have been those of East Asia' (10 May 1986: 15). This had not always been the case. In the period after 1945, the rapid disintegration of European colonialism in the region left a multitude of heterogeneous new states in Pacific Asia exposed to the vagaries of the Cold War and the evolving superpower rivalry between the USSR and America. This rivalry, moreover, had a disturbing habit of flaring into hot war in the Asian peripheries of this conflict for global supremacy. After 1960, the split between the previously aligned communist regimes of China and the USSR further complicated superpower rivalry in Pacific Asia and distorted the emerging character of the region. It was in the interstices of this conflict that the HPAEs eked out a fraught existence and formulated their subsequent economic, political and international outlook. What we need to examine, therefore, is how the contingent international security environment that governed the emergence of the HPAEs after 1950 affects their international political and economic conduct, and what implications this conduct has for the emergence of an interdependent Pacific economic and security community in the post-Cold War era.

In international relations terms, it was their disposition in the Cold War as military and economic clients of the United States that determined the subsequent fortunes of the HPAEs and initially moulded both their political understanding and international behaviour. More recently, the emergence of Japan, itself dependent upon the United States for its security, as both a model and a source of direct foreign investment to the region has complicated the character of American hegemony in the 1990s. The triangular pattern of Pacific trade, 'where Japan plays supplier to the United States absorber' (Higgott et al. 1993: 312) and where the HPAEs depend upon export-led, growth, has evident implications for further regional economic and political integration in the context of the disorderly new world that has emerged since 1991; a disorder additionally complicated by the fact that although the Asian miracle occurred under an American nuclear security umbrella, it was largely informed by such 'Asian values' as rule by men, not by law, consensus, harmony and the priority of collective over individual interest.

When in the course of the 1980s an institutional structure for accommodating emerging regional interdependence was first raised, the problem of specifically Asian understandings of democracy and foreign relations did not seem to present a problem (Keohane and Nye 1974; Gilpin 1987; Stubbs 1994). Nor was this entirely surprising given that the promotion of a way of life 'distinguished by free institutions, representative government, free elections, guarantees of individual liberty . . . and freedom from political oppression' (Kissinger 1994a: 118) constituted the foundation of American regional engagement after 1950, had received epistemological validation by scientistic theories of modernization since the early 1970s, and was rather reluctantly assumed to be an inevitable outcome of 'nation building' by a succession of Asian autocrats. Only in the course of the 1990s has it become apparent that the American-sponsored security and economic development on the Pacific Rim need not ineluctably promote an international order of equal, autonomous, self-determining nation states committed to constitutional freedoms. The evolving pattern of international relations consequently has complex ideological, historical, political and economic roots. In order to uncover them we shall initially examine the pattern of international dependence that evolved in the Cold War era, before subsequently considering the economic and ideological consequences of the end of the Cold War and their ramifications for the continued economic dynamism and institutional integration of contemporary Pacific Asia.

Pacific Asia and the Cold War, 1950–1992

It was the Truman Doctrine's assertion of the inexorable triumph of liberal over communist values that prompted the United States to adopt a policy of global containment after 1948. The policy assumed 'the age old American dream of a peace achieved by the conversion of the adversary' (Kissinger 1994b: 455). Communism, in this essentially Wilsonian view, contained within it the seed of its own inevitable demise. Its defeat consequently required 'a policy of firm containment, designed to confront the Russians with unalterable counter force at every point where they show signs of encroaching upon the interests of a peaceful and stable world' (Kennan 1947: 581). This extraodinarily American theory, as Henry Kissinger observes, 'assumed that the collapse of totalitarianism could be achieved in an essentially benign way. Although . . . formulated at the height of America's absolute power, it preached America's relative weakness.' Indeed 'containment allowed no role for diplomacy until the climactic final scene in which the men in the white hats accepted the conversion of the men in the black hats' (Kissinger 1994a: 130). The strategic pursuit of containment committed the United States to the defence of freedom in the 'hinterlands of the Soviet empire's extended periphery' (p. 123). Such a commitment effectively meant that America after 1950 had no permanent interests only permanent friends. Thus, when Mao's forces eventually overcame nationalist opposition on the Chinese mainland in 1949, it became the received wisdom in Washington that the new communist Sino-Soviet monolith had now to be contained at all costs.

More particularly, in terms of the Asia Pacific, the strategy initially required securing the Pacific as an American lake. Thus, in 1949, General Douglas MacArthur, Supreme Commander of America's Pacific Forces, defined America's Pacific 'line of defense', starting in the Philippines and continuing 'through the Ryukyu Archipelago, which includes its main bastion Okinawa. Then it bends back through Japan and the Aleutian Island chain to Alaska' (in Kissinger 1994b: 475). In order to guarantee the defence of the Pacific, the Americans embarked upon a series of bilateral mutual defence treaties with the non-communist states of East Asia. Indeed, by 1988, the United States had 'more bilateral alliances of one form or another in the Pacific than anywhere else' (Segal 1989: 239). Central to this security pattern of an American hub at the centre of bilateral Asian spokes was the alliance with Japan.

The United States – Japan alliance had its roots in the American postwar occupation and the San Francisco Peace Treaty of 1951 that returned full sovereignty to Japan. Under the terms of Article 9 of the American-inspired postwar constitution (1947), Japan renounced not only war but also the potential for war and belligerence. Simultaneously, Japan and America signed a Security Treaty in September 1951 'which allowed for American defence of Japan and the right to station forces there' (Segal 1989: 237). The Mutual Defence Pact of March 1954 subsequently modified this arrangement by permitting Japan to build a self-defence force. In 1960, a further renegotiation of the Security Treaty emphasized the United States' commitment to defend Japan against foreign aggression (Inoguchi 1991; Levin 1991: 76). In 1976, Prime Minister Takeo Miti's LDP government limited Japanese defence spending to 1 per cent of GNP. Even so, by the mid-1990s Japan was not only paying 73 per cent of the non-salary costs of the 44,000 Americans stationed in Japan, it also maintained a defence budget of $30 billion per annum, the world's third largest (Polomka 1991: 239; Satoh 1993: 73; Johnson 1996: 23). Moreover, by the late 1980s Japan had also developed the capacity to protect its sea lanes as far as Guam and established regional economic dominance through its command of high technology, its direct investment particularly in Southeast Asia, and its judicious use of financial aid that afforded the basis for a functionalist expansion of Japan's regional influence (Hughes 1996: 257). This notwithstanding, Japan's regional security role is both low-key and the subject of regional suspicion. Indeed, it was only gradually after 1951 that Japan finalized peace treaties with the newly independent states of Pacific Asia, concluding treaties with Taiwan in 1952, the Philippines in 1956, Indonesia in 1958 and South Korea only in 1965. For the first time since 1945, Japanese forces played a role in the United Nations peace keeping forces in Cambodia in 1992. Yet given the continuing inability of Japanese politicians to accept responsibility for war crimes committed by the Imperial Japanese Army between 1942 and 1945 or address the grievances of former comfort women in South Korea, Taiwan and the Philippines, any attempt to transform its economic power into regional hegemony immediately evokes uncomfortable memories of the Greater East Asian Co-prosperity Sphere of 1942–5.

Significantly, it is the former colony of Korea, the dagger pointed at the Japanese heart, that views Japan's mounting economic and military power with some reservation. This is somewhat ironic given that America extended its postwar security blanket to cover South Korea in order to cement its 1951 alliance with Japan. Indeed, the implications of the containment strategy for the putative HPAEs received its clearest manifestation on the Korean peninsula after 1950.

Security dilemmas in Northeast Asia

The Korean flashpoint   The end of World War II in Asia saw Korea divided between a Soviet-controlled North and an American-governed South at the thirty-eighth parallel. Whilst the Cairo Conference (1943) had envisaged the emergence of a free and independent Korea 'in due course', the evolving frigidity of the first Cold War saw the United States recognizing Syngman Rhee's presidency of a Republic of Korea (ROK) south of the thirty-eighth parallel in 1948, and the Soviet-sponsored, Kim Il Jung establishing the Democratic People's Republic of Korea (DPRK) in the North.

Interestingly, in January 1950, the United States Secretary of State, Dean Ascheson, declared both Korea and Taiwan outside the American defence perimeter and 'abjured any intention of guaranteeing areas located on the mainland of Asia' (Kissinger 1994b: 475). However, when DPRK troops invaded the South in June 1950, the Secretary of State rapidly reversed his earlier decision and committed MacArthur's Pacific Asia forces, under cover of a United Nations resolution, to the defence of 'free' Korea. The peace eventually concluded at Panmunjom in June 1953 saw Korea still effectively divided at the thirty-eighth parallel, but at a cost of 3 million Korean lives.

Korea has remained both divided and a potential flashpoint ever since. On 1 October 1953, the United States concluded a Mutual Security Treaty with South Korea in which both parties recognized that 'an armed attack in the Pacific area on either of the parties now under their respective administrative control . . . would be dangerous to its own peace and safety' (Lee 1993: 56). On this basis, the United States stationed 39,000 men, materiel and, after 1960, battlefield nuclear weapons on the Korean peninsula. Even in the 1990s, over one million 'men in uniform . . . confront each other daily across the 150-mile demilitarized zone' (Ye 1993: 38). Meanwhile, between 1953 and 1988 North Korea assiduously cultivated its ties with both Beijing and Moscow and cleverly played off the two bordering fellow communist powers after the Chinese–Soviet split in 1960. The North Koreans also developed an interesting line in state-sponsored terrorism, 'blowing up the South Korean cabinet in a bomb attack in Rangoon in 1983 and a South Korean passenger aircraft in mid-air in 1987' (Segal 1989: 207).

Despite the conclusion of the Cold War in Europe and the establishment of diplomatic ties between Russia and China and between the two formerly communist powers and South Korea, the Korean peninsula remains a source of international tension. Much of the responsibility for this continuing uncertainty resides with the peculiarly introverted and paranoid regime established in Pyŏngyang by the founder of the DPRK, Kim Il Sung, and continued uncertainly by his evidently confused son, Kim Jong Il, who succeeded him in July 1994 (*Far Eastern Economic Review*, 19 January 1995: 24). Despite the attempt of Chun Doo Hwan's government to launch a reconciliatory *Nordpolitik* after 1987, and the decline in superpower tension in the region in the course of the 1980s, North Korea has maintained a studied ambivalence towards both the South and détente. This ambivalence manifested itself most recently in the negotiations since 1991 to denuclearize the Korean peninsula. Indeed, it came as something of a surprise in December 1991 when both sides announced a Joint Declaration for Denuclearization of the Korean Peninsula, 'covering both reconciliation and provisions for realising mutual non-aggression' (Mack 1993: 3; Cotton 1993: 290). This was followed in 1992 by the North's decision to sign a safeguards agreement with the International Atomic Energy Agency (IAEA), whilst South Korea simultaneously announced the cancellation of the annual 'US–ROK Team Spirit exercise, which the North had long denounced as highly provocative' (Mack 1993: 4).

Nevertheless, as the IAEA pursued its inspection of North Korean facilities and discovered evidence of nuclear reprocessing of weapons-grade plutonium at the Yongbyon nuclear plant, North Korea once again retreated into its more familiar stance of hermetically sealed paranoia. In March 1993, North Korea announced its withdrawal from the Nuclear Non-Proliferation Treaty. However, after United Nations intervention in May 1993, North Korea began bilateral talks with the United States that eventually led to a Framework Agreement in October 1994 for a Korean Energy Development Organization (KEDO) that would replace the Yongbyon nuclear plant with a light water reactor. As Edward Neilan observes, 'the most impressive part of the KEDO arrangement forged by the Americans was to make it seem as though the US, South Korea and Japan were sharing its leadership and cost' (*Straits Times*, 13 March 1995). None the less, in April 1995, the North Koreans once more complicated the agreement by refusing to take a South Korean nuclear reactor. The face-conscious North Koreans, it would seem, 'are working for a peace treaty with the US without Seoul's participation' (*Far Eastern Economic Review*, 18 May 1995). In view of the increasing bilateral tensions between Japan, the United States and South Korea's President Kim, who wants North Korea 'punished' for intransigence (*Straits Times*, 25 March 1995), this is a ploy not without strategic merit. By 1996, the nuclear issue remained unresolved, whilst the North Korean regime's international isolation and internal difficulty in feeding its population has occasioned increasingly volatile international behaviour. It would seem that it is only a matter of time before North Korea collapses. The question remains, however, whether the process will be of mere internal significance or involve military and even nuclear conflict with South Korea.

The problems of Greater China   A different but equally problematic ambivalence characterizes the international status of Taiwan and its relations with both China and the United States. Prior to 1949, the Chinese Communist Party had expressed no interest in Taiwan and in the 1930s Mao Ze Dong had acknowledged the Japanese colony to be a separate entity (Copper 1994: 28). After 1945, however, the defeated Japanese returned Taiwan to the Nationalist Republic of China (ROC), and in 1949 Chiang Kai-shek's Nationalist forces retreated there after losing the mainland to the Communists. In early 1950, Mao, therefore, decided to revive China's historical claim to the island, invade Taiwan and extirpate the last vestiges of Chinese nationalism. Yet, just as the invasion of Korea inspired the United States to extend its defence perimeter to South Korea, Mao's threatened invasion in the spring of 1950 persuaded Ascheson to interpose the Seventh Fleet in the Taiwan Straits and extend America's protectorate to Indochina (Chang 1994: 150). The Korean War, thus, 'effectively drew the lines of the "grand area" in East Asia' (Cumings 1994: 226). By defending Taiwan, President Truman defended what the United States maintained until 1971 was the legitimate Chinese government. This, together with increased aid to Vietnam, 'appeared to Beijing as capitalist encirclement' (Kissinger 1994b: 479).

After 1950, therefore, there existed two claimants to the *de jure* authority for all China. Throughout the 1950s the KMT under the patriarchal 'leadership' of Chiang Kai-shek (Tsang 1993: 61) promoted a resolutely anticommunist stance, sought international support to recover the mainland, and sustained its role as the representative of all China in international affairs, most notably at the United Nations, in order to deny recognition to Mao's People's Republic of China. The Mutual Security Treaty agreed with the United States in 1954, together with US aid between 1950 and 1968, not only offered the basis for economic growth, but also secured national defence enabling Taiwan to withstand the PRC's attempt to take the offshore island of Quemoy by force in 1954 and again in 1958 (Yang 1994: 72).

By the late 1950s Taiwan had survived the first round of the Cold War in Pacific Asia, but its international position was increasingly compromised. John Foster Dulles, President Eisenhower's Secretary of State, persuaded Chiang Kai-shek, as the second Straits crisis drew to a close in 1958, to renounce the use of force to recover the mainland whilst retaining the ROC's 'sacred mission' of restoring 'freedom to its people' (Tsang 1993: 55). Subsequently, the KMT devoted itself to developing Taiwan into a model of Nationalist development, thereby vindicating Sun Yat-sen's 'three principles of the people' and shaming the PRC with the scale of Taiwan's economic achievement (p. 55). Externally, moreover, the Sino–Soviet split of 1960, occasioned by Khrushchev's decision to pursue peaceful co-existence with the US and not supply China with atomic technology, rendered Taiwan's survival in the 1960s less precarious (Spence 1991: 588).

At the same time, however, Taiwan's continuing claim to represent the Chinese mainland in international fora became increasingly unsustainable. In particular, the aftermath of the Nixon doctrine announced at Guam in 1969 illustrated the growing international isolation of Taiwan and its clientelist dependence on US support. The doctrine redefined US relations with its Pacific Asian clients in general and Taiwan in particular, requiring 'threatened countries to assume a larger burden of their own conventional defense' (Kissinger 1994b: 708), withdrew US forces from Asia, and dramatically altered the character of Sino–US relations. This 'geopolitical' reassessment of American commitments in Asia enabled Nixon to visit Beijing in February 1972 and issue, with Mao, a joint communiqué from Shanghai. The Shanghai Communiqué noted that the Chinese government opposed any 'activities which aim at the creation of . . . "two Chinas"' whilst the Americans acknowledged there is 'but one China and that Taiwan is part of China' (Spence 1991: 632).

The subsequent evolution of the Nixon doctrine cost Taiwan its seat in the United Nations in 1971 when the PRC was admitted as China's legitimate representative. The loss of diplomatic ties internationally followed the humiliating ejection from the UN and persuaded Taipei to adopt a policy of economic diplomacy, converting former embassies into trade missions. Taiwan's international position weakened further in 1979 when the Carter administration decided to 'normalize' US relations with China and recognize the 'government of the PRC as the sole government of China' (Spence 1991: 667). On the question of Taiwan's future, after 1979, Secretary of State Cyrus Vance acknowledged that the United States continued 'to have an interest in the peaceful resolution of the Taiwan issue', but the Chinese understood the agreement to mean that the 'way of bringing Taiwan back to the embrace of the motherland . . . is entirely China's internal affair' (p. 667). Particularly threatening to the continuation of the Taiwanese 'entity' was the US offer to withdraw all military personnel from the island within four months, supply no new offensive arms to Taiwan, and abrogate the mutual security treaty of 1954. In April 1979, the US Congress responded to Taiwan's mounting concern at the State Department's decision to abandon the island by passing a highly supportive Taiwan Relations Act (TRA). The Act promised to supply Taiwan 'with arms of a defensive character', required that 'the future of Taiwan . . . be determined by peaceful means', and considered 'boycotts and embargoes' by the PRC against Taiwan 'a threat to the peace and security of the western Pacific' (p. 671).

The TRA apart, Taiwan's eventual integration with China appeared inevitable after 1980 as the post-Mao leadership of the PRC adopted a policy of increasing economic openness. Deng Xiaoping sought a 'pragmatic' resolution of the problem (Kuo 1994: 115). In September 1981, Beijing promulgated a Nine-Point Proposal outlining a 'one country, two systems' approach to eventual integration. This proposal envisaged Taiwan as a special administrative region with a 'high degree of autonomy' (p. 115), retaining economic relations with the rest of the world, but none the less a provincial government of a country whose national capital was Beijing.

Taiwan's response to the proposed accommodation with Beijing was politely ambivalent. The official response to the Nine Point Proposal was the 'three no's' policy, namely no contact, no negotiations and no compromise. In practice, however, the KMT permitted visits to the mainland, and trade and investment in the Fujian Special Economic Zone across the Taiwan Straits. At the same time, declining international credibility prompted the KMT to embark upon domestic democratic reform and Taiwanization in order to bolster its legitimacy. Particularly after the accession of the indigenous Lee Teng-hui to the presidency in 1988, the KMT began to consider more carefully the formerly proscribed opposition policy of political reform leading to a democratic and independent Taiwanese state. Taiwan's economic strength has facilitated this policy, permitting the KMT to break out of its diplomatic isolation and expand its international participation. The ROC after 1986 developed important trade and investment links with the emerging economies of Southeast Asia and is now the largest investor in the developing Vietnamese economy (T.Y. Cheng 1994: 64). Despite losing its last formal diplomatic tie with South Korea in 1992, the ROC has steadfastly promoted its flexible economic diplomacy, which, together with the promotion of democracy, has secured Taiwan's continuing membership of the Asian Development Bank (ADB) and acceptance in APEC under the rubric of 'Chinese Taipei' (p. 68). Meanwhile, the combination of Taiwanese democratization and the negative international reaction to the events of July 1989 in Tiananmen Square unwittingly enhanced Taiwan's international credibility as 'the first Chinese democracy' (Chao and Myers 1994).

Nevertheless, despite oscillations in the international perception of Taiwan, the island's fundamentally anomalous status has not altered. This anomaly has been further complicated since 1989, both by growing international concern about the policy of the PRC after the death of Deng Xiaoping in 1997, and by the increasing economic interdependence of Taiwan, Hong Kong and the mainland Special Economic Zones. The fact that Hong Kong and Macau will have returned to the 'motherland' by the turn of the century exacerbates mainland pressure on the 'rebellious province'.

As with the two Koreas, negotiations between the two Chinas proceed schizophrenically. On the one hand, Taiwanese investment in Fujian and increasing intergovernmental contact suggest the possibility of eventual integration in a Greater China. From a functionalist perspective, such economic ties could 'spill over' into political accommodation. Thus the Koo–Wang talks between the two governments meeting as 'private organizations' in Singapore in April 1993 intimated ways in which 'new avenues of "direct and peaceful" relations' could resolve issues of smuggling, investment protection and illegal migration. Such low-level cooperation, by engendering trust, might, it was argued, pave the way for greater economic cooperation, leading eventually to full assimilation (Chang 1994: 162).

On the other hand, a history of mutual suspicion, exacerbated by growing regional political and economic uncertainty, renders prospects of peaceful accommodation increasingly unlikely. Taiwan has used its major international asset, its wealth, as a powerful inducement 'to win over new friends and persuade old ones to test the limits of a one China policy' (Cheng 1994: 121). Its financial and trading role in developing the Asia Pacific gives Taiwan an influence in the WTO, the World Bank and APEC that arouses Beijing's suspicion about the KMT's ultimate intentions. The PRC suspects that the KMT has covertly devised a new mainland policy, 'one country, two equal governments', to resolve the growing incompatibility between the Taiwanese democratization process and the one-China principle.

Ultimately, the end of the Cold War in Europe and the departure of Russia from the Asia Pacific after 1988 have altered fundamentally the balance of economic and strategic power in Pacific Asia and added to the anxiety of an already uncertain Chinese leadership. Thus although the regional strategy pursued by the post-Deng leadership of China remains central to the stability of the Asia Pacific, its international significance, especially for Western Europe and the United States, has declined. This has not only afforded Taiwan scope for diplomatic manoeuvring, it has also exacerbated PRC concern about Taiwan's intentions, and more particularly those of its western supporters. These fears escalated in June 1995 when both President Lee Teng-hui and Prime Minister Lien Chan undertook unofficial visits to the United States and Europe. Increasing international recognition, coupled with continuing fears of Taiwanese democratic reforms, 'triggered an abrupt shift in Beijing's basic policies' (*Far Eastern Economic Review*, 14 September 1995: 20). In June 1995, Beijing cancelled cross-Straits talks inaugurated in Singapore in 1993. This was followed in July by Chinese ballistic missile tests in a 'target area 150 kilometres north of Taipei' (p. 122) and in March tensions reached Cold War levels when the PRC decided to conduct ground-to-ground missile tests in the Straits of Taiwan during Taiwan's first democratic presidential election contest (*Far Eastern Economic Review*, 14 March 1996, 21 March 1996). The evident implication that Beijing would not rule out the use of force to reclaim Taiwan indicates that the peaceful resolution of the two-Chinas problem is not a foregone conclusion.

Indeed, the PRC's strategic use of the military threat to undermine Taiwanese independence resembles its successful tactics to forestall 'fledgling efforts to build democracy' in Hong Kong prior to its return to mainland rule in July 1997 under the terms of the 'one country, two systems' formula that Deng also proposes for Taiwan. The continuing uncertainty governing Beijing–Taipei relations inevitably leads us to a brief consideration of Beijing's relations with that other anomalous Chinese entity, the British colony of Hong Kong.

Significantly, it was in the context of the normalization of Sino–American relations and the opening of the mainland economic zones that the United Kingdom concluded the Sino–British Joint Declaration that effectively ended the 150 years of British administration of Hong Kong. Under the terms of that agreement Hong Kong becomes a Chinese Special Administrative Region when Britain's lease on the New Territories expires on 1 July 1997. The agreement signed by Deng Xiaoping and Margaret Thatcher in December 1984 ensures that 'the territory will enjoy the same capitalist lifestyle, the same legal and economic systems and the distinctive cultural identity it did under British rule' (Patrikeeff 1991: 143). More precisely, the Basic Law mini-constitution governing Hong Kong during a fifty-year transition to full assimilation with the mainland was intended to preserve the rule of British common law from erosion by 'Chinese style cronyism, influence peddling and disorder' (*Far Eastern Economic Review*, 26 January 1995: 18).

Events since 1984 have severely eroded the credibility of what at the time appeared to be a masterpiece of diplomacy. In particular, the aftermath of Tiananmen Square prompted the formation of a Democracy Movement in Hong Kong (Scott 1993: 63). This, combined with Beijing's negative reaction to British Governor Chris Patten's decision to democratize the colony's Legislative Council (Legco), further escalated tensions between Hong Kong and the mainland. The PRC subsequently established its own Hong Kong and Macau Affairs Office, and in 1993 set up a preliminary Working Committee to oversee the transition. By the time the first direct democratic Legco elections occurred in October 1995, relations with the colonial administration had deteriorated to such an extent that Beijing and London had to negotiate directly the arrangements governing the eventual transfer of sovereignty. As Daniel Wong, secretary-general of the Hong Kong Association for Democracy and People's Livelihood, observed, 'it appears that Beijing's "one country two systems" formula will apply only to economics' (*Far Eastern Economic Review*, 26 January 1995).

Unlike the question of the two Chinas and the two Koreas, it is fairly safe to surmise that the problem of Hong Kong 's status will have been resolved in 1997. What is also certain is that the KMT will observe closely the 'one country, two systems' model as it operates in Hong Kong. Indeed, as a number of recent commentators have observed, there exists a striking disjunction between the economic and political aspects of a China that is evidently both changing shape and threatening to evolve into a Greater China (Goodman and Feng 1994; Shambaugh 1995: 3). Whilst the former 'creates pressures for integration', the latter promote 'separate national identitites' (Shambaugh 1995: 3). It is also evident that Beijing's relationship with Taiwan, Hong Kong and the Special Economic Zones will depend increasingly upon informal *guanxi* networks rather than formal legal, institutional and contractual arrangements. As Michael Yahuda observes, the evolution of politics in Beijing, Hong Kong and Taipei will ultimately determine 'the realization of Greater China' (Yahuda 1993; 1995: 35) Post-Cold War Northeast Asia has witnessed growing Chinese irredentism, the inability to resolve Cold War flashpoints, the continuing Japanese inability to project a regional security presence and a confusion in US foreign policy during the Clinton administration that has created an environment of increasing insecurity and unresolved tension. What, we might next consider, of regional developments in Southeast Asia?

Evolving insecurity in Southeast Asia, 1948–1967

Like their Northeast Asian counterparts, the Southeast Asian countries that in 1967 came to constitute the founder members of ASEAN – Indonesia, the Philippines, Thailand, Malaysia and Singapore (Brunei joined in 1984 and Vietnam in 1995) – were profoundly affected by both the US doctrine of containment and an enduring fear of an external and internal communist threat.

Over a period of twenty-one years, the European and American colonial powers that returned to Southeast Asia in 1945 decided on both ideological and practical grounds to abandon their colonial pretensions. One of the more remarkable features of this decolonization was that the territories arbitrarily carved out by French Empire builders in Indo-China and British and Dutch merchant adventurers in Malaya, Borneo and Indonesia substantially retained their colonial shape after independence. This remained the case in spite of the fact that there was no very evident historical, cultural, religious or linguistic basis upon which to construct the new states that emerged after 1945. Indeed, not only were these new nation building states the outcome of decisions taken in London, Paris, Geneva, Washington and the Hague, the term 'Southeast Asia' itself was the product of the Quebec Conference of August 1943 that established the South East Asian Command under Lord Louis Mountbatten for the purpose of liberating the area from

Japanese occupation (Stockwell 1992: ch. 6). In the immediate postwar period three factors affected the international relations of the new states in Southeast Asia: the evolving relationship with the former colonial power; the conduct of the new state in terms of superpower rivalry, particularly the policy of containment as it affected Southeast Asia; and, after 1967, the evolving pattern of intraregional cooperation.

The first of the new Southeast Asian states to 'obtain independence was the Philippines in July 1946. The last to do so was Singapore' (Leifer 1974: 7), which seceded from the recently formed Malaysian Federation in August 1965. As Michael Leifer observes, 'the process of independence within Southeast Asia was a mixed activity involving widely differing experiences. There were both compliant and dogged colonials and the manner of attainment of independence had a direct bearing on national attitudes to foreign policy' (p. 7).

Indonesia, 1949–1967   Indonesia, like Vietnam, which experienced a more acute form, suffered from 'dogged' colonialism. The Japanese had announced their intention to grant Indonesia independence in March 1944. Preparation for a transfer of power, however, only emerged a week before Japanese capitulation in March 1945. In August 1945, the nationalist leaders Sukarno and Hatta proclaimed the independence of Indonesia as a sovereign unitary state with jurisdiction over the former territory of the Netherlands East Indies. The returning Dutch colonial power refused to accept the new arrangement and after a bitter struggle Dutch and Republican forces negotiated a federal order at Linggadjati in March 1947. The arrangement proved inoperable and after further fighting, the Dutch, in response to US pressure, relinquished authority to a unitary Indonesian state in December 1949. The new state did not initially comprise the territory of the Netherlands East Indies, the Dutch retaining control of this western portion of New Guinea, and it reverted to Indonesia, as Irian Jaya, only in August 1962. The Indonesian New Order subsequently extended its archipelagic empire, absorbing the former Portuguese colony of East Timor by invasion in 1975, ostensibly to prevent a communist coup.

In the course of the 1950s, particularly during the years of President Sukarno's charismatic Guided Democracy, Indonesia pursued an increasingly eccentric, anti-western and anti-colonial foreign policy. The country successfully cultivated its neutral, non-aligned credentials by hosting a conference of newly decolonized states at Bandung in April 1955, and Indonesia henceforth cultivated its image as a founder member of the Non-Aligned Movement (NAM). A direct outcome of the Bandung Conference was the development of good relations with the PRC and a shift from international neutrality to an emphasis on what Sukarno termed the 'New Emerging

Forces' (*Nefos*) that would sweep aside the outmoded former colonial powers. Sukarno's ideology consequently favoured escalating confrontation (*konfrontasi*) with the former colonial 'Old Established Forces' in the region. Its most striking manifestation occurred in January 1963, when Foreign Minister Subandrio formally adopted confrontation as the official Indonesian policy towards the recently formed entity of Malaysia (Fifield 1979: ch. 1; Suryadinata 1996: ch. 2). There followed a formal diplomatic breach between Jakarta and Kuala Lumpur, a recourse to terrorist insurgency in Sarawak, and the successful attempt to deny Malaysia a place at the Second Conference of Non-Aligned Countries in 1964. Confrontation was eventually resolved with the attempted coup and subsequent military counter-coup in Indonesia which led to the effective retirement of Sukarno in 1966 and the emergence of General, subsequently President, Suharto's New Order in 1967. In the course of 1966, the new regime, shaken by internal disturbances which it blamed on the communist PKI, negotiated an end to the confrontation.

The new establishment was virulently anti-communist and shared this antipathy with the Marcos regime in Manila, the Sarit regime in Thailand, UMNO in Malaysia and Lee Kuan Yew's PAP in Singapore. This commonly perceived threat constituted the basis for regional *rapprochement* after 1967 (Suryadinata 1996: ch. 5).

The problem of Malaysian federation, 1948–1967   Malaysia explored a different path to decolonization under largely benign British supervision, beginning in 1946 when Whitehall in conjunction with the Malay Sultans announced the Union of Malaya. Shortly afterwards Singapore achieved crown colony status. Widespread opposition to the Union, particularly amongst the Malays, led both to the formation of UMNO and the subsequent negotiation of a Federation of Malaya, formally announced on 1 February 1948 (Omar 1993: ch. 4). The new Federation had scarcely been announced before a largely Chinese communist revolt plunged the peninsula into a state of emergency which lasted officially from June 1948 to 1960, although the last members of the officially proscribed Malay Communist Party only surrendered in 1993. As the emergency abated, Malaya eventually attained independence in February 1957 along the federal constitutional lines announced in 1948. Meanwhile, in 1959 Singapore achieved full internal self-government and elected the first of many subsequent PAP governments. As Mary Turnbull argues, 'Malaya's success in achieving *merdeka* [freedom] drove Singapore to seek a similar independence, but the state seemed too small to be viable, so all responsible Singapore parties aimed to achieve independence through merger with the Federation' (Turnbull 1989: 252).

At the same time, crown colony rule had brought steady development to the Bornean states of North Borneo (Sabah), Sarawak and Brunei. After granting independence to the Federation of Malaya, Britain proposed a North Borneo Federation comprising Sarawak, North Borneo and Brunei, an arrangement ultimately rejected by Brunei's enigmatic Sultan Omar because he considered Brunei's interests closer to peninsular Malaya (p. 255). Subsequently, in May 1961, Tunku Abdul Rahman, the Prime Minister of Malaya, proposed to incorporate the Borneo territories and Singapore into a Malaysian Federation (Leifer 1974: 56). Such an arrangement appealed both to Britain's need to reduce its commitments East of Suez, to the UMNO leadership of the *Barisan Nasional* government of Malaya, which wished to offset the influence of Chinese Singapore with the Malays of Brunei, to Singapore because of its fear that newly independent Malaya and Indonesia might sever regional trading links, and to the Bornean dependencies threatened with potential assimilation into Sukarno's *Indonesia Raya* (pp. 254–5).

However, upset with the federal tax proposals for his oil-rich Sultanate, Sultan Omar of Brunei opted out of the proposed arrangement in 1962. This notwithstanding, Singapore, Sabah and Sarawak signed the Malaysia Agreement in July 1963. Almost at once the new Malaysian Federation attracted both intense regional antipathy and internal difficulties. Its threat to Indonesia's regional hegemony provoked a three-year *konfrontasi*. The former US dependency of the Philippines, granted independence in 1946, also became involved in the acrimonious diplomacy surrounding the Malaysian settlement. In 1962, President Macagapal claimed the former British North Borneo colony on the grounds that it originally constituted part of the former Sultanate of Sulu. As the independent Philippines incorporated the vestigial Sultanate in 1946, Macagapal maintained that Sabah should now be returned to Philippine rule. Meanwhile, the process of negotiating the entry of Singapore into Malaysia 'was distinguished by hard bargaining . . . marred by ill-feeling' and disrupted by inter-ethnic rivalry (Leifer 1974: 64–5). The determination of Singapore's Prime Minister, Lee Kuan Yew, to conduct himself as an equal head of state further exacerbated difficulties with Kuala Lumpur after 1963.

Underlying suspicion metamorphosed into outright conflict when Lee Kuan Yew entered the PAP in peninsular Malay elections in 1964, unleashing a process of inter-ethnic polarization that eventuated in Singapore's expulsion from the Federation in August 1965. This unhappy beginning subsequently conditioned Singapore's approach to foreign relations. The city state thus started its 'international existence as an encircled entity, distinguished from neighbouring antagonists by its ethnic identity' (p. 66) and worried that any *rapprochement* between Indonesia and Malaysia might occur at Singapore's expense.

Nevertheless, despite these unpromising foundations, the Malaysian Federation and Singapore have maintained the same territorial boundaries for thirty years. This emerging spirit of diplomatic tolerance may be attributed in part to changes in the leadership of Indonesia and the Philippines that facilitated accommodation with Kuala Lumpur after 1965, and in part to the shared perception of an external communist threat to Southeast Asian security that promoted the emergence of a security complex regionally aligned to the United States after 1967 (Acharya 1991: 173).

Thailand, 1950–1967   This shift from confrontation to cooperation drew the former colonies into an evolving relationship with Thailand and covert or overt acceptance of an American presence to inoculate the region against the seemingly inexorable spread of communism. Thailand had enjoyed an anomalous, but highly conditional regional independence as a buffer between French Indochina and British Burma and Malaya. In 1941, Thailand had allied itself militarily with Japan. In January 1942, Phibun had declared war against the western Allies and subsequently enriched Thailand territorially at their expense. With the unexpected surrender of Japan in August 1945, Thai politics assumed a brief constitutional civilian hue in order to gain American sympathy and deflect British and French claims for territorial compensation. This tactic effectively maintained the independence of Thailand at its 1942 boundaries and drew its leaders into the postwar American strategy of containment. After 1950, American policy considered both Thailand and its former colony of the Philippines as independent states to be defended against communism. Thailand particularly was 'to be wooed to the cause of containing communism in the region [and] . . . was the first Asian state to send troops to fight with the United Nations in Korea' (Wyatt 1984: 271).

Within the context of containment, the threat posed to its traditional hegemony in Indochina by the emerging power of Vietnamese- and Chinese-sponsored communism and the prospect of a united Vietnam achieving an ascendancy in the strategically important Mekong Delta particularly exercised Thai foreign relations. The crushing defeat of French forces by General Giap's Vietminh at Dienbienphu in March 1954 brought the French *mission civilisatrice* in Indochina to a dramatic conclusion. The Indochina settlement reached subsequently at Geneva in 1954 divided Vietnam at the seventeenth parallel between Ho Chi Minh's independent communist Democratic Republic of Vietnam (DRV) and a South Vietnam led by the ascetic Confucian nationalist Ngo Dinh Diem. The four powers at Geneva (France, Britain, the United States and China) envisaged the division to be temporary prior to unifying elections in 1956. In fact Geneva constituted a brief prelude to a civil war that necessitated escalating US involvement during the Kennedy presidency. Indeed, by the early 1960s, the South had become inured to American military and financial aid (Kolko 1985: ch. 8; Karnow 1988: ch. 5).

The premiss for US involvement was of course the doctrine of containment now adumbrated by the domino theory. This curious proposition, first promulgated in a National Security Council document of 1952, held that not only did the presence of a Communist China constitute a continuing threat to Indochina, but that the loss of a single Southeast Asian country would facilitate 'a relatively swift submission to or an alignment with communism by the remainder' (Kissinger 1994b: 627). On this basis, the United States after 1955 became increasingly embroiled in the Vietnamese War. Vietnam, J.F. Kennedy maintained, was to be the 'proving ground for democracy in Asia' (p. 639).

The evolution of ASEAN, 1967–1991

It was as a direct consequence of the domino theory, moreover, that Thailand, the Philippines and subsequently the other ASEAN states became integrated in a bi-polar Cold War world order. In August 1951, the United States had committed itself to a treaty of mutual security with the Philippines pledging assistance in the case of armed attack. Despite the odd profession of nationalism, the Philippines increasingly 'acquired a reputation for being a spokesman for American interests' (Leifer 1974: 11). The provision of extensive facilities for the Seventh Fleet at the Subic Bay and Clark bases gave credence to the growing impression that the Philippines was essentially an American client.

More significant, however, in terms of American strategic theory was the security of Thailand. Whilst Laos and particularly Cambodia, under its elusive and increasingly absolutist ruler, Prince Sihanouk, pursued a non-aligned stance, Thailand became 'the regional cornerstone' of American policy (Wyatt 1984: 271). In September 1954 John Foster Dulles convened the South-East Asia Collective Defense Treaty in Manila, which was subsequently signed by the United States, Thailand, the Philippines, Pakistan, the United Kingdom, New Zealand and Australia. The treaty protocol extended its scope to include Cambodia, Laos and South Vietnam. In 1955 the signatories established a permanent secretariat in Bangkok and called it the South-East Asian Treaty Organization (SEATO) (Haas 1989: 32–6). Thailand particularly welcomed SEATO because it entailed a formal alliance with the United States. Importantly, 'such an alliance brought considerable material benefits, especially to the military establishment which dominated the government of Thailand' well into the 1980s (Leifer 1974:

43; Wyatt 1984). As the Vietnam War intensified in the course of the 1960s, the western-aligned Southeast Asian states considered SEATO, together with the Five Power Defence Agreement (FPDA) between Singapore, Malaysia, the United Kingdom, Australia and New Zealand, and the Australian, New Zealand, United States defence treaty (ANZUS), central to regional security against communist incursion.

This mixture of overlapping treaties between American containers, decolonizing Britons, forward defensive Australians and New Zealanders and the new states offered at least the prospect of an external guarantee to regional security. The somewhat provisional nature of these arrangements also provided an incentive for finding a common basis for regional understanding. What Suharto termed 'internal resilience' (Acharya 1991: 162) and the shared perception of an external threat constituted the basis of a regional identity premissed on established territorial boundaries and economic growth that formed the background to the one peculiarly indigenous regional arrangement to emerge and survive the Cold War era, ASEAN.

ASEAN's roots lay in a number of abortive regional experiments of the early 1960s like the Thai, Philippine and Malayan attempt to form the Association of Southeast Asia (ASA) in 1961 and *Maphilindo*, an organization embracing Malaysia, the Philippines and Indonesia which disappeared in the *konfrontasi* of 1963–6. With the end of confrontation and the improvement in regional bilateral ties a new institutional expression of regional association both became a distinct possibility and possessed the added attraction of affording 'some recognition of the regional standing of Indonesia' whilst simultaneously containing 'any propensities on its part for a hegemonial position' (Leifer 1974: 95). Although the ostensible purpose for founding ASEAN 'was to promote economic, social and cultural co-operation . . . regional security was the prime preoccupation of its founders' (Leifer 1989: 1, Acharya 1991: 161–3). The promotion of 'regional peace and stability' formed the cornerstone of the 1967 Bangkok declaration and this founding statement represented 'an effort directly related to creating regional order among its members' (Snitwongse 1995: 519). By entering into regional cooperation the governments of Thailand, Malaysia, the Philippines, Indonesia and Singapore sought to promote 'regional internal security' (Leifer 1989: 3). Central to the philosophy of ASEAN were the related understandings of non-interference in the internal arrangements of member states, the solution of domestic stability through economic growth and the avoidance of external adventurism. As Michael Leifer explains, 'the contagion of internal political disorder would be prevented from spreading from an infected state to contaminate the body politic of regional partners, and from providing a point of entry to South-East Asia for competing external powers' (p. 3). National resilience would promote regional resilience and, as the Bangkok declaration maintained, ensure 'stability and security from external interference' (p. 5). Yet convergence of outlook did not initially entail a consensus on how to proceed. ASEAN began as a 'very modest intergovernmental exercise' (p. 30). A rotating annual assembly of foreign ministers assumed responsibility for all policy guidelines for the Association, but meetings convened only 'as required'.

The first Heads of Government meeting convened in Bali in 1976 almost at the end of ASEAN's first decade. This only occurred because the Philippines guaranteed it would not raise its continuing claim to Sabah. The next Heads of Government meeting in Manila convened in 1986 after the deposition of Philippine President Marcos. Both intragovernmental consensus and institutionalization evolved extremely slowly. Only in 1977 did the members agree to establish a permanent secretariat in Jakarta. Moreover, the evolving structure made no provision for collective defence against an external aggressor. Defence cooperation was limited to bilateral arrangements. Indeed, informal ties leading to corporate decision-making without loss of face and facilitated by innumerable rounds of bad golf characterized the apparently *ad hoc* ASEAN way well into the 1990s.

In fact it was anxiety about the prospects for regional security that forced ASEAN to develop into a regional embryo of good citizenship (Leifer in *Asian Wall Street Journal*, 10–11 March 1995). This embryo dates from the time of British withdrawal east of Suez and the ASEAN decision to declare itself in 1971 a Zone of Peace, Freedom and Neutrality (ZOPFAN) free from external interference. This pretentious and misguided description actually reflected regional concern over the changing Cold War environment after the Vietcong's Tet Offensive of 1968, the Nixon doctrine and the subsequent *rapprochement* with China that eventually led to American withdrawal from Vietnam by 1975. The Shanghai communiqué (1972) 'paved the way for the end of the Vietnam war because containing China in Vietnam had lost its *raison d'être*' (Leifer 1993: 58).

Such American strategic reappraisal, however, only served to establish the battle lines for a new round of conflict in Indochina over the putative next domino, Cambodia. The Cambodian conflict evolved after 1975 with the fall of Saigon and the foundation of a one-party communist state in reunited Vietnam. Phnom Penh fell to the Chinese-backed forces of Pol Pot's Khmer Rouge on 17 April 1975 (Chandler 1992: 194). The Democratic Republic of Vietnam soon fell out with the Chinese-supported Democratic Kampuchea and in the course of 1978 signed a treaty of friendship and cooperation with the Soviet Union. On Christmas Day 1978, the Vietnamese forces, confident of Soviet support, defeated the Khmer Rouge and replaced Pol Pot's genocidal regime with Heng Samrin's Vietnamese-sponsored People's Republic of Kampuchea.

By a curious mutation of the containment strategy, the United States and China now came informally to cooperate in Indochina against the Soviet Union and its Vietnamese client. This may be explained by the fact that, after 1975, the Vietnamese extended reconnaissance and naval facilities to the Russians at Da Nang and Cam Ranh Bay, thus threatening the American capability to police the Pacific. Meanwhile, the Chinese failure to teach the Vietnamese a 'limited lesson' in a short border war (1980) initiated an escalation in regional tension and the arrival of the second Cold War in Pacific Asia (Halliday 1989: ch. 8).

It was Vietnam's evolving Indochinese hegemony, together with the prospect of American withdrawal of military support, that concentrated ASEAN's collective mind after 1975. In 1976, after several years of drift, trade differences and concern over the legitimacy of Indonesia's invasion of East Timor in 1975, which violated the spirit of the Bangkok declaration, the five ASEAN Heads of Government agreed to a Treaty of Amity and Cooperation (TAC). The treaty established a code of conduct for regional interstate relations, reaffirmed the integrity of territorial sovereignty of member states, and established this self-denying ordinance as the basis of regional order (Leifer 1989: 69). However, it was the advent of a Chinese-supported, but formally independent, Kampuchea after 1975, interposed between Thailand and Vietnam, which both provided the basis for a brief inter-communist balance of power and increased the international prominence of ASEAN. The ASEAN states, in other words, were the unintended beneficiaries of this balance. Australia and New Zealand observed the 1977 ASEAN Heads of Government meeting in Kuala Lumpur in 1977, whilst Japan's Prime Minister, Takeo Fukuda, attempted to build a 'heart to heart relationship' (Olsen 1970: 200). The Fukuda doctrine envisaged an equal partnership with ASEAN and constituted the basis for evolving political dialogue between Japan and the Association (Hughes 1996: 257). Thus, although in practical terms the Kuala Lumpur meeting in 1977 moved little beyond the largely rhetorical reassertion of ZOPFAN as a joint endeavour to manage regional order, its international status had dramatically improved.

With the Vietnamese invasion of Kampuchea in 1978 and the subsequent question mark over the status of the Vietnam-backed Heng Samrin regime, the international importance of ASEAN increased again, not because of anything it actually did, but because Vietnam's Cambodian adventure had upset both the Nixon doctrine and Beijing's regional hegemony. ASEAN was consequently given face. The Cambodian crisis vividly illustrated both the limited strengths and significant weaknesses of what local scholars and diplomats consider 'the ASEAN way'. The crisis provided a basis for regional solidarity. The fact that Vietnam had violated Cambodia's national sovereignty constituted a clear breach of the public philosophy of ASEAN elaborated in both the Bangkok Declaration and the TAC. The fact that the Vietnamese invasion terminated the genocidal regime of Pol Pot's Khmer Rouge was, of course, irrelevant. An emergency meeting held by the foreign ministers of the ASEAN states in January 1979 formally insisted upon 'respect for national sovereignty' and refused to countenance 'changes of government brought about by military intervention across internationally recognized borders' (Leifer 1989: 101), a non-negotiable position that rather conveniently overlooked Indonesia's violation of East Timor's territorial integrity three years earlier.

This posturing, however, gave ASEAN an identity as a diplomatic community evolving a collegial style and practice in response to a commonly perceived threat to the balance of power in the region, whilst leaving its actual contribution to regional security somewhat vague. This self-apppointed regional security role as a 'diplomatic gamekeeper posting warning signs, but without wielding a shotgun' (p. 119), moreover, achieved some diplomatic success. ASEAN played a significant role in forming and supporting a coalition government of Democratic Kampuchea in exile under the presidency of former Prince Sihanouk and including Khmer Rouge representation in the form of vice president Khieu Samphan (p. 124). Even more astonishingly, given the well-documented genocidal credentials of the Khmer Rouge (Chandler 1992: 179–80), ASEAN succeeded by 1982 in 'securing overwhelming endorsement at the United Nations (UN) for the international representation of Kampuchea by its nominee'. It capitalized upon this by 'insisting on a UN role in a political settlement of the Kampuchean conflict which meant, in effect, a settlement on ASEAN terms' (Leifer 1989: 125). Indeed, the UN agreement brokered in Paris in 1991 that led to the resolution of the Cambodian conflict substantially reflected ASEAN's desire to provide for an interim coalition government led by Prince Sihanouk prior to UN-sponsored multiparty elections in May 1993 and by so doing reinforce its commitment to the territorial integrity of Southeast Asia.

Yet although it had formed an effective international pressure group on regional security, ASEAN's conduct of the Kampuchea crisis graphically illustrated its profound dependence upon external actors and the illusory character of its attempt to erect a *cordon sanitaire* around the region. Paradoxically, by involving itself in a coalition directed at Vietnam's Indochinese hegemony it became an unwitting party to the Sino-Soviet split that originated in the 1960s and was exacerbated by the Soviet incursion into Pacific Asia as Vietnam's ally in 1978. In defining a shared external threat, ASEAN chose alignment with China and the United States in 'a regional expression of their global competition with the USSR' (p. 138), a strategy in fact that contradicted the Association's ostensible vision of the region as a Zone of Peace, Freedom and Neutrality.

Moreover, even within the ASEAN consensus on the restoration of Cambodian boundaries to the *status quo ante* 1975, differences began to emerge over the means to prosecute this end. Thailand, whose 'strategic environment' was most compromised by Vietnamese hegemony, favoured close cooperation with China. The Thai military elite openly abetted and gave some legitimacy to the guerilla warfare waged on the Thai–Cambodian border by the Khmer Rouge. Malaysia, too, favoured closer ties with China. Indeed, as early as May 1974 Malaysia had broken ranks with the rest of ASEAN and established diplomatic links with the PRC, a move imitated by Thailand and the Philippines in the course of 1975. By contrast, Indonesia's relations with China remained frosty after the PRC supported the abortive coup by the PKI in October 1965. Thus while Thailand and, to a lesser extent, Malaysia sought to use China as a means of curtailing Vietnam's ascendancy in Indochina, Indonesia saw the utility of a Vietnamese buffer against a potential Chinese hegemony in Southeast Asia.

In the actual evolution of the Cambodian crisis, these incoherences in the perception of external threat failed to materialize. Nevertheless, the actual resolution of the Cambodian crisis illustrated ASEAN's limited influence over its security environment. The end game to the Cambodian crisis constituted the regional manifestation of the collapse of Soviet global ambition. In July 1986, Gorbachev launched a new phase in Soviet–Chinese and Soviet–Asian relations. In August 1988, Igor Rogachev began discussions in Beijing over border disputes and the Cambodian issue. In December 1988, Gorbachev announced the withdrawal of 'the major portion of Soviet forces in Mongolia' (Kissinger 1994b: 792) and in April 1989 Hanoi agreed 'to withdraw all its forces from Cambodia by the end of that year' (Mackintosh 1993: 24). The rapid retreat of Russia from Pacific Asia after 1988, together with the normalization of relations with China after 1989 and South Korea in 1990, left Vietnam cruelly exposed to the indifference of a United States that refused to recognize it and a China that wished to teach it a 'limited lesson'.

Indeed, it was China, the emerging regional hegemon, that determined the terms for resolving the Cambodian issue. Although Heng Samrin's eventual replacement as Prime Minister and leader of the People's Revolutionary Party of Kampuchea (PRPK), Hun Sen, had begun talks with Sihanouk's coalition in exile in Paris in 1987 and a UN sponsored framework for settling the Cambodian crisis was agreed in 1990, the final resolution required Beijing's support. Thus, Prince Sihanouk reached an accommodation with Hun Sen on the coalition that would rule Cambodia prior to multiparty elections in May 1993 only when Beijing sanctioned the arrangement in June 1991. The actual implementation of the agreement further required Sino–Vietnamese *rapprochement* secured when the upstart

Vietnamese performed an act of tributary deference in October 1991 (*Straits Times*, 10 July 1991; Yahuda 1993: 45). In November 1991, Sihanouk returned to Phnom Penh as the head of a multiparty coalition and officially 'the Indochina problem . . . ceased to exist' (Leifer 1993: 56).

The problem of Indochina was a particular manifestation of the balance of power in Pacific Asia, which since the 1950s had been distorted by the contortions of the Cold War and the doctrine of containment. As the Cold War closed in Asia, 'the pattern of external influences' changed dramatically (Leifer 1993: 66; 1996: 17). This rapid transformation in the international political and economic relations of Pacific Asia after 1991 has drawn attention both to the changing balance of power in Pacific Asia and to the role that ASEAN occupies within it.

By the beginning of the 1990s, ASEAN was well established as a regional actor and enjoyed growing international prestige. In many ways this is somewhat surprising, for despite its thirty-year existence, its Heads of Government have met at only four ASEAN summits and its 'evolution . . . proceeded in the absence of frequent multilateral contacts' (Leifer 1989: 147). ASEAN had, in fact, sustained 'quasi-friendships' which served common security interests (p. 158). It might at best be considered a security community, but had failed to evolve into anything more than this. ASEAN foreign ministers never tired of proclaiming strong bilateral ties, but there was no evidence of any broader multilateral cooperation (Acharya 1991: 173; 1992: 15; Huxley 1996: 220). Nevertheless, ASEAN had survived the Cold War and has gradually widened its membership. The oil-rich Sultanate of Brunei joined the group in 1984, and in 1991 Laos and Cambodia signed the TAC and became official observers at ASEAN meetings. Observer status was extended to Myanmar (Burma) in 1995. More suprisingly, Vietnam, against which ASEAN defined its collective identity between 1978 and 1991, both signed the TAC and became the seventh member in July 1995.

Since 1991, moreover ASEAN has sedulously attempted to broaden both its economic and its security role, thereby engendering regional integration 'free from . . . Great Power interference' (Sopiee 1992: 131). This pursuit of regional autonomy was early manifest in the notion of ZOPFAN and reinforced by successive attempts since 1985 to declare the region a Nuclear Weapons Free Zone. This ASEAN vision moved closer to realization with the decision in 1993 to establish a multilateral forum to discuss matters of regional security. This 'milestone leap', as the *Straits Times* explained in Singlish, was embodied in the Singapore Declaration of January 1993, which sought to 'engage member states in new areas of cooperation in security matters' (*Straits Times*, 29 January 1993; 1 February 1993) and led to the first meeting of the ASEAN Regional Forum (ARF) in

Bangkok in July 1994. Essentially, ARF reflects ASEAN's preferred strategy of gradually building regional consensus through interpersonal ties and avoiding embarrassing loss of face. Regional harmony, ASEAN scholars and diplomats maintain, can be secured through 'preventive diplomacy'. To this end ARF, which includes the ASEAN states and its twelve dialogue partners, including China, Laos, Cambodia, South Korea, Burma, Canada, the United States and Australia, seeks to create a cooperative Pacific Asian diplomatic community.

In effect, then, ASEAN has achieved its regional standing through an ability to manage problems rather than solve them, an approach that has also extended into the realm of economic cooperation with the ASEAN economic ministers, decision in 1991 to establish an ASEAN Free Trade Area (AFTA) within fifteen years. Broadening membership, dialogue partners and economic and security concerns through the multilateral framework of AFTA and ARF all serve a broader managerial purpose. This purpose is to secure multilateral regional ties through consultation, cooperative security, transparency and confidence building measures (Leifer 1996: 27).

However, despite its well-honed interpersonal networks of cooperation, ASEAN has achieved only minimal institutional deepening (Chin 1995: 433). In part this is a product of the collective insecurity which constituted ASEAN's foundation. A common external threat from 1967 to 1991 meant that tensions between member states could be temporarily ignored, whilst promoting economic development would, it was assumed, erode the pertinence of territorial claims.

ASEAN, then, places its faith in the good relationships established over time between regional political representatives and the cultivation of close bilateral ties. The officially agreed philosophy, therefore, requires a studied indifference to the internal affairs of neighbouring countries, and means that ASEAN has had astonishingly little impact on the intramural disputes that troubled its formation prior to 1967. Consequently, a number of unresolved conflicts remain to threaten the credibility of ASEAN as a uniquely cohesive, Asian solution to regional security. The Philippine claim to the Malaysian state of Sabah has remained unresolved since 1965 and continues to trouble relations between Manila and Kuala Lumpur. The Third ASEAN summit meeting in Manila in 1987 was delayed for a decade because President Marcos insisted on introducing the Sabah claim. Moreover, the interpersonal rivalry between Mahathir and Suharto over leadership of NAM, together with Malaysia and Indonesia's competing claims for the West Malaysian islands of Ligitan and Sipidan, periodically cloud relations between Jakarta and Kuala Lumpur. Meanwhile, Singapore's relations with Malaysia, Indonesia and more recently the Philippines have at times been acerbic and anxious rather than harmoniously consensual. Politicians on both sides of the causeway between Johor and Singapore frequently pronounce on matters relating to internal domestic affairs. Such comment achieved a particularly strident level when Israeli Prime Minister Chaim Herzog visited Singapore officially in November 1986. Mahathir condemned the visit, claiming it outraged Islamic sensibilities, and tried to veto it. In 1996, Lee Kuan Yew and subsequently Goh Chok Tong aggravated Malaysian ire by intimating that Singapore might have to consider re-merger if its economy lost competitiveness (*The Economist* 14 September 1996: 23). Again in March 1997, injudicious remarks about the state of Johor by Lee Kuan Yew required an 'unreserved apology' before the increasingly fractious ties between Singapore and Malaysia were restored (*Straits Times*, 29 March 1997). Moreover, despite a dialogue that has so far lasted thirteen years, the two states have failed to resolve Malaysia's claim to the Singapore-administered island of Pedra Branca (Chin 1995: 430). At different times, Singapore's implacable insistence on its stern but fair judicial system has particularly alienated regional sensibilities. The execution of two Indonesian commandos in the aftermath of confrontation in 1968 caused the suspension of bilateral relations between Singapore and Jakarta until 1973. Analogously, the decision to execute the Filipina maid Flor Contemplaçion on somewhat questionable grounds led to the downgrading of diplomatic ties between Singapore and Manila in May 1995.

The inability to resolve regional disputes, coupled with the practice of non-interference in the domestic affairs of neighbouring states, has also fostered festering claims to autonomy by disappointed regional minorities. Thus, in southern Thailand and Mindanao in the Philippines, Islamic separatism has assumed an increasingly fundamentalist hue that poses a growing threat to regional stability, whilst human rights abuses in East Timor continue to undermine Indonesia's international credibility (Human Rights Watch 1994). Analogously, ASEAN's widely advertised promotion of regional stability at the expense of human rights has also favoured a questionable policy of constructive engagement with the State Law and Order Council (SLORC), which arbitrarily rules Myanmar. ASEAN's decision to admit Myanmar to observer status at its meetings prior to the extension of full membership in 1998 exacerbated relations with the European Union and the United States at the ASEAN Regional Forum meeting in Jakarta in July 1996 and caused growing uncertainty within ASEAN over the wisdom of constructive engagement (*The Australian*, 27–28 July 1996).

Moreover, despite the region being a Zone of Peace, Freedom and Neutrality, conflict has simmered not only over land, but also over sea limits between these neighbouring states. Inter-ASEAN disputes over responsibility for the strategically vital Straits of Malacca between Indonesia, Malaysia and Singapore required the intervention of external powers insisting on a 'liberal regime of transit passage', subsequently incorporated in the UN Law of the Sea Convention (1982). Only a powerful external alignment 'served to safeguard Singapore's position making it possible for the island-state to avoid serious public contention with Indonesia and Malaysia' (Leifer 1989: 61; Prins 1993: 27–9). Illustrative of the burgeoning gap between the widely advertised theory of a distinctively harmonious Asian approach to security issues and the actual practice of the ASEAN states, the most recent ASEAN summit in Bangkok (December 1995) found its members endorsing the treaty first proposed by Indonesia in 1985 declaring ASEAN, together with Laos, Cambodia and Myanmar, a nuclear-free zone, whilst at the same time their various governments considered the US provision of a naval regional presence, including nuclear warships, vital to the continuation of regional stability.

The commitment to consensus whilst at the same time failing to address let alone resolve issues of environmental pollution, regional free trade, human rights issues in East Timor and Myanmar and territorial disputes within the region indicates both the fragility of ASEAN and the incoherence of its public philosophy, a public philosophy sustained in the period of the Cold War and its immediate aftermath only by the rigid media controls of ASEAN governments and the tacit support extorted from the western press.

The problematic balance of power in Pacific Asia in the post-Cold War era

With the end of the Cold War a number of unresolved economic and security issues have, thus, emerged to cast growing doubt upon the harmonious development of both ASEAN and Northeast Asia in what many commentators nevertheless continue to view as the 'new Pacific century' (*The Economist*, 5 January 1996). Optimists, nevertheless, draw attention to the achievement of ASEAN in Southeast Asia and the success of the structure of American security treaties, most notably the pivotal US–Japan treaty, in maintaining regional stability in Northeast Asia. This optimism draws sustenance from the progressive resolution of conflict in Pacific Asia since 1975, and sees a confident and prosperous Pacific Asia occupying an increasingly prominent place in the global trading order envisaged by the WTO. In this positive account, economic growth will render territorial disputes otiose. Pan-Asian fora promoting economic interdependence and multilateral security ties like APEC, AFTA and ARF will build regional confidence, as former communist regimes in China, Pacific Russia, Vietnam, Laos and Cambodia experience the benign consequences of foreign direct investment and export-oriented growth. Moreover, the serendipitous conjunction of specifically Asian values of consensus, thrift and harmony, with the globalization of the post-GATT world economy will facilitate both increased inter-Asian trade and cooperation, and, invisible handedly, create a 'borderless world' rendering the territorial and resource-based conflicts of the era of the nation state redundant (Ohmae 1991). This 'synergy' of Asian values with the extended order of the market constitutes the foundation of a new 'Asian Age' (Jin 1995: 273, Naisbitt 1995). This optimistic scenario emphasizes Pacific Asian economic strength and its seemingly effortless capacity both to sustain and to integrate economic growth at a regional and an international level. In this idealistic view, arrangements that promote economic interdependence like ASEAN, AFTA, PECC and APEC form the building blocks of Asia Pacific economic cooperation. In this context, APEC in particular has been invested with great expectations in promoting, through a process of spillover from economic and 'epistemic' interdependence, growing confidence that in turn will establish a new multilateral regional security order (see Kahler 1990: 395; Sato 1990; Aggarwal 1994; Alagappa 1994; Garnaut 1994; Harris 1994; Wolfowitz 1994).

From the perspective of evolving interdependence, arrangements like ASEAN, ARF and AFTA initially facilitate confidence, followed in time by low-level regional cooperation, leading inexorably to broader economic and security cooperation. The emerging sense of a broader regional identity is analogously intimated by a loose non-governmental regional grouping like the Pacific Economic Cooperation Council, which in the course of the 1980s facilitated the Australian-sponsored but Japanese-inspired APEC. Those who favour an emerging global order premised upon globalization, functionalist interdependence and increasingly open markets present APEC as the basis not only of open regionalism, but of a new, rational and essentially liberal multilateral security order.

Those of a more sanguine disposition offer a more pessimistic interpretation of Pacific Asian security. Whilst recognizing the considerable success of conflict resolution in Pacific Asia since 1975 and the abatement of the Soviet threat in both Northeast Asia and Indochina since 1986, commentators of a realist persuasion point to an emerging set of factors not evidently amenable to liberal multilateral solutions. In this context it is important to observe that the Cold War ended more ambiguously in Pacific Asia than in Europe and left in its aftermath both unresolved conflict and a new range of issues likely to trouble the new world order in the Pacific Basin. Thus in Northeast Asia, the continuing difficulty in resolving nuclear weapons on the Korean peninsula, and the unresolved conflict between an increasingly nationalist China, Hong Kong and the rebellious province of Taiwan, continue to vex the regional economic and security order.

Added to continuing and unresolved territorial claims across the region, the intensifying friction over Pacific Asian trade and issues of human rights has precipitated a notable cooling in the attitude of the various branches of the US government to engagement with Pacific Asia generally and the key regional powers of China and Japan in particular. China's burgeoning trade surpluses with the United States and its intransigence on human rights issues since Tiananmen and more recently with the prosecution of dissidents like Wei Jinsheng has occasioned a mounting chorus of American disapproval. Coterminously, growing economic tension between Japan and the United States over market access has deleteriously affected the pivotal US Japanese security treaty. An increasingly isolationist and protectionist US Senate has become frustrated with East Asian economic practice generally, and in particular Japanese free-riding upon US-financed security and open access to the comparatively free American market. Friction between the United States and Japan exacerbated by incidents like the rape of an Okinawan schoolgirl by American servicemen in September 1995 provoked discussion on both sides of the Pacific about the continuing utility of the Cold War structure of alliances that provided the security framework for Pacific Asian growth (Johnson 1996: 23–9). Although President Clinton and Japanese Prime Minister Hashimoto reconfirmed the security treaty in September 1996, its premiss is looking decidedly uncertain. As Chalmers Johnson maintains, throughout the Cold War era the United States tolerated Japanese mercantilism in return for the American base in Okinawa and Japan's passive support for 'American foreign policy in East Asia' (p. 23). Japanese nationalists, in particular, have become increasingly frustrated with this *nichibei* (Japan–US) relationship. More important in terms of regional diplomacy is the Japanese government's evolution of an autonomous Basic Defence policy. In the course of the 1980s, Japan's Ministry for Foreign Affairs and Defence Agency gradually expanded the Fukuda doctrine and actively sponsored multilateral sub-regional security dialogue particularly through its trade and investment links with ASEAN and the ASEAN Regional Forum (Hughes 1996: 231).

Pacific Asian concern over the continued US hegemony in the Pacific has also facilitated both a regional arms race and the worrying emergence of a nationalist and increasingly developed Greater China. The rapid economic development of China has facilitated a new irredentism amongst the PRC leadership that has provisionally replaced an increasingly redundant Maoism. China it seems seeks to reassert its role as the Central Kingdom and in so doing reclaim its historical boundaries at the height of the fifteenth-century Ming dynasty. National assertiveness coupled with irredentist stridency lends a curiously nineteenth-century flavour to Chinese foreign policy (Dibb 1995: 42–3). This irredentism has cast a shadow over China's dealings with Taiwan and Hong Kong. It has also provoked a potentially disturbing clash with Japanese nationalists over the *Diaoyutai*, or Senkaku Islands, as they are known to the Japanese, in the East China Sea. Interestingly, the attempt to secure the potentially oil-rich islands has united Taiwanese and Hong Kong nationalists behind Beijing's claim in a way that gives increasing credibility to the view that Europe's past may be Asia's future.

Burgeoning nationalism has also affected China's relationship with ASEAN through its historical claim, if not to its historical tributary states of *Nanyang*, at least to their territorial waters. In the course of the 1990s China has vigorously reasserted its territorial claim to treat the South China Sea as a Chinese lake, a claim that Taiwan, as the *soi-disant* 'nationalist' government, reinforces. By so doing, Beijing has escalated competing claims to the Spratly (*Nansha*), Paracel and Natuna Islands to 'a defining crisis for the period' (*Asian Wall Street Journal*, 10–11 March 1995). The potentially rich oil and natural gas resources that lie beneath the South China Sea further fuel China's vigorous reassertion of its *amour propre* and ancient rights. The fact that China is now a net importer of oil and that Indonesia's Sumatran oil fields will expire early in the next century, whilst Japan and the NIEs have no natural resources, means that Pacific Asia is running on empty (Calder 1996a: 56). Kent Calder suggests that as Pacific Asia becomes increasingly dependent on oil imports to sustain its high growth, contentious claims to sea lanes and unresolved difficulties over resources in the South and East China seas will exacerbate both regional tension and the recourse to nuclear power for both domestic energy and weapons use (Calder 1996b: ch. 1).

Escalating regional tension over energy and territory has also exposed the frailty in both the ASEAN approach to diplomacy, the liberal functionalism that invests so much faith in multilateral international cooperation and the potentially explosive regional costs of growing American economic and political detachment from Pacific Asia. The Spratly dispute in particular constitutes an ironic consequence of Russo–American détente. The Russian withdrawal from Cam Ranh Bay and its treaty obligations to Vietnam after 1988 made possible the resolution of Indochinese hostility, facilitated the reduction of US forces in Pacific Asia, and inspired a nationalist Philippine senate in 1992 to close the US Clark air and Subic Bay naval facilities which had previously guaranteed the sea lanes of the South China sea. This in turn made possible the projection of the recently strengthened Chinese navy into the South China Sea (Sheng 1995: 27). China's 'creeping assertiveness' manifested itself first in 1988 when a short naval engagement removed the Vietnamese from the Paracel Islands. Subsequently, the Chinese began placing markers throughout the South China Sea and, more threateningly, built new structures on Mischief Reef 135 kilometres from the Philippine island of Palawan. China, foreign minister Qian Qichen observes, is thus merely reimposing an irrrefutable sovereignty to the sea and its mineral resources that dates back over almost two millennia to the Song and Han dynasties, or, as Singapore's Senior Minister explained graphically and perhaps more accurately, 'it is like a big dog going up against a tree, lifting his leg to mark the tree so that smaller dogs will know that a big dog has been there' (*Asian Wall Street Journal*, 12–13 March 1995).

Moreover, although China is a signatory to the United Nations Convention governing the Law of the Sea (UNCLOS) which officially allows all signatory states a twelve nautical mile border and a two hundred mile economic exclusion zone, China does not accept that the UN convention overrides its historical sovereignty (Sheng 1995: 19–20). As a Chinese foreign ministry spokesman explained in March 1995, 'China possesses indisputable sovereignty over the *Nansha* islands [and] has every right to set up markers.' Indeed, Article 2 of its Sea Law (1992) states unequivocally China's claim to Taiwan and the *Nansha* islands and 'reserves the right to use military force to prevent any violation of its sovereign territory' (*Straits Times*, 3 March 1995). This view necessarily conflicts with the interpretation of the Vietnamese, Malaysian, Philippine, Brunei and Indonesian governments, all of whom claim sovereignty over their own territorial waters according to UN convention.

Characteristically, the ASEAN countries, with the increasingly active support of Japan, would prefer to resolve the conflict according to its face-saving, consensual, 'step by step approach' (Wanandi, *Far Eastern Economic Review*, 3 August 1995: 17; Lee 1995: 8). Accordingly, the ASEAN Regional Forum was established in 1994 as an informal group of nineteen Pacific Asian countries, including China, Japan, Russia, the United States, the European Union, South Korea, Australia and New Zealand, as the first step in building confidence, subsequently facilitating 'preventive diplomacy' and leading ultimately to conflict resolution (*Far Eastern Economic Review*, 3 August 1995; Lee 1995; Leifer 1996: 23). ARF has met annually since 1993 and ASEAN has convened a number of 'informal' regional workshops on the South China Sea in order to establish confidence. The intention is twofold: 'to educate an irredentist China in the canons of good regional citizenship and to sustain the active engagement of the US in regional affairs' (Leifer, *Far Eastern Economic Review*, 30 November 1995). ARF, like ASEAN, seeks to create a milieu either where problems do not arise or, if they do, provides a procedure to manage them. ARF seeks to extend the ASEAN way of consultative diplomacy across the Pacific, a consensual strategy that particularly appeals to the Japanese Defence Agency given Japan's investment in maintaining the economic status quo in both Northeast and Southeast Asia (Dibb 1995: 29; Hughes 1996: 235). Yet while this

TABLE 4.1 Defence expenditure, 1995

Country	Defence spending ($USm.)	GDP (%)
Indonesia	1,800	1.40
Japan	45,800	1.02
Malaysia	2,600	4.03
North Korea	5,300	25.50
Philippines	600	1.22
PRC – China	28,400	5.40
ROC – Taiwan	11,400	4.90
Singapore	2,260	3.90
South Korea	13,500	3.90
Thailand	3,500	3.22

Source: Jane's Sentinel http://www.thomson.com/janes/scsreg.html, Newsweek, 21 June 1995

strategy served ASEANs purposes during the the Cold War, it seems unlikely to meet the changed circumstances of the 1990s. ASEAN's low-key diplomatic approach in the Cold War era assumed a balance of power in Pacific Asia, but it is precisely this balance that an irredentist greater China threatens. Indeed, despite a shared sense of 'Asianness', the PLA and the foreign ministry of the PRC seem reluctant to learn the lessons of regional good citizenship when it affects an irrefragable issue of sovereignty. Thus at various informal workshops and at the ARF meetings in Bangkok (1994), Brunei (1995) and Jakarta (1996), the Chinese delegation studiously refused any attempt to 'internationalize' the Spratly issue or address it within a multilateral framework. China, in fact, will deal with competing claims to the Spratly and Natuna Islands on a bilateral basis only, rendering ARF multilateralism redundant. As Shen Guofeng, a Chinese foreign ministry official, informed the ASEAN states in Brunei, 'ARF has no business discussing claims for the Spratlys' (*The Melbourne Age*, 3 July 1995).

Given the limitations of ARF and APEC in building and sustaining a new Pacific Asian community, it is not surprising to find that across Pacific Asia, developing economies have dramatically expanded their armed forces (see tables 4.1 and 4.2). Thus Indonesia bought the remaindered East German navy in 1994, Singapore invests heavily in high-tech weaponry to transform itself into a 'poison shrimp', and Malaysia shops for British Hawk trainers and cut price MiG–29s from Russia. In Northeast Asia Taiwan's defence expenditure has increased to 5 per cent of GDP as the threat from China has intensified, South Korea builds United States F–16C/D fighters under licence, and Japan, currently leading the world in arms expenditure, plans to import United States AWACs 19 P–3 submarine and hunting patrol

TABLE 4.2 Armed forces, 1995

Country	Tanks	Combat aircraft	Combat vessels
Indonesia	305	126	44
Japan	1,160	650	85
Malaysia	26	117	15
North Korea	4,200	820	415
Philippines	41	155	44
PRC – China	10,000	5,913	975
ROC – Taiwan	1,414	513	134
Singapore	350	175	12
South Korea	1,900	509	164
Thailand	763	220	50
USA (regional)	240	273	12

Source: Newsweek, 21 June 1995

aircraft and awaits delivery of 130 FS–X aircraft (*Straits Times*, 11 July: 94). Meanwhile China continues to test its nuclear weaponry, expand its navy with the purchase of four cut-price *Kilo*-class nuclear submarines from Russia, and is in the market for a refurbished nuclear-powered aircraft carrier in order to enhance its blue-water capacity and enforce its claims in the South China Sea (*International Herald Tribune*, 29 November 1995; *Far Eastern Economic Review*, 10 October 1996: 20). Between 1988 and 1992, American companies alone exported more than $14.6 billion worth of weaponry to Pacific Asia (*Guardian Weekly*, 15 March 1992). In the 1990s entrepreneurial Singapore hosted an annual air show, sales from which kept a number of ailing European and American aerospace groups in business as Asian defence procurement reached $130 billion by 1995 (*Straits Times*, 21 February 1994; *Jane's Sentinel* 1995: 1–3) Indeed, as the Pacific Asian economies have boomed, so too has military expenditure. The annual average percentage arms expenditure across Pacific Asia rose between 2 per cent and 6 per cent of GDP between 1984 and 1995. Significantly, it has been the weaker economies whose outlay on defence has stagnated since 1984, like Vietnam and the Philippines, that have been targeted by an irredentist China.

In this context, it is interesting to observe that those Asian statesmen ostensibly most committed to the notion of a new Pacific Asian regional order and a borderless world have by no means abandoned national self-defence in pursuit of their vision. This paradoxical state of affairs that affects both economic interdependence and regional security in Pacific Asia leads us finally to consider the viability of the Asian values widely promulgated by Asian scholars and diplomats as the basis of both economic and political development and regional order in Pacific Asia in the twenty-first century. This is no idle speculation when it is becoming increasingly apparent that the tacit acceptance of American hegemony is no longer sustainable in the emerging new world disorder, whilst there does not appear to be the necessary regional resources to sustain a 'Pax Asiana' (*Sunday Times* (Singapore), 5 February 1995).

Conclusion

As we discussed in chapter 1, Pacific Asian development occurred under ethical influences and historical circumstances vastly different from those that shaped the modernization of Europe and the United States. Moreover, the ruling elites of late developing Pacific Asian states are increasingly reluctant to embrace either the content or even the forms of political practice often bequeathed to them by their former western colonial masters. Indeed, to contemporary pan-Asianists like Mahathir Mohamad, Shintaro Ishihara, Goh Chok Tong or Kishore Mahbubani the promotion of equal rights and civil liberties has in fact brought about western economic stagnation, inner-city chaos and monstrous regiments of single-parent families (Goh, *Straits Times*, 22 August 1994; Mahathir and Ishihara 1995; Mahbubani 1994: 6–7). Their subsequent promotion in Pacific Asia would potentially constitute an insidious ploy to undermine, or, worse, recolonize, the recently established Pacific Asian states (Mahathir, *Straits Times*, 31 August 1993, 7th October 1993). Instead, the new Pacific Asia places its faith in what might be described as essentially post-Confucian characteristics, adumbrated in Malaysia, Indonesia and Thailand by a syncretic overlay of post-Islamic and post -Buddhist values such as 'self-confidence, social cohesion, subordination of the individual, bureaucratic tradition and moralising certitude', which as Roderick Macfarquhar observed in 1980, offered a 'potent combination for development purposes' (*The Economist*, 6 October 1994). Such Asian values, together with the traditional emphasis on family, hierarchy, order, consensus, harmony and balance, constitute the ideological foundation of Asian development. Moreover, the successful translation of traditional high cultural values of Islamic, Buddhist and Islamic provenance into programmes of mass education and bureaucratic practice offers the prospect of a potentially enduring but Asian modernity that effectively synergizes the extended order of the market with the 'bounded governance' structures of classical culture that afford Pacific Asian states a competitive advantage (Gellner 1994: ch. 27; Jin 1995: 276).

Paradoxically, however, this Asian model and the values it promotes secured order and promoted development under the benign aegis of American containment, a policy which was premised upon entirely different ideological preoccupations. Can the Asian values that American hegemony inadvertently facilitated now sustain a new Pacific Asian order? Those infatuated by Pacific Asia's economic development maintain that this is indeed the case and emphasize the utility of a uniquely Asian approach to problem solving. Noordin Sopiee, Director of the Malaysian Institute of Strategic and International Studies (ISIS), maintains that whilst the western approach to negotiation is 'Cartesian' and the 'Cartesian way emphasises legalistic forms, agreements, contracts, institutions and structures', the Asian approach, by contrast, 'relies more on the meeting of minds and hearts, on consensus building, peer pressure, and on unilateral good and proper behaviour' (Sopiee, *Straits Times*, 1 September 1994, 11 September 1994, 1992: ch. 12). Whilst Asia has no supranational institutions comparable to NATO or the European Union, it has, instead, informal 'networks that are inclusive rather than exclusive' (Mahbubani 1995: 107). Asian values and the inclusive networks they build have, it is maintained, made possible the emergence of a new Pacific community (p. 107) that Singapore Minister for the Arts B.G. Yeo terms a 'common cultural area in East Asia' (*Straits Times*, 14 September 1992) that heralds 'a return to the time when Asia was the cradle of civilization' (*Straits Times*, 2 May 1994). East Asia's 'moment in history' has, it would seem, 'come' (Mahbubani 1995: 106).

Yet, curiously, the security of this 'autonomous, integrated, exemplary and purposeful' (p. 106) new actor in world affairs requires the continued naval presence of the otherwise decadent United States. Although the more consistent pan-Asian nationalists like Mahathir and Ishihara see little need for a continuing American security presence, more pragmatic Asian politicians, in both Northeast and Southeast Asia, wish to preserve American bases in Japan and South Korea and even restore them to the Philippines. Thus, B.G. Yeo maintains the United States 'must remain engaged in the region in both economic and military terms in order to complete a new triangular balance of power in East Asia that is vital for the continued prosperity and stability of the region' (*Straits Times*, 14 September 1992).

However, the new and as yet ill-defined triangular balance between Japan, China and the United States requires that America not only practise the Asian approach to international relations but also 'absorb the best of Asian civilization' both to reform its moral decline and build a Pacific 'two way street' (Mahbubani 1995: 107). As American scholars like Don Emmerson observe, Asian values seems to assume that 'economic cooperation begins at home while military security involves including powers from abroad including partners such as the United States who can, in the long run, balance

China and Japan' (*Straits Times*, 2 May 1994; Emmerson 1995). Indeed, growing uncertainty over the stability of the US–Japanese security treaty, Chinese expansionism and the evident ineffectiveness of flexible consensus in solving intractable trade and territorial disputes through multilateral arrangements like ASEAN, AFTA and APEC has prompted the Philippines to renegotiate its security links with America and Indonesia to sign a security pact with 'caucasian' Australia in December 1995, much to the consternation of both pan-Asian nationalists like Mahathir and western democrats concerned at Australian recognition of Indonesia's occupation of East Timor (*The Economist*, 5 January 1996).

Paradoxically, it would appear that the United States, which entered Pacific Asia after 1945 to contain communism and nurture freedom, self determination and civil liberties, must, in order to remain in Asia, learn the Asian lessons of balance, harmony and flexible consensus. Meanwhile, these same values, so useful in ordering the internal arrangements of hierarchical, growth-driven, enterprise associations, have proved singularly ineffectual in resolving regional security, or promoting market opening or an acceptable world trade order. Indeed, at the end of the Cold War, Pacific Asia has no agreed balance of power or any overarching collective security arrangement. Swept away by euphoria over economic growth, Pacific Asian leaders and a variety of western commentators have promulgated the view that the major strategic problems of international relations have been solved and that economic interdependence will guarantee peace. Recent events in the Spratlys, the Taiwan Straits, the Senkaku Islands and North Korea suggest such optimism is unsustainable. Ironically, if a multilateral security community does emerge from the brave new world disorder, it would be, much to the consternation of Pacific Asian scholar-bureaucrats, an anarchical one.

Conclusion

In one of many interviews given to Singapore's state-licensed *Straits Times*, Singapore's Senior Minister and sole political theorist of note, Lee Kuan Yew, observed that within twenty years East Asia would 'coin its own political vocabulary' (*Straits Times*, 6 February 1995). The argument of this book is that East Asia already has developed a distinctive, although not necessarily coherent, political vocabulary which reflects the non-liberal political culture that informs governmental practice, shapes economic development and affects the internal and external relations of the various Pacific Asian states. As we have shown in chapter 1, traditional high cultural understandings that in the nineteenth and early twentieth century seemed to have failed the test of modernization have been revised and revived by modernizing elites both to legitimate rule, sustain social cohesion and mobilize the population towards collectively achievable social and economic targets. High cultural values suitably syncretized with the requirements of modernization offer a plausible alternative developmental ethic to the freedom, pluralism and spontaneously generated order of Anglo–American liberalism. As Ernest Gellner has observed, 'neither the lack of political and intellectual liberty . . . nor the perpetuation of a Confucian family spirit seems bound to inhibit economic performance' (Gellner 1994: 199). Indeed, much to the consternation of western liberals and social democrats, the case of the HPAEs gives empirical weight to Gellner's contention that 'the deadly angel who spells death to economic efficiency is not always at the service of liberty' (p. 199).

The contemporary Asian polities of Pacific Asia, thus, emerged under a significantly different ethic from that of the Anglo–American world, in contingently different historical circumstances with an ambivalently anti-individualist approach to the market. These factors in turn shaped a distinctively Pacific Asian understanding of authority and political obligation, political identity and civil society and economic and international statecraft.

Let us review what this approach entails for the state, civil society, the market and international relations.

The liberal democratic view of the state that we discussed in chapter 1 assumes that governments respect the equal rights of citizens to choose, enact and revise their conception of the good life in a world of incommensurable values. By contrast, modernized Pacific Asian political theory, drawing upon a revised tradition, maintains that government may justifiably intervene in most aspects of socio-economic life in order to promote an officially predetermined conception of the good. In contemporary Pacific Asia this good is presented in technocratic, developmentalist terms. The state constitutes an enterprise to be rationally managed towards bureaucratically determined goals. For ideological purposes, the state technocracy often associates this developmental good with a yet to be realized religious and national mission. In order to steer the people towards this collective unity, the post-colonial technocratic elite establishes economic and social outcomes and draws selectively upon traditional Asian values to promote socially cohesive development.

This developmental mission informs the emerging Pacific Asian view of democracy. Regular elections offer an important source of feedback on elite initiatives. In fact the strength of the relatively autonomous state manifests itself most clearly when the election represents a test of the ruled rather than the rulers. The ruled pass the test when they confirm the rational rule of the dominant technocratically minded party elite.

The absence in Pacific Asia of any clear distinction between political office and the person of the office holder further facilitates an understanding of technocratic guidance. Without such a distinction, it is difficult to establish either the concept of a loyal opposition or the notion of checks and balances upon political power so central to constitutional rule in western democracies. In the Pacific Asian understanding of constitutionalism, law represents not a check on power, but rather an extension of administrative technique. Consequently, Pacific Asian rule is inherently apolitical. In place of a constitutional understanding that articulates an evolving association in terms of law, in Pacific Asia we find legalistically prescribed performances with little space for critical interrogation of what these performances might entail. It is the state elite, moreover, who possess the necessary skill to adjust mutable laws and constitutions to the demands of the latest growth plan.

Political communication in this view is a monologue facilitated by the state control of media and state licensing of interest groups rather than a dialogue between autonomous social actors. In Pacific Asia, strong state technocracies develop policy autonomously and without reference, except informally, to a public or civil realm (Scalapino 1996: 127). These ruling apolitical technocracies, moreover, seek to manage the emerging social, economic, ethnic and religious groups spawned by urbanization and economic growth and channel their activities along state-determined lines. Yet, such omnicompetent managerialism only rarely causes tension between the ruling elite and the new, educated middle-class groups produced by thirty years of economic growth and urbanization. Social and political associations, media and non-governmental organizations that evolve under technocratic guidance remain effectively in its thrall. Constant exposure to state education, Asian values and programmes of collective mobilization inures these associations to narrow specialism and habits of group loyalty inimical to autonomous activity and facilitates an essentially ersatz civil society that craves the management that techno-paternalism affords.

Consequently, political change in Pacific Asia neither constitutes an authoritarian response to pressure from civil society nor reflects an emerging demand for the polymorphous delights of an independent media and political pluralism. Rather, change represents the anxious and often proactive attempt by a virtuous rulership to maintain harmony, balance and economic growth in a world that always threatens to dissolve into uncertainty. An Asian understanding of power as the capacity to syncretize difference and project an ethical understanding has facilitated this managerial project. Traditionally the power of the ruler rested in his capacity to absorb difference and maintain consensus. In this context, the military autocratic style popular in Taiwan, South Korea, Indonesia and Thailand in the early phase of modernization disturbingly intimated the actual or potential threat of violence. The potential recourse to a military solution signifies not only a lack of sophistication but also an absence of consensus and moral authority. Consequently, in the course of the 1980s East and Southeast Asian states devised a series of managerial strategies of a more democratic character not only to maintain the authority of the state, but also to assuage the anxieties of emerging middle-class groups and thus render them both more visible and more politically pliable. In this context, Asian constitutions represent the mutable by-products that eventuate from the search for new 'men of prowess' modified to the current requirements of an apolitical technocracy.

The economic strategies selected by the elite technocracies and the contingent international circumstances that made such strategies plausible further facilitated the successful translation of an Asian ethic into a modern political practice. This was particularly the case with the strong state technocracies in South Korea and Taiwan and the efficient import-replacing city states of Singapore and Hong Kong that effectively exploited the embedded liberalism of the postwar international trading order. The Northeast Asian states in particular effectively protected domestic manufacturing markets and groomed industrial winners in order to capture market share in both America and Europe. As Dengjian Jin has argued, these polities synthesized a particularist concern with personal ties and connections of an Asian provenance with an international system of impersonal and generalized rules (Jin 1995: 264). The success of South Korea, Taiwan and Singapore, in particular, resided in a technocratic capacity to link an Asian 'connectual structure' to the international market through an export-oriented development strategy. The technocratic focus on exports avoided destructive, zero sum domestic competition, whilst the system of generalized rules in international markets provided externally validated criteria that pushed domestic firms 'to improve their products and processes' (p. 273). In Jin's view this synergy of Asian bounded governance with export-led growth facilitated by the character of the international trade order constitutes in economic terms a comparative cultural advantage, reflected in the high rates of growth, high savings rates and education-hungry populations of South Korea, Taiwan and Singapore.

By contrast, the weaker technocratic management of Thailand, Malaysia and Indonesia rendered them less successful in picking industrial winners and generating the switch from resource dependence and agriculture to higher value-added manufacturing production. The Southeast Asian economies have instead been notable since the 1980s for their relatively deregulated financial markets and openness to FDI. This strategy, coinciding with the revaluation of the yen and the other Northeast Asian currencies after 1985, fortuitously opened these later developing HPAEs to Japanese, Hong Kong, Singaporean, Taiwanese and South Korean investment on an unprecedented scale. Northeast Asian conglomerates in particular use Thailand, Malaysia and Indonesia as low-cost manufacturing bases for low-level technology and subsequent export that requires a cheap, pliable and low skilled workforce. Growth in these economies, low-level manufacturing apart, has occurred in areas like financial services, retail and tourism, which gives Southeast Asian economic development a curiously ersatz and technologyless flavour.

A notable consequence of export-led growth has not only occasioned two distinctive types of Pacific Asian development, a Northeast and a Southeast Asian model, it has also left these economies exposed to changes in the external trading and international environment. As we saw in chapter 2, a distinctive pattern of trade between Japan, the Northeast Asian economies, the ASEAN economies and the large and relatively open US market largely accounts for the impressive export-induced growth of Pacific Asia. A characteristic Pacific Asian trading pattern established itself in the course of the 1980s whereby Japan ran trade surpluses with the United States, South Korea, Taiwan and the Southeast Asian economies, whilst the Asian NIEs and ASEAN economies maintained trade surpluses with the United States and deficits with Japan.

However, the growing frustration of western manufacturers with the continuing impermeability of the Japanese market, the tariff and non-tariff mechanisms restricting access to the domestic markets of the HPAEs and the consequent trade imbalances established in favour of the Pacific Asian economies vis-à-vis the United States and Western Europe has occasioned demands to modify the international trading order. Yet, the attempts to reform the international trade regime in Pacific Asia have assumed a contradictory character. On the one hand, we have seen the attempt to promote liberalization through international agencies like the World Trade Organization and enhanced economic cooperation through APEC. The problem with these voluntarist arrangements is that, whilst strong on the rhetoric of cooperation and globalization, they have so far failed to generate a meaningful rule-based approach to Pacific Asian trade with sanctions for non-compliance. This failure has prompted the US government in particular to doubt the merits of multilateral arrangements and resort instead to a mixture of sanctions through Section 301 of the US Trade Act and managed trade designed to allocate US manufacturers a share in Japanese and HPAE domestic markets. Such a strategy, as Ruggie observes, ultimately undermines the international trade regime largely established by the Americans after 1945 (Ruggie 1993: 37).

Changes in the international trading environment deleterious to the continued viability of an export-led growth strategy also reflect changes in the international political order as it affects the Asia Pacific. During the Cold War, to combat the appeal of communism in Asia and to reduce the temptation of neutralism on the part of the Pacific Asian states within the American sphere of influence, the United States tolerated the rigging of domestic markets. As the communist threat receded in the course of the 1980s, an emergent irredentist China, combined with Pacific Asian mercantilism, growing resentment at western demands for market access and criticism of illiberal political practice, has both complicated and confused international relations in the Asia Pacific. Anxiously evolving in the interstices of the Cold War, both Japan and the HPAEs grew accustomed to the security umbrella afforded by the United States along the Pacific littoral after 1950. The collapse of the Russian protectorate over Vietnam in the course of the 1980s inspired a US reassessment of its regional security role and a re-evaluation in both Japan and the HPAEs of the nature of their security ties to Washington. An emerging sentiment of pan-Asian nationalism that either, like Mahathir and Ishihara, resented an American hegemony or, like other Asian nationalist leaders, required that presence on Asian terms further complicated the US security role in Pacific Asia.

Closure of the American bases in the Philippines and pressure on the continued American presence in Okinawa have cast doubt over the continued American commitment to its Cold War allies and uncertainty over the US–Japanese security treaty that stabilized the Northeast Pacific after

1950. Concern about US commitment has led Japan and the Southeast Asian states to develop closer ties through the notably Asian diplomatic machinery of the ASEAN Regional Forum. ASEAN had served as a useful Cold War proxy for promoting American and, to a lesser extent, Chinese policy to contain Soviet ambitions in Southeast Asia in the period after 1975.

However, the recently expanded ASEAN forum, with its strategy of engendering cooperation and consensus through consultative mechanisms, like its economic equivalent APEC, seems an oddly impotent arrangement in the post-Cold War era. In particular it has demonstrated a notable inability to restrict a China that is changing shape as that irredentist regional power seeks to reassert ancient territorial claims and a traditional hegemony over Pacific Asia. Greater Chinese nationalism, motivated by a historical sense of grievance over unequal nineteenth-century treaties and animated after 1997 by the return of Hong Kong, has demonstrated a notable disregard for international conventions in asserting claims to the potential mineral-rich seas surrounding the Senkaku and Spratly Islands in the East and South China Seas.

This concatenation of trade and what Henry Kissinger would term 'geopolitical' considerations presents obvious problems for the continued development of the HPAEs. The nature of their growth strategies and their historical reliance upon an American security umbrella render them peculiarly vulnerable to a combination of American economic protectionism and military retreat from Pacific Asia. At the same time, specifically Asian mechanisms like the ASEAN Regional Forum or the EAEC seem ill suited for dealing with issues of economic or territorial concern in the New World Order as it affects Pacific Asia. In other words, the external circumstances that facilitated the rapid growth and development of the Pacific Asian states and enabled them to evolve practices that rendered them economically competitive and internally cohesive have altered dramatically in the 1990s. It is doubtful whether the modified traditional practices syncretized with the demands of the international market that proved so successful in the Cold War era of the American protectorate from 1945 to 1990 will continue to succeed in the more uncertain Pacific Asian context of the new century.

Bibliography

Abeysinghe, T., Ng, H.G. and Tan, L.Y. 1994: E.S.U. Forecasts of the Singapore Economy. In A. Chin and N.K. Jin (eds), *Outlook for the Singapore Economy*. Singapore: Trans Global Publishing.

Acharya, A. 1991: The Association of South East Asian Nations: 'Security Community' or 'Defence Community'? *Pacific Affairs* 64, 2, 159–77.

Acharya, A. 1992: Regional Military–Security Cooperation in the Third World: A Conceptual Analysis of the Relevance and Limitations of ASEAN (Association of South East Asian Nations). *Journal of Peace Research* 29, 7–21.

Aggarwal, V. 1994: Comparing Regional Cooperation Efforts in the Asia-Pacific and North America. In A. Mack and J. Ravenhill (eds), *Pacific Cooperation: Building Economic and Security Regimes in the Asia-Pacific Region*. St Leonards: Allen and Unwin.

Ahn, Chung-Si 1993: Democratization and Political Reform in South Korea: Development, Culture and Institutional Change. *Asian Journal of Political Science*, 1, 2, 93–110.

Akamatsu, K. 1962: Historical Pattern of Economic Growth in Developing Countries. *Developing Economies* 2, March/August, 3–25.

Akamatsu, K. 1965: *Sekai Keizairon* (World Economics). Tokyo: Kunimoto Shobu.

Alagappa, M. 1994: Regionalism and Security: A Conceptual Investigation. In A. Mack and J. Ravenhill (eds), *Pacific Cooperation: Building Economic and Security Regimes in the Asia-Pacific Region*. St Leonards: Allen and Unwin.

Ali, A. 1994: Japanese Manufacturing Investment in Malaysia. In K.S. Jomo (ed.), *Japan and Malaysian Development in the Shadow of the Rising Sun*. London: Routledge.

Almond, G. and Verba, S. 1963: *The Civic Culture*. Princeton: Princeton University Press.

Amsden, A. 1989: *Asia's Next Giant: South Korea and Late Industrialization*. Oxford: Oxford University Press.

Anatory, M. and Jomo, K.S. 1994: Japanese Multinational Intra-Firm Trade Transfer Pricing Practices in Malaysia. In K.S. Jomo (ed.), *Japan and Malaysian Development in the Shadow of the Rising Sun*. London: Routledge.

Anazawa, M. 1994: Japanese Manufacturing Investment in Malaysia. In K.S. Jomo (ed.), *Japan and Malaysian Development in the Shadow of the Rising Sun*. London: Routledge.

Anderson, B. 1990: *Language and Power: Exploring Political Cultures in Indonesia*. Ithaca: Cornell University Press.

Anderson, B. and McVey, R. 1971: *A Preliminary Analysis of the October 1st 1965 Coup in Indonesia*. Ithaca: Modern Indonesia Project, Cornell University Press.

Andrews, J.C. 1991: *The Asian Challenge*. Hong Kong: Longman.

Arendt, H. 1971: *On Revolution*. London: Penguin.

Asher, M. 1993: Planning for the Future: The Welfare System in a New Phase of Development. In G. Rodan (ed.), *Singapore Changes Guard*. Melbourne: Longman.

Asher, M. 1994: *Social Security in Malaysia and Singapore: Practices, Issues and Reform Directions*. Kuala Lumpur: Institute of Strategic and International Studies.

Asia Watch Report 1989: *Silencing All Critics: Human Rights Violations in Singapore*. Asia Watch: New York.

Aslam, M. and Piei, M.H. 1994: Malaysia–Japan: Unequal Trade Partners. In K.S. Jomo (ed.), *Japan and Malaysian Development in the Shadow of the Rising Sun*. London: Routledge.

Back, Jung Gook 1992: Elections as Transformation: Explaining the Reorganization of a Ruling Coalition. In D.C. Shin, M.H. Zoh and M. Chey (eds), *Korea in the Global Wave of Democratization*, Seoul: National University Press.

Baik, Bong 1973: *Kim Il Sung Biography*, vol. III. Beirut: Dar Al-Talia.

Baum, J. 1994: The Money Machine. *Far Eastern Economic Review*, 11 August, 62–6.

Beetham, D. 1993: Liberal Democracy and the Limits of Democratization. In D. Held (ed.), *Prospects for Democracy: North, South, East, West*. Cambridge: Polity Press.

Berlin, I. 1975: *Four Essays on Liberty*. Oxford: Oxford University Press.

Binder, L., Coleman, J., LaPalombara, J., Pye, L., Verba, S. and Weiner, M. 1971: *Crises and Sequences in Political Development*. Princeton: Princeton University Press.

Bosco, J. 1994a: Factions Versus Ideology: Mobilization Strategies in Taiwan's elections. *China Quarterly*, 13, 7, 28–61.

Bosco, J. 1994b: Taiwan Factions: *Guanxi*, Patronage and the State in Local Politics. In M.A. Rubinstein (ed.), *The Other Taiwan: 1945 to the Present*. Armonk, NJ: M.E. Sharpe Inc.

Bowie, A. 1994: The Dynamics of Business–Government Relations in Industrialising Malaysia. In A. Macintyre (ed.), *Business and Government in Industrialising Asia*. St Leonards: Allen and Unwin.

Bresnan, J. 1993: *Managing Indonesia: The Modern Political Economy*. New York: Columbia University Press.

Brown, D. 1994: *The State and Ethnic Politics in Southeast Asia*. London: Routledge.

Buchanan, J. 1975: *The Limits of Liberty Between Anarchy and Leviathan*. Chicago: University of Chicago Press.

Budiman, A. 1994: From Lower to Middle Class: Political Activities Before and After 1988. In D. Bourchier and J. Legge (eds), *Democracy in Indonesia: 1950s and 1990s*. Clayton: Monash University Press.

Calder, K.E. 1993: *Strategic Capitalism: Private Business and Public Purpose in Japanese Industrial Finance*. Princeton: Princeton University Press.

Calder, K.E. 1996a: Asia's Empty Tank. *Foreign Affairs*, 75, 6, 53–70.

Calder, K.E. 1996b: *Asia's Deadly Triangle: How Arms, Energy and Growth Threaten to Destabilise Asia Pacific*. London: Nicholas Brealy.

Campos, J. 1993: Leadership and the Principle of Shared Growth: Insights into the Asian Miracle. *Asian Journal of Political Science*, 1, 2, 1–39.

Cardoso, F.H. and Faletto, E. 1979: *Dependency and Development in Latin America*. Berkeley: University of California Press.

Chalmers, I. 1991: Indonesia 1990: Democratization and Social Forces. In S. Siddique and C.Y. Ng (eds), *Southeast Asian Affairs 1991*. Singapore: ISEAS.

Chan, Heng Chee 1989: The PAP and the Structuring of the Political System. In K. Singh and P. Wheatley (eds), *The Management of Success: The Moulding of Modern Singapore*. Singapore: Institute of Southeast Asian Studies.

Chan, Heng Chee 1991: Political Developments 1965–1979. In E. Chew and E. Lee (eds), *A History of Singapore*. Oxford: Oxford University Press.

Chan, Heng Chee 1993: Democracy, Evolution and Implementation. In R. Bartley, H.C. Chan, S. Huntington and S. Ogata (eds), *Democracy and Capitalism: Asian and American Perspectives*. Singapore: Institute of Southeast Asian Studies.

Chan, Wing Tsit 1973: *A Source Book in Chinese Philosophy*. Princeton: Princeton University Press.

Chandler, D. 1992: *Brother Number One: A Political Biography of Pol Pot*. Boulder, CO: Westview Press.

Chang, D.W. 1994: Taiwan's Unification with Mainland China: Problems and Prospects. *Asian Journal of Political Science*, 2, 1, 149–68.

Chao, L. and Myers, R. 1994: The First Chinese Democracy: Political Development of the Republic of China on Taiwan, 1986–1994. *Asian Survey*, xxxiv, 3, 213–30.

Cheah, Hock Beng 1993: Responding to Global Challenges: The Changing Nature of Singapore's Incorporation into the International Economy. In G. Rodan (ed.), *Singapore Changes Guard: Social, Political and Economic Directions in the 1990s*. St Leonards: Allen and Unwin.

Chee, Soon Juan, 1994: *Dare to Change: An Alternative Vision for Singapore*. Singapore: The Singapore Democratic Party.

Cheng, Chung-ying 1991: *New Dimensions of Confucian and Neo-Confucian Philosophy*. New York: State University of New York Press.

Cheng, R.L. 1994: Language Unification in Taiwan Present and Future. In M.A. Rubinstein (ed.), *The Other Taiwan: 1945 to the Present*. Armonk, NJ: M.E. Sharpe Inc.

Cheng, Tung Jen 1989: Democratising the Quasi-Leninist Regime in Taiwan. *World Politics*, 41, 4, 471–99.

Cheng, T.Y. 1994: The R.O.C.'s Changing Role in the Asia-Pacific Region. In G. Klintworth (ed.), *Taiwan in the Asia-Pacific in the 1990s*. St Leonards: Allen and Unwin.

Cheong, A. 1994: 'Property Sector' Performance and Challenges Ahead. In A. Chin and N.K. Jin (eds), *Outlook for the Singapore Economy*. Singapore: Trans Global Publishing.

Chew, M. 1995: Human Rights in Singapore: Perceptions and Problems. *Asian Survey* xxxiv, 11, 933–49.

Chey, M. and Shin, D.C. 1992: The Experience of Democratization and Quality of Life among the Korean Mass Public. In D.C. Shin, M.-H. Zoh and M. Chey (eds), *Korea in the Global Wave of Democratization*. Seoul: National University Press.

Chiang Kai-shek 1943: *The Voice of China: Speeches of Generalissimo and Madame Chiang Kai-shek between December 7, 1941 and October 10, 1943*. London: Hutchinson.

Chin, Kin Wah 1995: ASEAN Consolidation and Institutional Change. *Pacific Review* 8, 3, 424–39.

Chowdhury, A. and Islam, I. 1993: *The Newly Industrialised Economies of East Asia*. London: Routledge.

Chu, Hsi (Zhu, Xi) and Lu, Tsu Ch'un 1967: *Reflections on Things Close at Hand*. New York: Columbia University Press.

Chu, J.J. 1996: Taiwan: A Fragmented Middle Class in the Making. In R. Robison and D.S.G. Goodman (eds), *The New Rich in Asia: Mobile Phones, McDonald's and Middle Class Revolution*. London: Routledge.

Chu, Yun-han 1992: *Crafting Democracy in Taiwan*. Taipei: Institute for National Policy Research.

Chu, Yun-han 1994: Social Protests and Political Democratization in Taiwan. In M.A. Rubinstein (ed.), *The Other Taiwan*. Armonk, NJ: M.G. Sharpe Inc.

Chua, Beng Huat 1995: *Communitarian Ideology and Democracy in Contemporary Singapore*. London: Routledge.

Clad, J. 1991: *Behind the Myth: Business Money and Power in Southeast Asia*. London: Grafton.

Clark, C. 1989: *Taiwan's Development: Implications for Contesting Political Paradigms*. Westport, CT: Greenwood Press.

Clark, D. (ed.) 1993: *Korea Briefing: Festival of Korea*. Boulder, CO: Westview Press.

Coedes, G. 1971: *The Indianized States of Southeast Asia*. Hawaii: University Press of Hawaii.

Cook, N. 1990: Thai Identity in the Astrological Tradition. In C.J. Reynolds (ed.), *National Identity and its Defenders: Thailand 1939–1989*. Clayton: Monash University Press.

Copper, J. 1994: *Taiwan: Nation State or Province?* Boulder, CO: Westview Press.

Cotton, J. 1991: On the Identity of Confucianism: Theory and Practice. *Political Theory Newsletter* 3, 13–26.

Cotton, J. 1993: The Two Koreas and Rapprochement: Foundations for Progress? In J. Cotton (ed.), *Korea under Roh Tae Woo*. St Leonards: Allen and Unwin.

Cotton, J. and Kim H.A. van Leest 1992: Korea: Dilemmas for the Golf Republic. *Pacific Review* 5, 4, 360–8.

Crick, B. 1971: *Essays in Political Theory*. London: Penguin.

Crouch, H. 1993: Authoritarian Trends, the UMNO Split and the Limits to State Power. In J.S. Kahn and F.K.W. Loh (eds), *Fragmented Vision: Culture and Politics in Contemporary Malaysia*. St Leonards: Allen and Unwin.

Cumings, B. 1987: The Origins and Development of the Northeast Asian Political Economy: Industrial Sectors, Product Cycles, and Political Consequences. In F.C. Deyo (ed.), *The Political Economy of the New Asian Industrialism*. Ithaca: Cornell University Press.

Cumings, B. 1989: *The Origins of the Korean War: Vol. 1, Liberation and the Emergence of Separate Regimes, 1945–1947; Vol. 2, The Roaring of the Cataract, 1947–1950*. Princeton: Princeton University Press.

Cumings, B. 1994: Japan and the Asian Periphery. In M.P. Leffler and D.S. Painter (eds), *The Origins of the Cold War: An International History*. London: Routledge.

Dahl, R. 1971: *Polyarchy: Participation and Opposition*. New Haven: Yale University Press.

Dahl, R. 1989: *Democracy and Its Critics*. New Haven: Yale University Press.

de Bary, T. 1981: *Neo-Confucian Orthodoxy and the Learning of Mind-and-Heart*. New York: Columbia University Press.

Denker, M.S. 1994: The Evolution of Japanese Investment in Malaysia. In K.S. Jomo (ed.), *Japan and Malaysian Development in the Shadow of the Rising Sun*. London: Routledge.

Deyo, F.C. 1987: State and Labor: Modes of Political Exclusion in East Asian Development.

Dibb, P. 1995: *Towards a New Balance of Power in Asia*. Adelphi Paper 295, Oxford: Oxford University Press.

Doner, R.F. 1991: Approaches to the Politics of Economic Growth in Southeast Asia. *Journal of Asian Studies* 50, 4, 818–49.

Dong, W.M. 1993: The Democratisation of South Korea: What Role Does the Middle Class Play? In J. Cotton (ed.), *South Korea under Roh Tae Woo*. St Leonards: Allen and Unwin.

Dunn, J. 1991: *Western Political Theory in the Face of the Future*. Cambridge: Canto.

Dunn, J.A. 1989: The Asian Auto Imbroglio: Patterns of Trade Policy and Business Strategy. In S. Haggard and Chung-in Moon (eds), *Pacific Dynamics: The International Politics of Industrial Change*. Boulder, CO: Westview Press.

Duyvendak J.L. 1928: *The Book of Lord Shang*. London: Probstain.

Eberstadt, N. 1991: Some Comments on Democracy and Development in East Asia. In T.W. Robinson (ed.), *Democracy and Development in East Asia: Taiwan, South Korea and the Philippines*. Washington: AEI Press.

Eden, L. and Molot, M.A. 1993: Fortress or Free Market NAFTA and Its Implications for the Pacific Rim. In R. Higgott, R. Leaver and J. Ravenhill (eds), *Pacific Economic Relations in the 1990s: Cooperation or Conflict?* St Leonards: Allen and Unwin.

Elman, B. 1987: Confucianism and Modernization: A Reevaluation. In J.P.L. Jiang (ed.), *Confucianism and Modernization: A Symposium*. Taipei: Freedom Council.

Elvin, M. 1986: The Double Disavowal: Attitudes of Radical Thinkers to the Chinese Tradition. In S.Y. Ming (ed.), *China and Europe in the Twentieth Century*. Chengchu: Chengchu University Press.

Emmerson, D.K. 1995: Region and Recalcitrance: Rethinking Democracy in Southeast Asia. *Pacific Review*, 8, 2, 223–48.

Emmerson, D.K. and Simon, S.W. 1993: *Regional Issues in Southeast Asian Security: Scenarios and Regimes*. Seattle: National Bureau of Asian Research.

England, J. and Rear, J. 1980: *Industrial Relations and Law in Hong Kong*. Hong Kong: Oxford University Press.

Etzioni, A. 1994: *The Spirit of Community: Rights, Responsibilities and the Communitarian Agenda*. Washington: George Washington University Press.

Fallows, J. 1994: *Looking at the Sun: The Rise of the New East Asian Economic and Political System*. New York: Pantheon.

Fifield, R. 1979: *National and Regional Interests in ASEAN: Competition and Cooperation in Regional Politics*. Occasional Paper 57, Singapore: Institute of South East Asian Studies.

Fingarette, H. 1972: *Confucius: The Secular and the Sacred*. New York: Harper.

Fishburn, T. (ed.) 1994: *The World in 1995*. London: *The Economist*.

Foucault, M. 1984: On the Genealogy of Ethics: An Overview of Work in Progress. In P. Rabinow (ed.), *The Foucault Reader*. London: Penguin.

Frank, B., Markowitz, J., McKay, R. and Roth, K. 1991: The Decline of the Rule of Law in Malaysia and Singapore Parts I and II. Report of the Committee on International Human Rights of the Association of the Bar of New York. *The Record*, 45, 8 and 46, 1, 5–90.

Fukuda, S. 1995: *With Sweat and Abacus: Economic Roles of Southeast Asian Chinese on the Eve of World War II* (ed. G. Hicks). Singapore: Select Books.

Fukuyama, F. 1992: *The End of History and the Last Man*. London: Hamish Hamilton.

Fukuyama, F. 1995a: Democracy's Future: The Primacy of Culture. *Journal of Democracy* 6, 1, 3–15.

Fukuyama, F. 1995b: Confucianism and Democracy. *Journal of Democracy* 6, 2, 20–34.

Garnaut, R. 1994: Options for Asia-Pacific Trade Liberalization (A Pacific Free Trade Area?). In S.Y. Chia (ed.), *APEC: Challenges and Opportunities*. Singapore: Institute of Southeast Asian Studies.

Geertz, C. 1960: *The Religion of Java*. Glencoe, IL: Free Press.

Geertz, C. 1993: *The Interpretation of Cultures: Selected Essays*. London: Fontana.

Gellner, E. 1987: *Culture, Identity and Politics*. Cambridge: Cambridge University Press.

Gellner, E. 1988: *Plough, Sword and Book: The Structure of Human History*. London: Collins.

Gellner, E. 1994: *Conditions of Liberty: Civil Society and its Rivals*. London: Hamish Hamilton.

Gilpin, R. 1987: *The Political Economy of International Relations*. Princeton: Princeton University Press.

Girling, J. 1981: *Thailand: Society and Politics*. Ithaca: Cornell University Press.

Gold, T.B. 1993: Taiwan's Quest for Identity in the Shadow of China. In S. Tsang (ed.), *In the Shadow of China: Political Development in Taiwan since 1949*. London: Hurst and Company.

Goldsmith, J. 1994: *Le Piège: Entretiens avec Yves Messarovitch sur quelques idées reçues*. Paris: Fixot.

Gomez, E.T. 1994: *Political Business: Corporate Involvement of Malaysian Political Parties*. Townsville: James Cook University Press.

Goodman, D.S. and Feng, Chongyi 1994: Guangdong, Greater Hong Kong and the New Regionalist Future. In D.S. Goodman and G. Segal (eds), *China Deconstructs: Politics, Trade and Regionalism*. London: Routledge.

Government of Singapore 1991: *The Next Lap*. Singapore: Times Press.

Gullick, J.M. 1991: *Malay Society in the Late Nineteenth Century*. Kuala Lumpur: Oxford University Press.

Haas, M. 1989: *The Asian Way to Peace: A Story of Regional Cooperation*. New York: Praeger.

Habermas, J. 1976: *Legitimation Crisis* (trans. T. McCarthy). London: Heinemann.

Habermas, J. 1987: *The Theory of Communicative Action* (trans. T. McCarthy), 2 vols. Boston: Beacon Press.

Haggard, S. 1990: *Pathways from the Periphery: The Politics of Growth of the Newly Industrializing Countries*. Ithaca: Cornell University Press.

Hall, D.G. 1991: *A History of South-East Asia*. London: Macmillan.

Halliday, F. 1989: *The Making of the Second Cold War*. London: Verso.

Han, Fei Tzu 1964: *Basic Writings* (trans. B. Watson). New York: Columbia University Press.

Han, Sung Joo 1989: South Korean Politics in Transition. In L. Diamond, J.J. Linz and S.M. Lipset (eds), *Democracy in Developing Countries*. Boulder, CO: Lynne Reiner.

Harris, S. 1994: Conclusion: The Theory and Practice of Regional Cooperation. In A. Mack and J. Ravenhill (eds), *Pacific Cooperation: Building Economic and Security Regimes in the Asia-Pacific Region*. St Leonards: Allen and Unwin.

Hayek, F. 1960: *The Constitution of Liberty*. London: Routledge and Kegan Paul.

Heine-Geldern, R. 1956: Concepts of State and Kingship in Southeast Asia. *Southeast Asia Program Data Papers*. Ithaca: Cornell University Press.

Held, D., 1993: *Prospects for Democracy: North, South, East, West*. Cambridge: Polity Press.

Helleiner, E. 1994: From Bretton Woods to Global Finance: A World Turned Upside Down. In R. Stubbs and G. Underhill (eds), *The Political Economy and the Changing Global Order*. London: Macmillan.

Henderson, G. 1968: *Korea: The Politics of the Vortex*. Cambridge, MA: Harvard University Press.

Heng, Peck Koon 1993: The Chinese Business Elite of Malaysia. In R. McVey (ed.), *Southeast Asian Capitalists*. Ithaca: Southeast Asia Program, Cornell University Press.

Hewison, K., 1985: The State and Capitalist Development in Thailand. In R. Higgott and R. Robison (eds), *Essays in the Political Economy of Structural Change*. London: Routledge.

Hewison, K. 1996: Emerging Social Forces in Thailand: New Political and Economic Roles. In R. Robison and D.S.G. Goodman (eds), *The New Rich in Asia: Mobile Phones, McDonald's and Middle Class Revolution*. London: Routledge.

Hewison, K., Robison, R. and Rodan, G. 1993: Political Power in Industrialising Capitalist Societies: Theoretical Approaches. In B. Hewison, R. Robison and G. Rodan (eds), *Southeast Asia in the 1990s: Authoritarianism, Democracy and Capitalism*. Sydney: Allen and Unwin.

Higgott, R., Leaver, R. and Ravenhill, J. 1993: The Pacific Economic Future: Towards

Conventions of Moderation. In R. Higgott, R. Leaver and J. Ravenhill (eds), *Pacific Economic Relations in the 1990s: Cooperation or Conflict?* St Leonards: Allen and Unwin.

Hill, H. 1994: The Economy. In H. Hill (ed.), *Indonesia's New Order: The Dynamic of Socio-Economic Transformation.* St Leonards: Allen and Unwin.

Hill, M. and Lian, Kwen Fee 1995: *The Politics of Nation Building and Citizenship in Singapore.* London: Routledge.

Ho, W.M. 1989: Value premises underlying the transformation of Singapore. In K. Singh and P. Wheatley (eds), *The Management of Success: The Moulding of Modern Singapore.* Singapore: Institute of Southeast Asian Studies.

Hobsbawm, E. 1983: Introduction. In E. Hobsbawm and T. Ranger (eds), *The Invention of Tradition.* Cambridge: Cambridge University Press.

Hoston, G. 1994: *The State, Identity, and the National Question in China and Japan.* Princeton: Princeton University Press.

Hsiao, M. 1992: Emerging Social Movements and the Rise of a Demanding Civil Society in Taiwan. In T.J. Cheng and S. Haggard (eds), *Political Change in Taiwan.* Boulder, CO: Lynne Reiner.

Hsu, L. 1935: *The Political Philosophy of Confucius.* New York: Dutton.

Huff, W.G. 1994: *The Economic Growth of Singapore: Trade and Development in the Twentieth Century.* Cambridge: Cambridge University Press.

Hughes, C.W. 1996: Japan's Sub-Regional Security and Defence Linkages with ASEANs [*sic*], South Korea and China in the 1990s. *Pacific Review* 9, 2, 229–50.

Human Rights Watch 1994: *Human Rights in Indonesia and East Timor: The Limits of Openness.* New York: Human Rights Watch.

Huntington, S. 1991: *The Third Wave: Democratization in the Late Twentieth Century.* Norman: University of Oklahoma Press.

Huntington, S. 1993a: The Clash of Civilizations? *Foreign Affairs* 72, 3, 22–49.

Huntington, S. 1993b: American Democracy in Relation to Asia. In R. Bartley, H.C. Chan, S. Huntington and S. Ogata (eds), *Democracy and Capitalism: Asian and American Perspectives.* Singapore: Institute of Southeast Asian Studies.

Hutton, W. 1995: *The State We're In.* London: Vintage.

Huxley, T. 1996: Southeast Asia in the Study of International Relations: The Rise and Decline of a Region. *Pacific Review* 9, 2, 199–228.

Inoguchi, T. 1991: *Japan's Foreign Relations.* London: Pinter.

Ishii, Y. 1993: Religious Patterns and Economic Change in Siam in the Sixteenth and Seventeenth Centuries. In A. Reid (ed.), *Southeast Asia in the Early Modern Era: Trade, Power and Belief.* Ithaca: Cornell University Press.

Jackson, P.A. 1991: Thai Buddhist Identity: Debates on the Thaiphung Phra Rwang. In C.J. Reynolds (ed.), *National Identity and its Defenders.* Monash Papers on Southeast Asia 25, Clayton: Monash University Press.

Jacobs, B. 1985: *The Korean Road to Urbanization and Development.* Urbana: University of Illinois Press.

Jacobs, J. 1984: *Cities and the Wealth of Nations: Principles of Economic Life.* New York: New York.

Jesudason, J.V. 1990: *Ethnicity and the Economy: The State, Chinese Business and Multinationals in Malaysia.* Singapore: Oxford University Press.

Jesudason, J.V. 1995: Statist Democracy and the Limits of Civil Society in Malaysia. *Journal of Commonwealth and Comparative Politics* 33, 3, 335–56.

Jin, Dengjian 1995: Bounded Governance within Extended Order: The Confucian Advantage of Synergy under Generalized Constitutional Rules. *Constitutional Political Economy* 6, 3, 261–77.

Jitsuchon, S. 1991: *Retrospects and Prospects of Thailand's Economic Development*. Working Paper No 2, Tokyo: Economic Planning Agency.

Johnson, C. 1982: *MITI and the Japanese Miracle: The Growth of Industrial Policy 1925–1975*. Stanford: Stanford University Press.

Johnson, C. 1996: The Okinawan Rape Incident and the End of the Cold War in East Asia. *Quadrant* March, 23–9.

Jomo, K.S. 1994a: Malaysian Forests, Japanese Wood. In K.S. Jomo (ed.), *Japan and Malaysian Development in the Shadow of the Rising Sun*. London: Routledge.

Jomo, K.S. 1994b: The Proton Saga: Malaysian Car, Mitsubishi Gain. In K.S. Jomo (ed.), *Japan and Malaysian Development in the Shadow of the Rising Sun*. London: Routledge.

Jones, E. 1994: Predicting Asia's Fate. *The National Interest* Spring, 18–28.

Kahan, A. 1992: *Aristocratic Liberalism: The Social and Political Thought of Jacob Burckhardt, J.S. Mill and Alexis de Tocqueville*. Oxford: Oxford University Press.

Kahler, M. 1990: Organizing the Pacific. In R.A. Scalapino, S. Sato, J. Wanandi and S.-J. Han (eds), *Regional Dynamics: Security, Political and Economic Issues in the Asia-Pacific Region*. Jakarta: Centre for Strategic and International Studies.

Kahler, M. 1994: Institution-Building in the Pacific. In A. Mack and J. Ravenhill (eds), *Pacific Cooperation: Building Economic and Security Regimes in the Asia–Pacific Region*. St Leonards: Allen and Unwin.

Kahn, J.S. 1994: Subalternity of Malay Identity. In A. Gomes (ed.), *Modernity and Identity: Asian Illustrations*. Melbourne: La Trobe University Press.

Karnow, S. 1988: *Vietnam: A History*. London: Penguin.

Kennan, G. [X] 1947: The Sources of Soviet Conduct. *Foreign Affairs* 25, 4, 560–83.

Keohane, R. and Nye, J. 1974: *Power and Interdependence: World Politics in Transition*. Boston: Little, Brown and Company.

Kessler, C. 1993: Archaism and Modernity: Contemporary Malay Political Culture. In J. Kahn and F. Loh (eds), *Fragmented Vision: Culture and Politics in Contemporary Malaysia*. St Leonards: Allen and Unwin.

Khoo, K.J. 1993: The Grand Vision: Mahathir and Modernisation. In J. Kahn and F. Loh (eds), *Fragmented Vision: Culture and Politics in Contemporary Malaysia*. St Leonards: Allen and Unwin.

Kim, Chong Lim 1990: Potential for Democratic Change in a Divided Nation. In I.J. Kim and Y.W. Kihl (eds), *Political Change in South Korea*. New York: Paragon House.

Kim, Jae Yul 1993: Democratisation in South Korea. In J. Cotton (ed.), *Korea under Roh Tae Woo*. St Leonards: Allen and Unwin.

Kissinger, H. 1994a: Reflections on Containment. *Foreign Affairs* 73, 3, 113–32.

Kissinger, H. 1994b: *Diplomacy*. New York: Simon and Schuster.

Klintworth, G. (ed.) 1994: *Taiwan in the Asia-Pacific in the 1990s*. St Leonards: Allen and Unwin.

Koentjaraningrat 1990: *Javanese Culture*. Singapore: Oxford University Press.

Kolko, G. 1985: *Vietnam: Anatomy of a War, 1940–1975*. London: Unwin Hyman.

Koo, Hagen 1991: Middle Class Democratization and Class Formation. *Theory and Society* 20, 486–94.

Krugman, P. 1994: The Myth of Asia's Miracle. *Foreign Affairs* 73, 6, 62–78.

Kuo, Shirley W.Y. 1994: The Taiwanese Economy in the 1990s. In G. Klintworth (ed.), *Taiwan in the Asia-Pacific in the 1990s*. St Leonards: Allen and Unwin.

Kuo, Tai Chun and Myers, R. 1988: The Great Transition: Political Change and the Prospects for Democracy in the Republic of China on Taiwan. *Asian Affairs* 15, 3, 115–35.

Kymlicka, W. 1995: *Multicultural Citizenship*. Oxford: Oxford University Press.
Laothamatas, A. 1992. *Business Associations and the New Political Economy of Thailand*. Boulder, CO: Westview.
Laothamatas, A. 1994: From Clientilism to Partnership: Business–Government Relations in Thailand. In A. Macintyre (ed.), *Business and Government in Industrialising Asia*. St Leonards: Allen and Unwin.
Lapidus, I. 1991: *A History of Islamic Societies*. Cambridge: Cambridge University Press.
Lasch, C. 1985: *The Minimal Self: Psychic Survival in Troubled Times*. London: Picador.
Lee, Boon Hiok 1990: Political Contestation in Singapore. In N. Mahmood and Z. Ahmad (eds), *Political Contestation: Case Studies from Asia*. Singapore: Heinemann Asia.
Lee, Hongkoo 1993: The End of the Cold War and the Prospect for Korean Unification. In T.B. Millar and J. Walter (eds), *Asian-Pacific Security after the Cold War*. St Leonards: Allen and Unwin.
Lee, Lai To 1995: ASEAN and the South China Seas Conflict. *The Pacific Review* 8, 3, 531–43.
Lee, Wing-on and Bray, M.K. 1995: Education: Evolving Patterns and Challenges. In J.Y.S. Cheng and S.S.H. Lao (eds), *From Colony to SAR: Hong Kong's Challenges Ahead*. Hong Kong: University of Hong Kong Press.
Legge J. (ed.) 1893: *The Great Learning*, Vol. 1 of *The Chinese Classics* (7 vols), Oxford and London: Spottiswoode.
Legge, J.D. 1972: *Sukarno: A Political Biography*. Sydney: Allen and Unwin.
Leifer, M. 1974. *The Foreign Relations of the New States*. London: Longman.
Leifer, M. 1989: *ASEAN and the Security of Southeast Asia*. London: Routledge.
Leifer, M. 1993: The Indochina Problem. In T.B. Millar and J. Walter (eds), *Asian-Pacific Security after the Cold War*. St Leonards: Allen and Unwin.
Leifer, M. 1995: *Dictionary of the Modern Politics of South East Asia*. London: Routledge.
Leifer, M. 1996: *The ASEAN Regional Forum: Extending ASEANs Model of Regional Security*. Adelphi Paper 302, Oxford: Oxford University Press.
Leudde-Neurath, R. 1988: State Intervention and Export-oriented Development: Neoclassical Theory and Taiwanese Practice. In G. White (ed.), *Developmental States in East Asia*. London: Macmillan.
Levenson J.R. 1965: *Confucian China and its Modern Fate* (3 vols). London: Routledge and Kegan Paul.
Levin, N.D. 1991: Japan's Defense Policy: The Internal Debate. In H. Kendall and C. Joewono (eds), *Japan, ASEAN and the United States*. Berkeley: University of California Press.
Lim, C.P. and Gomez, E.T. 1994: Malaysian *Sogoshoshas*: Superficial Cloning, Failed Emulation. In K.S. Jomo (ed.), *Japan and Malaysian Development in the Shadow of the Rising Sun*. London: Routledge.
Lim, Linda Y.C. 1989: Social Welfare. In K.S. Sandhu and P. Wheatley (eds), *Management of Success: The Moulding of Modern Singapore*. Singapore: Institute of Southeast Asian Studies.
Lim, Linda Y.C. 1994: Economic Outlook 1996: ASEAN Region. In H.C. Chan (ed.), *Regional Outlook Southeast Asia 1996*. Singapore: Institute of Southeast Asian Studies.
Lim, Yun-Chin and Kim, Byung-Kook 1992: Labour and Democratization in Korea: A Search for a Social Pact. In D.C. Shin, M.H. Zoh and M. Chey (eds), *Korea in the Global Wave of Democratization*. Seoul: National University Press.
Ling, Sieh Lee Mei 1993: The Transformation of Malaysian Business Groups. In R. McVey (ed.), *Southeast Asian Capitalists*. Ithaca: Southeast Asia Program, Cornell University Press.

Lipset, S.M. 1963: *Political Man: The Social Basis of Politics.* New York: Anchor.

List, F. 1983: *The National System of Political Economy* (trans. W.O. Henderson). London: Frank Cass (originally published 1837).

Lloyd, P. and Sandilands, R. 1988: The Trade Sector in a Very Open Re-export Economy. In C.Y. Lim and P. Lloyd (eds), *Singapore: Reasons for Growth.* Singapore: Oxford University Press.

Lo, Shiu-hing 1996: Hong Kong: Post-Colonialism and Political Conflict. In R. Robison and D.S.G. Goodman (eds), *The New Rich in Asia: Mobile Phones, McDonald's and Middle Class Revolution.* London: Routledge.

Lodge, G. 1991: *Two Public Lectures.* Singapore: National University of Singapore Press.

Low, L. 1993: The Public Sector in Contemporary Singapore: In Retreat? In G. Rodan (ed.), *Singapore Changes Guard: Social, Political and Economic Changes in the 1990s.* St Leonards: Allen and Unwin.

Lu, Ya-li 1991: Political Developments in the Republic of China. In T. Robinson (ed.), *Democracy and Development in East Asia: Taiwan, South Korea and the Philippines.* Washington, DC: AEI Press.

Macintyre, A. 1994: Power, Prosperity and Patrimonialism: Business and Government in Indonesia. In A. Macintyre (ed.), *Business and Government in Industrialising Asia.* St Leonards: Allen and Unwin.

Mack, A. 1993: Security and the Korean Peninsula in the 1990s. In A. Mack (ed.), *Asian Flashpoint: Security and the Korean Peninsula.* St Leonards: Allen and Unwin.

Mackie, J. 1995: Economic Systems of the Overseas Chinese. In L. Suryadinata (ed.), *Southeast Asian Chinese and China: The Politico-Economic Dimension.* Singapore: Times Academic Press.

Mackintosh, M. 1993: The Soviet Union in the Pacific: Force Structure and Regional Relations. In T.B. Millar and J. Walter, *Asian Pacific Security after the Cold War.* St Leonards: Allen and Unwin.

McVey, R. 1993: The Materialization of the Southeast Asian Entrepreneur. In R. McVey (ed.), *Southeast Asian Capitalists.* Ithaca: Southeast Asia Program, Cornell University Press.

McVey, R. 1994: The Case of the Disappearing Decade. In D. Bourchier and J. Legge (eds), *Democracy in Indonesia: 1950s and 1990s.* Clayton: Monash University Press.

Mahathir Mohamad 1989: *The Malay Dilemma.* Singapore: Times Press.

Mahathir Mohamad 1993a: *The Challenge.* Petaling Jaya: Pelanduk Publishing.

Mahathir Mohamad 1993b: Views and Thoughts of Dr Mahathir Mohamad. In A.S.A. Hamid (ed.), *Malaysia's Vision 2020: Understanding the Concept, Implications and Changes.* Sleangor: Pelanduk Publishing.

Mahathir Mohamad and Ishihara, S. 1995: *The Voice of Asia: Two Leaders Discuss the Coming Century.* Tokyo: Kodansha International.

Mahbubani, K. 1994: The United States: Go East Young Man. *Washington Quarterly* 17, 2, 5–23.

Mahbubani, K. 1995: The Pacific Way. *Foreign Affairs* 74, 1, 100–11.

Mahmood, N. 1990: Political Contestation in Malaysia. In N. Mahmood and Z. Ahmad (eds), *Political Contestation: Case Studies from Asia.* Singapore: Heinemann.

Marcuse, H. 1969: *One-Dimensional Man: The Ideology of Industrial Society.* London: Routledge and Kegan Paul.

Matthews, T. and Ravenhill, J. 1994: Strategic Trade Policy: The Northeast Asian Experience. In A. Macintyre (ed.), *Business and Government in Industrialising Asia.* St Leonards: Allen and Unwin.

Mauzy, D.K. 1983: *Barisan Nasional: Coalition Government in Malaysia.* Kuala Lumpur: Mancan.

Mencius 1970: *Mencius* (trans. D.C. Lau). London: Penguin.

Metraux, D. 1990: *Taiwan's Political and Economic Growth in the Late Twentieth Century.* Lampeter: Edwin Mellen Press.

Metzger, L. 1994: *Les Sultanats de Malaise: Un regime monarchique au XXe siècle.* Paris: Editions L'Harmattan.

Metzger, T. 1977: *Escape from Predicament: Neo-Confucianism and China's Evolving Political Culture.* New York: Columbia University Press.

Mill, J.S. 1970: *Utilitarianism, On Liberty and Essay on Bentham* (ed. M. Warnock). London: Fontana.

Milne, R. and Mauzy, D. 1990: *Singapore: The Legacy of Lee Kuan Yew.* Boulder, CO: Westview Press.

Milner, A. 1994: *The Invention of Politics in Colonial Malaya: Contesting Nationalism and the Expansion of the Public Sphere.* Cambridge: Cambridge University Press.

Miners, N. 1991: *The Government and Politics of Hong Kong.* Hong Kong: Oxford University Press.

Minogue K.R. 1987: Loquocentricity and Democracy: The Communicative Theory of Modern Civil Unity in B. Parekh (ed.), *Political Discourse: Explorations in Indian and Western Political Thought.* New Delhi: Sage.

Moon, Chung-in 1994: Changing Patterns of Business–Government Relations and Regime Transition in South Korea. In A. Macintyre (ed.), *Business and Government in Industrialising Asia.* St Leonards: Allen and Unwin.

Moore, B. 1966: *The Social Origin of Dictatorship and Democracy.* Boston: Beacon Press.

Moore, M. 1988: Economic Growth and the Rise of Civil Society: Agriculture in Taiwan and South Korea. In G. White (ed.), *Developmental States in East Asia.* London: Macmillan.

Munro, D. 1977: *The Concept of Man in Contemporary China.* Ann Arbor: University of Michigan Press.

Myrdal, G. 1968: *Asian Drama: An Enquiry into the Poverty of Nations.* London: Penguin.

Naisbitt, J. 1995: *Megatrend Asia: The Eight Megatrends That Are Changing the World.* London: Nicholas Brealy.

Needham, J. 1978: *The Shorter Science and Civilization of China* (2 vols). Cambridge: Cambridge University Press.

Neher, C.D. 1994: *Southeast Asia in the New International Era.* Boulder, CO: Westview Press.

Nitisastro, W. 1994: A-Once-For-All Settlement of Foreign Debt. *Indonesian Business Weekly* II, 38, 18–20.

Oakeshott, M. 1981: *Rationalism in Politics and Other Essays.* Oxford: Oxford University Press.

O'Donnell, G., Schmitter, P. and Whitehead, L. 1986: *Transitions from Authoritarian Rule: Prospects for Democracy.* Baltimore: Johns Hopkins University Press.

Ogata, S. 1993: Capitalism, the Market Mechanism and the State in Economic Development. In R. Bartley, C.H. Chan, S. Huntington and S. Ogata (eds), *Democracy and Capitalism: Asian and American Perspectives.* Singapore Institute of Southeast Asian Studies.

Ohmae, K. 1991: *The Borderless World: Power and Strategy in the International Economy.* New York: Harper.

Okimoto, D. 1989: *Between MITI and the Market: Japanese Industrial Policy for High Technology.* Stanford: Stanford University Press.

Okita, S. 1989: The Future of the Asian-Pacific Region and the Role of Japan. In

M. Shinohara and F. C. Lo (eds), *Global Adjustment and the Future of the Asian Pacific Economy*. Tokyo: Institute of Developing Economies and Asia-Pacific Development Center.

Olsen, L. 1970: *Japan in Post-War Asia*. London: Pall Mall Press.

Omar, A. 1993: *Bangsa Melayu: Malay Concepts of Democracy and Community 1945–50*. Kuala Lumpur: Oxford University Press.

Ozari, R. and Arnold W. (eds) 1985: *Japan's Foreign Relations: A Global Search for Economic Security*. Boulder, CO: Westview.

Pacific Economic Cooperation Council (PECC) 1994a: *Pacific Economic Development Report: Advancing Regional Integration*. Singapore: PECC.

Pacific Economic Cooperation Council (PECC) 1994b: *Pacific Economic Outlook 1994–1995*. San Francisco: The Asia Foundation.

Palliser, J. 1991: *Politics and Policy in Traditional Korea*. Cambridge, MA: Harvard University Press.

Park, M.K. 1987: Interest Representation in South Korea: The Limits of Corporatist Control. *Asian Survey* 27, 8, 903–12.

Park, S.H. 1994: *Japan's Economic Role in the Dynamic Growth of Asian Economies: A Summary of Issues*. Research Paper No. 19, Department of Japanese Studies, Singapore: National University of Singapore Press.

Pasuk, P. and Baker, C. 1995: *Thailand: Economy and Politics*. Kuala Lumpur: Oxford University Press.

Pasuk, P. and Sungsidh, P. 1994: *Corruption and Democracy in Thailand*. Bangkok: Chulalongkorn University Press.

Patrick, H.T. and Park, Y.C. (eds) 1994: *The Financial Development of Japan, Korea and Taiwan: Growth, Repression and Liberalization*. Oxford: Oxford University Press.

Patrikeeff, F. 1991: Hong Kong – A Contract Revisited. In S. Harris and J. Cotton (eds), *The End of the Cold War in Northeast Asia*. St Leonards: Allen and Unwin.

Peyrefitte, A. 1993: *The Collision of Two Civilizations: The British Expedition to China 1792–4*. London: Harrill.

Plunk, D. 1991: Political Development in the ROK. In T. Robinson (ed.), *Democracy and Development in East Asia: Taiwan, South Korea and the Philippines*. Washington, DC: AEI Press.

Polomka, P. 1991: Commentary. In S. Harris and J. Cotton (eds), *The End of the Cold War in Northeast Asia*. St Leonards: Allen and Unwin.

Potter, D. 1993: Democratization in Asia. In D. Held (ed.), *Prospects for Democracy: North, South, East, West*. Cambridge: Polity Press.

Prins, G. 1993: Maritime Security and Common Security. In A. Mack (ed.), *A Peaceful Ocean? Maritime Security in the Pacific in the Post Cold-War Era*. St Leonards: Allen and Unwin.

Przeworski, A. 1992: *Democracy and the Market*. Cambridge: Cambridge University Press.

Pye, L. 1966: *Aspects of Political Development*. Boston: Little, Brown and Company.

Pye, L., with Pye, M. 1985: *Asian Power and Politics: The Cultural Dimensions of Authority*. Cambridge, MA: Harvard University Press.

Pye, L. 1988: *The Mandarin and the Cadre: China's Political Cultures*. Ann Arbor, MI: Center for Chinese Studies.

Quah, J.S.T. (ed.) 1990: National Values and Nation Building: Defining the Problem. In J.S.T. Quah (ed.), *In Search of Singapore's National Values*. Singapore: Times Academic Press.

Quah, J.S.T. (ed.) 1994: Political Consequences of Rapid Economic Development: The Singapore Case. In S. Nagel (ed.), *Asian Development and Public Policy*. London: Macmillan / St Martins.

Ramage, D. 1996: *Politics in Indonesia: Democracy, Islam and the Ideology of Tolerance.* London: Routledge.

Rao, V.V.B., Daquila, T.C. and Pau Woo Yuen 1994: *ASEAN: External Debt Perspectives.* Singapore: Times Academic Press.

Redding, S.G. 1993: *The Spirit of Chinese Capitalism.* Berlin: Walter de Gruyter.

Reid, A. 1993a: A Time and a Place. In A. Reid (ed.), *Southeast Asia in the Early Modern Era: Trade, Power and Belief.* Ithaca: Cornell University Press.

Reid, A. 1993b: *Southeast Asia in the Age of Commerce 1450–1680: Vol. 2, Expansion and Crisis.* New Haven: Yale University Press.

Rhee, J.-C. 1994: *The State and Industry in South Korea: The Limits of the Authoritarian State.* London: Routledge.

Rieff, P. 1987: *The Triumph of the Therapeutic: The Uses of Faith after Freud.* Chicago: University of Chicago Press.

Riggs, F. 1966: *Thailand: The Modernization of a Bureaucratic Polity.* Honolulu: East–West Center Press.

Robinson, T., with Arnold, J.A. and Shime, P.J. (1991) Introduction. In T. Robinson (ed.), *Democracy and Development in East Asia: Taiwan, South Korea and the Philippines.* Washington, DC: AEI Press.

Robison, R. 1989: Authoritarian States, Capitalist Owning Classes and the Politics of Newly Industrializing Countries: The Case of Indonesia. *World Politics* 41, 1, 52–74.

Robison, R. 1990: *Power and Economy in Suharto's Indonesia.* Manila: *Journal of Contemporary Asia* Publishers.

Robison, R. 1993: Indonesia: Tensions in State and Regime. In K. Hewison, R. Robison and G. Rodan (eds), *Southeast Asia in the 1990s: Authoritarianism, Democracy and Capitalism.* St Leonards: Allen and Unwin.

Rodan, G. 1992: Singapore's Leadership Transition: Erosion or Refinement of Authoritarian Rule? *Bulletin of Concerned Asian Scholars* 24, 1, 13–19.

Rodan, G. 1993a: The Growth of Singapore's Middle Class. In G. Rodan (ed.), *Singapore Changes Guard: Social, Political and Economic Directions in the 1990s.* St Leonards: Allen and Unwin.

Rodan, G. 1993b: Preserving the One Party State in Singapore. In K. Hewison, R. Robison and G. Rodan (eds), *Southeast Asia in the 1990s: Authoritarianism, Democracy and Capitalism.* St Leonards: Allen and Unwin.

Rodan, G. 1996a: Class Transformations and Political Tension in Singapore's Development. In R. Robison and D.S.G. Goodman (eds), *The New Rich in Asia: Mobile Phones, McDonald's and Middle Class Revolution.* London: Routledge.

Rodan, G. 1996b: Theorising Political Opposition in East and Southeast Asia. In G. Rodan (ed.), *Political Opposition in Industrialising Asia.* London: Routledge.

Rodner, M. 1995: APEC: The Challenges of Asia Pacific Cooperation. *Modern Asian Studies* 29, 2, 403–37.

Roff, W. 1994: *The Origins of Malay Nationalism.* Kuala Lumpur: Oxford University Press.

Rorty, R. 1989: *Contingency, Irony, and Solidarity.* Cambridge: Cambridge University Press.

Rostow, W.W. 1971: *Politics and the Stages of Growth.* Cambridge: Cambridge University Press.

Ruggie, J. 1993: Unravelling Trade: Global, Institutional Change and the Pacific Economy. In R. Higgott, R. Leaver and J. Ravenhill (eds), *Pacific Economic Relations in the 1990s: Cooperation or Conflict?* St Leonards: Allen and Unwin.

Ryan, M. 1995: USTRs Implementation of 301 Policy in the Pacific. *International Studies Quarterly* 39, 333–50.

Samudavanija, C.A. 1991: State-Identity Creation, State-Building and Civil Society 1939–1989. In C.J. Reynolds (ed.), *National Identity and its Defenders: Thailand, 1939–1989.* Monash Papers on Southeast Asia No. 25, Clayton: Monash University Press.

Santoso, A. 1992: Democracy and Parliament: Future Agenda. *The Indonesian Quarterly* xx, 1, 84–94.

Saravanamuttu, J. 1992: The State, Ethnicity and the Middle Class Factor: Addressing Non-violent Democratic Change in Malaysia. In K. Rupesinghe (ed.), *Internal Conflict and Governance.* London and New York: Macmillan and St Martin's Press.

Sato, S. 1990: The Interrelationship between Global and Regional Security Issues for the Asia-Pacific Region. In R.A. Scalapino, S. Sato, J. Wanandi and S.-J. Han (eds), *Regional Dynamics: Security, Political and Economic Issues in the Asia-Pacific Region.* Jakarta: Centre for Strategic and International Studies.

Satoh, Y. 1993: The Japanese Role. In T.B. Millar and J. Walter (eds), *Asian-Pacific Security after the Cold War.* St Leonards: Allen and Unwin.

Scalapino, R. 1996: Informal Politics in East Asia. *Asian Survey* xxxvi, 3, 227–37.

Schumpeter, J. 1943: *Capitalism, Socialism, and Democracy.* London: Allen and Unwin.

Schwarz, A. 1994: *Indonesia, a Nation in Waiting: Indonesia in the 1990s.* St Leonards: Allen and Unwin.

Scott, I. 1993. Legitimacy and its Discontents: Hong Kong and the Reversion to Chinese Sovereignty. *Asian Journal of Political Science* 1, 1, 55–75.

Segal, G. 1989: *Rethinking the Pacific.* Oxford: Clarendon Press.

Segal, G. 1994: Deconstructing Foreign Relations. In D.S. Goodman and G. Segal (eds), *China Deconstructs: Politics, Trade and Regionalism.* London: Routledge.

Semmel, B. 1993: *The Liberal Ideal and the Demons of Empire: Theories of Empire from Adam Smith to Lenin.* Baltimore: Johns Hopkins University Press.

Seow, F. 1994: *To Catch a Tartar: A Dissident in Lee Kuan Yew's Prison.* New Haven: Yale Southeast Asia Studies/Monograph 42.

Setyawan, D. (ed.) 1994: APEC Economic Leader's Declaration of Common Resolve. *The Indonesian Quarterly* xxii, 4, 378–80.

Shambaugh, D. 1995: The Emergence of Greater China. In D. Shambaugh (ed.), *Greater China.* Oxford: Clarendon Press.

Sheng, Lijun 1995: Beijing and the Spratlys. *Issues and Studies: Journal of Chinese Studies and International Affairs* 31, 7, 18–45.

Simon, D.F. 1994: The Orbital Mechanics of Taiwan's Technological Development: An Examination of the 'Gravitational' Pushes and Pulls. In G. Klintworth (ed.), *Taiwan in the Asia-Pacific in the 1990s.* St Leonard's: Allen and Unwin.

Skocpol, T. 1973: A Critical Review of Barrington Moore's *Social Origins of Dictatorship and Democracy: Politics and Society* 12, 2, 1–34.

Smail, J.R.W. 1989: Indonesia. In D. Steinberg (ed.), *In Search of Southeast Asia: A Modern History.* St Leonards: Allen and Unwin.

Snitwongse, K. 1995: ASEANs Security Cooperation: Searching for a Regional Order. *The Pacific Review* 8, 3, 518–30.

Soedjatmoko 1965: Cultural Motivations to Progress: The Exterior and Interior Views. In R.N. Bellah (ed.), *Religion and Progress in Modern Asia.* New York: Free Press.

Soetrisno, L. 1984: Pergeseran Dalam Golongan Menegah di Indonesia. *Prisma* 13, 2, 25–37.

Song, B.N. 1990: *The Rise of the Korean Economy.* Hong Kong: Oxford University Press.

Sopiee, N. 1992: The New World Order: What Southeast Asia Should Strive for. In R. Mahmood and T. Ramnath (eds), *Southeast Asia: The Way Forward.* Kuala Lumpur: Friedrich Ebert Stiftung.

Spence, J. 1991: *The Search for Modern China*. New York: Norton.
Springborg, P. 1992: *Western Republicanism and the European Prince*. Cambridge: Polity Press.
Steinberg, D. (ed.) 1989: *In Search of South East Asia: A Modern History*. Sydney: Allen and Unwin.
Steinberg, D. 1993: The Transformation of the South Korean Economy. In D.N. Clark (ed.), *Korea Briefing 1993*. Boulder, CO: Westview Press.
Stockwell, A.J. 1992: Southeast Asia in War and Peace: The End of European Colonial Empires. In N. Tarling (ed.), *The Cambridge History of Southeast Asia*, Vol. 2. Cambridge: Cambridge University Press.
Stubbs, R. 1994: The Political Economy of the Asia-Pacific Region. In R. Stubbs and R.D. Underhill (eds), *Political Economy and the Changing Global Order*. London: Macmillan.
Suehiro, A. 1992: Capitalist Development in Post-War Thailand: Commercial Banks, Industrial Elites and Agribusiness Groups. In R. McVey (ed.), *Southeast Asian Entrepreneurs*. Ithaca: Cornell University Press.
Suffian, Tun Mohammed 1979: *The Constitution of Malaysia and Its Development*. Kuala Lumpur: Oxford University Press.
Suh, Kuk Sang (ed.) 1983: *The Identity of the Korean People: A History of Legitimacy on the Korean Peninsula*. Seoul: National Unification Board.
Sukarno, A. 1964: The Liberating Effects of Nationalism in Asia. In L. Snyder (ed.), *The Dynamics of Nationalism: Readings in its Meaning and Development*. New York: D. van Nostrand Co.
Sun Yat-sen 1981: *Three Principles of the People*. Taipei: China Publishing Company.
Suryadinata, L. 1989: *Military Ascendancy and Political Culture: A Study of Indonesia's Golkar*. Athens: Ohio University Press.
Suryadinata, L. 1990: Political Contestation in Malaysia. In N. Mahmood and Z. Ahmad (eds), *Political Contestation: Case Studies from Asia*. Singapore: Heinemann.
Suryadinata, L. 1996: *Indonesia's Foreign Policy under Suharto: Aspiring to International Leadership* Singapore: Times Academic Press.
Tan, G. 1992: *The Newly Industrialising Countries of Asia*. Singapore: Times Academic Press.
Tarling, N. (ed.) 1992: *The Cambridge History of Southeast Asia*, Vol. 2. Cambridge: Cambridge University Press.
Taubert, A. 1991: Liberalism under Pressure in Indonesia. *South East Asian Affairs 1991*. Singapore: Institute of Southeast Asian Studies.
Taylor, C. 1992: *Sources of the Self: The Making of Modern Identity*. Cambridge: Cambridge University Press.
Terwiel, B.J. 1991. Thai Nationalism and Identity: Popular Themes in the 1930s. In C.J. Reynolds (ed.), *National Identity and its Defenders: Thailand 1939–1989*. Clayton: Monash University Press.
Thanet A. 1995: The Contour of Thai Rights. Paper delivered at ASEAN Inter-University Seminar on Social Development, Cebu, Philippines.
Thurow, L. 1996: *The Future of Capitalism*. St Leonards: Allen and Unwin.
Tien, Hung-ma 1992: Transformation of an Authoritarian State: Taiwan's Development Experience. In T.-J. Cheng and S. Haggard (eds), *Political Change in Taiwan*. Boulder, CO: Lynne Rienner.
Tien, Hung-ma 1993: Dynamics of Taiwan's Democratic Transition. In S. Tsang (ed.), *In The Shadow of China: Political Development in Taiwan since 1949*. London: Hurst and Company.
Tremewan, C. 1994: *The Political Economy of Social Control in Singapore*. London: Macmillan.

Tsang, S. 1988: *Democracy Shelved: Great Britain, China and Attempts at Constitutional Reform in Hong Kong 1945–52*. Hong Kong: Oxford University Press.

Tsang, S. 1993: Chiang Kai-shek and the Kuomintang's Policy to Reconquer the Chinese Mainland, 1949–1958. In S. Tsang (ed.), *In the Shadow of China: Political Developments in Taiwan since 1949*. London: Hurst and Company.

Tu, Wei-ming 1984: *Confucian Ethics Today: The Singapore Challenge*. Singapore: Federal Publications.

Tu, Wei-ming 1989: *Confucianism in an Historical Perspective*. Occasional Paper and Monograph Series No. 15, Singapore: Institute of East Asian Philosophies.

Tu, Wei-ming (ed.) 1991: *The Triadic Chord: Confucian Ethics, Industrial East Asia and Max Weber*. Singapore: Institute of East Asian Philosophies.

Turnbull, C.M. 1989: *A History of Malaysia, Singapore and Brunei*. Sydney: Allen and Unwin.

Turnbull, C.M. 1992: *A History of Singapore, 1819–1985*. Singapore: Oxford University Press.

Vanberg, V. 1994: *Rules and Choice in Economics*. London: Routledge.

Van Wolferen, K. 1989: *The Enigma of Japanese Power*. London: Macmillan.

Vasil, R. 1984: *Governing Singapore*. Petaling Jaya: Eastern Universities Press.

Vatikiotis, M. 1993: *Indonesian Politics under Suharto*. London: Routledge.

Vogel, E. 1991: *The Four Little Dragons*. Cambridge, MA: Harvard University Press.

Vogel, E. and Lodge, G. 1987: *Ideology and National Competitiveness: A Comparison of Nine Different Countries*. Boston: Harvard Business School Press.

Wade, R. 1990: *Governing the Market: Economic Theory and the Role of Government in East Asian Industrialization*. Princeton: Princeton University Press.

Wade, R. 1992: East Asia's Economic Success: Conflicting Perspectives, Partial Insights and Shaky Evidence. *World Politics* 44, 1, 270–320.

Wade, R. 1993: Taiwan and South Korea as Challenges to Economic and Political Science. *Comparative Politics* 25, 2, 147–67.

Wang, Yang Ming 1963: *Instructions for Practical Living*. New York: Columbia University Press.

Watanabe, T. 1992: *Asia: Its Growth and Agony*. Honolulu: University of Hawaii Press.

Weber, M. 1951: *Religion of China*. Glencoe, IL: Free Press.

White, G. and Wade, R. 1988: Developmental States and Markets in East Asia: An Introduction. In G. White (ed.), *Developmental States in East Asia*. London: Macmillan.

Wibisono, C. 1995: The Economic Role of the Indonesian Chinese. In L. Suryadinata (ed.), *South East Asian Chinese and China: The Politico-Economic Dimension*. Singapore: Times Academic Press.

Winckler, E.A. 1984: Taiwan from Hard to Soft Authoritarianism. *China Quarterly*, 4 September, 481–99.

Winckler, E.A. 1992: Taiwan Transition? In T.-J. Cheng and S. Haggard (eds), *Political Change in Taiwan*. Boulder, CO: Lynne Rienner.

Wittfogel, K.A. 1969: *Oriental Despotism: A Comparative Study of Total Power*. New Haven: Yale University Press.

Wolfowitz, P. 1994: The Asia-Pacific Region: Confidence-Building in the Post Cold-War Era. In S.Y. Chia (ed.), *APEC: Challenges and Opportunities*. Singapore: Institute of Southeast Asian Studies.

Wolters, O. 1982: *History, Culture, Religion in Southeast Asian Perspectives*. Singapore: Institute of Southeast Asian Studies.

Wong, J. 1994: *Explaining Southeast Asia's Dynamic Growth*. Papers in Japanese Studies No. 19, National University of Singapore: Department of Japanese Studies.

World Bank 1992: *World Economic Tables 1992*. Baltimore: Johns Hopkins University Press.

World Bank 1993a: *The East Asian Miracle: Economic Growth and Public Policy*. Oxford: Oxford University Press.

World Bank 1993b: K. Kim and D. Leipziger, *Lessons of East Asia: Korea: A Case of Government-Led Development*. Washington: World Bank.

World Bank 1993c: L.C. Chew, *Lessons of East Asia: Hong Kong: A Unique Case of Development*. Washington: World Bank.

World Bank 1993d: T.W. Soon and C.S. Tan, *Lessons of East Asia: Singapore: Public Policy and Economic Development*. Washington: World Bank.

World Bank 1993e: S. Christensen, D. Dollar, A. Siamwalla and P. Vichayanand, *Lessons of East Asia: Thailand: The Institutional and Political Underpinnings of Growth*. Washington: World Bank.

World Bank 1993f: I.M. Salleh and S.D. Meyanathan, *Lessons of East Asia: Malaysia: Growth, Equity and Structural Transformation*. Washington: World Bank.

World Bank 1993g: A. Bhattacharaya and M. Pangestu, *Indonesia Development, Transformation and Public Policy*. Washington: World Bank.

World Bank 1994: *East Asia's Trade and Investment: Regional and Global Gains from Liberalization*. Washington: World Bank.

World Bank 1996: *World Development Report*. Washington: World Bank.

Wright, M.C. 1957: *The Last Stand of Chinese Conservatism: The Tung Chih Restoration 1862–74*. Stanford: Stanford University Press.

Wyatt, D.K. 1984: *Thailand: A Short History*. New Haven: Yale University Press.

Wyatt, D.K. 1989: Thailand. In D. Steinberg (ed.), *In Search of Southeast Asia*. St Leonards: Allen and Unwin.

Xu, Xin-peng 1994: Taiwan's Economic Cooperation with Fujian and Guandong Province. In G. Klintworth (ed.), *Taiwan in the Asia-Pacific in the 1990s*. St Leonards: Allen and Unwin.

Yahuda, M. 1993: China: Will it Strengthen or Weaken the Region? In T.B. Millar and J. Walter, *Asia-Pacific Security after the Cold War*. St Leonards: Allen and Unwin.

Yahuda, M. 1995: The Foreign Relations of Greater China. In D. Shambaugh (ed.), *Greater China*. Oxford: Clarendon Press.

Ye, Ru'An 1993: Historic Transformation of the Korean Peninsula and China's Concerns. In A. Mack (ed.), *Asian Flashpoint: Security and the Korean Peninsula*. St Leonards: Allen and Unwin.

Yoshihara, K. 1988: *The Rise of Ersatz Capitalism in Southeast Asia*. Kuala Lumpur: Oxford University Press.

Yoshihara, K. 1994: *Japanese Economic Development*. Kuala Lumpur: Oxford University Press.

Yoshihara, K. 1995: The Ethnic Chinese and Ersatz Capitalism in Southeast Asia. In L. Suryadinata (ed.), *Southeast Asian Chinese and China: The Politico-Economic Dimension*. Singapore: Times Academic Press.

Young, A. 1992: A Tale of Two Cities: Factor Accumulation and Technical Change in Hong Kong and Singapore. In O. Blanchard and S. Fischer (eds), *N.B.E.R. Macroeconomics Annual 1992*. Cambridge, MA: MIT Press.

Young, A. 1995: The Tyranny of Numbers: Confronting the Statistical Realities of the East Asian Growth Experience. *The Quarterly Journal of Economics* cx, 3, 655–80.

Youngston, A.J. 1982: *Hong Kong Economic Growth and Policy*. Hong Kong: Oxford University Press.

Index

Compiled by Meg Davies (Registered Indexer)